Wiley CPAexcel® Exam Review
PRACTICE QUESTIONS

2019

FINANCIAL ACCOUNTING AND REPORTING

Wiley CPAexcel® Exam Review

PRACTICE QUESTIONS

2019

FINANCIAL ACCOUNTING AND REPORTING

Craig Bain, Ph.D., CPA
Meghann Cefaratti, Ph.D.
Donald R. Deis Jr., Ph.D., CPA, CFE
Pam Smith, Ph.D., CPA, MBA

Wiley Efficient Learning™

Table of Contents

Contents

Contents

Contents

Multiple Choice Questions

Conceptual Framework and Financial Reporting

Financial Accounting Standards Board (FASB)

Overview of U.S. GAAP

FASB and Standard Setting

AICPA.040201FAR-SIM

1. What group currently writes the Generally Accepted Accounting Principles?

   A. Internal Revenue Service.
   B. Securities and Exchange Commission.
   C. Financial Accounting Foundation.
   D. Financial Accounting Standards Board.

AICPA.040202FAR-SIM

2. The FASB is a(n):

   A. Private sector body.
   B. Governmental unit.
   C. International organization.
   D. Group of accounting firms.

AICPA.040206FAR-SIM

3. In reference to proposed accounting standards, the term "negative economic consequences" includes:

   A. The cost of complying with GAAP.
   B. The inability to raise capital.
   C. The cost of government intervention when not in compliance with GAAP.
   D. The failure of internal control systems.

AICPA.040207FAR-SIM

4. The FASB has maintained that:

   A. The interests of the reporting firms will be a primary consideration when developing new GAAP.
   B. GAAP should have little or no cost of compliance.
   C. New GAAP should be neutral and not favor any particular reporting objective.
   D. GAAP should result in the most conservative possible financial statements.

   For example, the requirement to expense all research and development costs is uniform across all firms and does not favor one firm over another.

AICPA.061231FAR

5. Which of the following statements best describes the operating procedure for issuing a new Financial Accounting Standards Board (FASB) statement?

   A. The emerging issues task force must approve a discussion memorandum before it is disseminated to the public.
   B. The exposure draft is modified per public opinion before issuing the discussion memorandum.
   C. A new statement is issued only after a majority vote by the members of the FASB.
   D. A new FASB statement can be rescinded by a majority vote of the AICPA membership.

AICPA.040208FAR-SIM

6. Which of the following will best protect investors against fraudulent financial reporting by corporations?

   A. Criminal statutes.
   B. The requirement that financial statements be audited.
   C. The fact that all firms must report the same way.
   D. The integrity of management.

aicpa.aq.fasb.ss.001_18

7. How are amendments incorporated into the FASB Accounting Standards Codification?

   A. By issuing an exposure draft
   B. By releasing an accounting standards update
   C. By producing a discussion paper
   D. By publishing a statement of financial accounting standards

Accrual Accounting

aicpa.aq.acc.acct.001_17

8. Dannon Co. reported its expenses of $35,200 on the cash basis. Corporate records revealed the following information:

Beginning prepaid expense	$1,300
Beginning accrued expense	1,650
Ending prepaid expense	1,800
Ending accrued expense	1,200

What amount of expense should the Dannon report on its books under the accrual basis?

A. $34,250
B. $35,150
C. $35,300
D. $36,150

AICPA.101044FAR

9. Young & Jamison's modified cash-basis financial statements indicate cash paid for operating expenses of $150,000, end-of-year prepaid expenses of $15,000, and accrued liabilities of $25,000. At the beginning of the year, Young & Jamison had prepaid expenses of $10,000, while accrued liabilities were $5,000. If cash paid for operating expenses is converted to accrual-basis operating expenses, what would be the amount of operating expenses?

A. $125,000
B. $135,000
C. $165,000
D. $175,000

AICPA.130726FAR

10. Ina Co. had the following beginning and ending balances in its prepaid expense and accrued liabilities accounts for the current year:

	Prepaid Expenses	Accrued Liabilities
Beginning balance	$5,000	$8,000
Ending balance	10,000	20,000

Debits to operating expenses totaled $100,000. What amount did Ina pay for operating expenses during the current year?

A. $83,000
B. $93,000
C. $107,000
D. $117,000

Financial Accounting Standards Codification

aicpa.aq.fasc.001_17

11. The FASB amends the Accounting Standards Codification through the issuance of

A. Accounting Standards Updates.
B. Statements of Financial Accounting Standards.
C. Technical Bulletins.
D. Staff Accounting Bulletins.

AICPA.100883FAR-SIM

12. Which of the following statements includes the most useful guidance for practicing accountants concerning the FASB Accounting Standards Codification.

A. The Codification includes only FASB Statements.
B. The Codification is the sole source of U.S. GAAP, for nongovernmental entities.
C. The Codification significantly modified the content of GAAP when it became effective.
D. An accountant can be sure that all SEC rules are included in the Codification.

AICPA.100884FAR-SIM

13. U.S. GAAP includes a very large set of accounting guidance. Choose the correct statement.

A. The FASB Accounting Standards Codification includes guidance about items that are not under the purview of the Generally Accepted Accounting Principles, such as the income tax basis of accounting.
B. Authoritative guidance from FASB Statements adopted before the FASB Accounting Standards Codification does not appear in the Codification.
C. There is an implied hierarchy within the FASB Accounting Standards Codification, with FASB Statements assuming the top level.
D. International accounting standards are not included in the FASB Accounting Standards Codification.

AICPA.130717FAR

14. Which of the following documents is typically issued as part of the due-process activities of the Financial Accounting Standards Board (FASB) for amending the FASB Accounting Standards Codification?

A. A proposed statement of position.
B. A proposed accounting standards update.
C. A proposed accounting research bulletin.
D. A proposed staff accounting bulletin.

Conceptual Framework of Financial Reporting by Business Enterprises

Objectives and Qualitative Characteristics

aicpa.aq.obj.qual.char.001_17

15. What is the primary objective of financial reporting?

    A. To provide economic information that is comprehensible to all users.
    B. To provide management with an accurate evaluation of their financial performance.
    C. To provide forecasts for future cash flows and financial performance.
    D. To provide information that is useful for economic decision making.

aicpa.aq.obj.qual.char.002_17

16. Within the context of the qualitative characteristics of accounting information, which of the following is a fundamental qualitative characteristic?

    A. Relevance
    B. Timeliness
    C. Comparability
    D. Confirmatory value

Assumptions and Accounting Principles

AICPA.120623FAR

17. Which of the following characteristics of accounting information primarily allows users of financial statements to generate predictions about an organization?

    A. Reliability.
    B. Timeliness.
    C. Neutrality.
    D. Relevance.

AICPA.061241FAR

18. Which of the following assumptions means that money is the common denominator of economic activity and provides an appropriate basis for accounting measurement and analysis?

    A. Going concern.
    B. Periodicity.
    C. Monetary unit.
    D. Economic entity.

AICPA.940503FAR-FA

19. Reporting inventory at the lower of cost or market is a departure from the accounting principle of:

    A. Historical cost.
    B. Consistency.
    C. Conservatism.
    D. Full disclosure.

Fair Value Framework

Fair Value Framework—Introduction and Definitions

aicpa.aq.fv.frame.intro.001_17

20. Which of the following statements is correct regarding fair value measurement?

    A. Fair value is a market-based measurement.
    B. Fair value is an entity-specific measurement.
    C. Fair value measurement does **not** consider risk.
    D. Fair value measurement does **not** consider restrictions.

AICPA.090416FAR-SIM

21. Which one of the following is not a purpose of the fair value framework as set forth in ASC 820, *Fair Value Measurement*?

    A. Provide a uniform definition of "fair value" for GAAP purposes.
    B. Provide a framework for determining fair value for GAAP purposes.
    C. Establish new measurement requirements for financial instruments.
    D. Establish expanded disclosures about fair value when it is used.

Recognition and Measurement

080107FAR-FVO

22. On January 15, 2008, Able Co. made a significant investment in the debt securities of Baker Co., which it intends to hold until the debt matures. Able's fiscal year-end is December 31. If Able Co. intends to measure and report its investment in Baker Co. debt securities at fair value as permitted by ASC 820 on which one of the following dates must Able elect to implement the fair value option?

    A. January 15, 2008
    B. January 31, 2008
    C. March 31, 2008
    D. December 31, 2008

AICPA.090425FAR-SIM

23. In which of the following circumstances, if any, would an auditor be concerned as to whether or not the price paid to acquire an asset was the fair value of the asset?

    I. The asset was acquired from the acquiring firm's majority shareholder.
    II. The asset was acquired in an active exchange market.

    A. I only.
    B. II only.
    C. Both I and II.
    D. Neither I nor II.

AICPA.120618FAR

24. Giaconda, Inc. acquires an asset for which it will measure the fair value by discounting future cash flows of the asset. Which of the following terms best describes this fair value measurement approach?

    A. Market
    B. Income
    C. Cost
    D. Observable inputs

Inputs and Hierarchy

aicpa.aq.inputs.001_17

25. Which of the following is a level three input to valuation techniques used to measure the fair value of an asset?

    A. Quoted prices in active markets for identical assets.
    B. Quoted prices for similar assets in active markets.
    C. Unobservable inputs for the asset.
    D. Inputs other than quoted prices that are observable for the asset.

AICPA.090431FAR-SIM

26. Which of the following statements concerning inputs used in ascertaining fair value is/are correct?

    I. Only observable inputs can be used.
    II. Inputs that incorporate the entity's assumptions may be used.

    A. I only.
    B. II only.
    C. Both I and II.
    D. Neither I nor II.

AICPA.090432FAR-SIM

27. Which of the following statements concerning the fair value hierarchy used in ascertaining fair value is/are correct?

    I. Quoted market prices should be adjusted for a "blockage factor" when a firm holds a sizable portion of the asset being valued.
    II. Quoted market prices in markets that are not active because there are few relevant transactions cannot be used.

    A. I only.
    B. II only.
    C. Both I and II.
    D. Neither I nor II.

AICPA.130735FAR

28. Each of the following would be considered a Level 2 observable input that could be used to determine an asset or liability's fair value, **except**

    A. Quoted prices for identical assets and liabilities in markets that are not active.
    B. Quoted prices for similar assets and liabilities in markets that are active.
    C. Internally generated cash flow projections for a related asset or liability.
    D. Interest rates that are observable at commonly quoted intervals.

Disclosure Requirements

AICPA.080120FAR-FVO

29. For a firm that elects to measure certain of its financial assets and financial liabilities at fair value, required financial statement disclosures are intended to facilitate which of the following comparisons?

    I. Comparisons between entities that use different measurement methods for similar assets and liabilities.
    II. Comparisons between assets and liabilities of a single entity that uses different measurement methods for similar assets and liabilities.

    A. Neither I nor II.
    B. I only.
    C. II only.
    D. Both I and II.

AICPA.090434FAR-SIM

30. Under U.S. GAAP, the disclosure requirements when fair value measurement is used are differentiated by which of the following classifications?

    A. Between assets measured at fair value and liabilities measured at fair value
    B. Between fair value measurements that result in gains and fair value measurements that result in losses
    C. Between items measured at fair value on a recurring basis and items measured at fair value on a nonrecurring basis
    D. Between items for which fair value measurement is required and items for which fair value measurement is elected

AICPA.090436FAR-SIM

31. Which one of the following is not a required disclosure in annual financial reports for an entity that uses fair value measurement?

    A. The level of the fair value hierarchy within which fair value measurements fall
    B. The valuation techniques used to measure fair value
    C. Combined disclosures about fair value measurements required by all pronouncements
    D. A discussion of any change from the prior period in valuation techniques used to measure fair value

International Financial Reporting Standards (IFRS)

IASB Accounting Standards

AICPA.101181FAR

32. When referring to IFRS, which of the following are NOT included?

    A. IASs.
    B. SEC.
    C. IFRICs.
    D. IFRS Interpretations.

TREPA-0098

33. According to the IASB Framework for the Preparation and Presentation of Financial Statements, the qualitative characteristic of faithful representation includes

    A. Timeliness, predictive value, and feedback value.
    B. Neutrality, completeness, and free from error.
    C. Predictive value, confirmatory value, and materiality.
    D. Comparability and consistency.

TREPA-0100

34. According to the IASB Framework, the financial statement element that is defined as increases in economic benefits during the accounting period in the form of inflows or enhancements of assets or decreases of liabilities that result in increases in equity, other than those relating to contributions from equity participants, is

    A. Revenue.
    B. Income.
    C. Profits.
    D. Gains.

IASB Framework

AICPA.101157FAR-SIM

35. According to the IASB Framework, the process of reporting an item in the financial statements of an entity is:

    A. Recognition.
    B. Statement of Financial Position.
    C. Disclosure.
    D. Presentation.

AICPA.101158FAR-SIM

36. Which of the following is a fundamental (primary) qualitative characteristic of useful financial information included in IASB's Framework?

    A. Comparability.
    B. Timeliness.
    C. Relevance.
    D. Understandability.

AICPA.101160FAR-SIM

37. When should an item that meets the definition of an element be recognized?

    A. The item has a cost or value that can be measured reliably.
    B. It is highly unlikely that any future economic benefit associated with the item will flow to the entity.
    C. Both A and B.
    D. Neither A nor B.

IFRS for SMEs

AICPA.100900FAR-OFS-SIM

38. Which of the following statements, if any, concerning IFRS for SMEs is/are correct?

    I. IFRS for SMEs is based on accrual basis accounting.
    II. Generally, IFRS for SMEs may be used as an alternative to using OCBOA.

    A. I only.
    B. II only.
    C. Both I and II.
    D. Neither I nor II.

AICPA.100901FAR-OFS-SIM

39. Under IFRS for SMEs, which of the following cost flow assumptions can be used for inventory valuation purposes?

	FIFO	LIFO	Weighted Average Cost
A.	Yes	Yes	Yes
B.	Yes	Yes	No
C.	Yes	No	Yes
D.	Yes	No	No

AICPA.100905FAR-OFS-SIM

40. Which one of the following is a characteristic of accounting under IFRS for SMEs?

    A. Interest incurred during construction must be capitalized.
    B. Earnings per share must be provided in the financial statements.
    C. Goodwill must be amortized.
    D. The LIFO cost flow assumption can be used in valuing inventories.

IFRS—General-Purpose Financial Statements

AICPA.101207FAR-SIM

41. IFRS requires a classified Statement of Financial Position. What are the required classifications?

    A. Cash; trade receivables and payables; property, plant and equipment; long-term assets and liabilities; and other assets and liabilities.
    B. Cash; trade receivables and payables; property, plant and equipment; and other assets and liabilities.
    C. Current, long-term, and other assets and liabilities.
    D. Current and non-current assets and liabilities.

AICPA.101212FAR-SIM

42. Which of the following items would not appear on the Income Statement prepared using IFRS?

    A. Discontinued operations.
    B. Gross Profit.
    C. Depreciation and amortization.
    D. All items would appear on the Income Statement when using IFRS.

Balance Sheet/Statement of Financial Position

AICPA.101198FAR-SIM

43. Reporting accounts receivable at net realizable value is a departure from the accounting principle of:

    A. Conservatism.
    B. Fair value.
    C. Market value.
    D. Historical cost.

AICPA.101201FAR-SIM

44. The following trial balance of JB Company at December 31, Year five, has been adjusted except for income taxes. The income tax rate is 30%.

	DR	CR
Accounts receivable, net	$725,000	
Accounts payable		250,000
Accumulated depreciation		125,000
Cash	185,000	
Contributed capital		650,000
Expenses	3,750,000	
Goodwill	140,000	
Prepaid taxes	225,000	
Property, plant, and equipment	850,000	
Retained earnings, 1/1/ year five		350,000
Revenues		4,500,000
	5,875,000	5,875,000

During year five, estimated tax payments of $225,000 were paid and debited to prepaid taxes. There were no differences between financial statement and taxable income for year five.

Included in accounts receivable is $400,000 due from a loyal customer. Special terms were granted to this customer to make payments of $100,000 semi-annually every March 1 and September 1.

In JB Company's December 31, year five Balance Sheet, what amount should be reported as current assets?

A. 710,000
B. 910,000
C. 935,000
D. 1,135,000

AICPA.101204FAR-SIM

45. Which of the following accounts is a contra account?

A. Accumulated depreciation, equipment.
B. Depreciation expense, office equipment.
C. Dividends.
D. Unearned revenue.

Income Statement

AICPA.101208FAR-SIM

46. In a multi-step Income Statement:

A. Total expenses are subtracted from total revenues.
B. Gross profit (margin) is shown as a separate item.
C. Cost of sales and operating expense are subtracted from total revenues.
D. Other income is added to revenue from sales.

AICPA.101211FAR-SIM

47. If the accountant forgets to record salary expense in the Statement of Income, what is the result?

A. Net income is too high.
B. Net income is too low.
C. Retained earnings is too low.
D. Retained earnings is correctly stated, as the omission only affects the Income Statement.

AICPA.110580FAR

48. A company's activities for year two included the following:

Gross sales	$3,600,000
Cost of goods sold	1,200,000
Selling and administrative expense	500,000
Adjustment for a prior-year understatement of amortization expense	59,000
Sales returns	34,000
Gain on sale of available-for-sale securities	8,000
Gain on disposal of a discontinued business segment	4,000
Unrealized gain on available-for-sale securities	2,000

The company has a 30% effective income tax rate. What is the company's net income for year two?

A. $1,267,700
B. $1,273,300
C. $1,314,600
D. $1,316,000

Statement of Comprehensive Income

assess.AICPA.020501FAR-FA_11_17

49. Rock Co.'s financial statements had the following balances at December 31:

Gain on the sale of equipment	$50,000
Foreign currency translation gain	100,000
Net income	400,000
Unrealized gain on the available-for-sale debt securities	20,000

What amount should Rock report as comprehensive income for the year ended December 31?

A. $400,000
B. $420,000
C. $520,000
D. $570,000

assess.AICPA.090633FAR-I-B_11_17

50. A company reports the following information as of December 31:

Sales revenue	$800,000
Cost of goods sold	600,000
Operating expenses	90,000
Unrealized holding gain on the available-for-sale debt securities, net of tax	30,000

What amount should the company report as comprehensive income as of December 31?

A. $30,000
B. $110,000
C. $140,000
D. $200,000

assess.AICPA.130719FAR_11_17

51. Palmyra Co. has net income of $11,000, a positive $1,000 net cumulative effect of a change in accounting principle, a $3,000 unrealized loss on available-for-sale debt securities, a positive $2,000 foreign currency translation adjustment, and a $6,000 increase in its common stock. What amount is Palmyra's comprehensive income?

A. $4,000
B. $10,000
C. $11,000
D. $17,000

Statement of Changes in Equity

AICPA.101238FAR-SIM

52. The Statement of Changes in Equity:

    A. Is one of the required financial statements under U.S. GAAP
    B. Includes accounts such as the retained earnings and common share accounts but not other comprehensive income items.
    C. Is used only if a corporation frequently issues common shares
    D. Reconciles all of the beginning and ending balances in the equity accounts.

AICPA.101239FAR-SIM

53. The Statement of Changes in Equity shows an increase in the common stock account of $2,000 and an increase in the additional paid-in capital account of $10,000. If the common stock has a par value of $2, and the only transactions affecting these accounts were these issues of common stock, what was the average issue price of the common stock during the year?

    A. $2
    B. $5
    C. $10
    D. $12

AICPA.101241FAR-SIM

54. Which of the following items would appear on the Statement of Owner's Equity?

	Notes Payable	Treasury Stock	Advertising Expense	Retained Earnings
A.	Yes	Yes	Yes	Yes
B.	No	Yes	Yes	Yes
C.	No	Yes	No	Yes
D.	No	No	No	No

Statement of Cash Flows

Sources and Uses of Cash

AICPA.040213FAR-SIM

55. Which of the following sets of financial statements generally cannot be prepared directly from the adjusted trial balance?

    A. Income Statement, Balance Sheet, Statement of Cash Flows
    B. Income Statement, Statement of Cash Flows
    C. Statement of Cash Flows
    D. Balance Sheet and Statement of Cash Flows

AICPA.061230FAR

56. New England Co. had net cash provided by operating activities of $351,000; net cash used by investing activities of $420,000; and cash provided by financing activities of $250,000.

    New England's cash balance was $27,000 on January 1. During the year, there was a sale of land that resulted in a gain of $25,000, and proceeds of $40,000 were received from the sale.

    What was New England's cash balance at the end of the year?

    A. $27,000
    B. $40,000
    C. $208,000
    D. $248,000

AICPA.070771FAR

57. Paper Co. had net income of $70,000 during the year. The dividend payment was $10,000. The following information is available:

Mortgage repayment	$20,000
Available-for-sale debt securities purchased	10,000 increase
Bonds payable—issued	50,000 increase
Inventory	40,000 increase
Accounts payable	30,000 decrease

What amount should Paper report as net cash provided by operating activities in its Statement of Cash Flows for the year?

    A. $0
    B. $10,000
    C. $20,000
    D. $30,000

Operating, Investing, and Financing Activities

AICPA.061224FAR

58. Which of the following items is included in the Financing Activities section of the Statement of Cash Flows?

    A. Cash effects of transactions involving making and collecting loans
    B. Cash effects of acquiring and disposing of investments and property, plant, and equipment
    C. Cash effects of transactions obtaining resources from owners and providing them with a return on their investment
    D. Cash effects of transactions that enter into the determination of net income

AICPA.110566FAR

59. Abbott Co. is preparing its Statement of Cash Flows for the year. Abbott's cash disbursements during the year included the following:

Payment of interest on bonds payable	$500,000
Payment of dividends to stockholders	300,000
Payment to acquire 1,000 shares of Marks Co. common stock	100,000

What should Abbott report as total cash outflows for financing activities in its Statement of Cash Flows?

A. $0
B. $300,000
C. $800,000
D. $900,000

AICPA.130711FAR

60. A company is preparing its year-end cash flow statement using the indirect method. During the year, the following transactions occurred:

Dividends paid	$300
Proceeds from the issuance of common stock	$250
Borrowings under a line of credit	$200
Proceeds from the issuance of convertible bonds	$100
Proceeds from the sale of a building	$150

What is the company's increase in cash flows provided by financing activities for the year?

A. $50
B. $150
C. $250
D. $550

Operating Cash Flows—Indirect Method

aicpa.aq.op.cash.flow.001_17

61. The following information pertains to Ash Co., which prepares its statement of cash flows using the indirect method:

Interest payable at beginning of year: $15,000

Interest expense during the year: $20,000

Interest payable at end of year: $5,000

What amount of interest should Ash report as a supplemental disclosure of cash flow information?

A. $10,000
B. $20,000
C. $30,000
D. $35,000

AICPA.08211239FAR-III

62. How should the amortization of a bond discount on long-term debt be reported in a Statement of Cash Flows prepared using the indirect method?

A. As a financing activities inflow
B. As a financing activities outflow
C. In operating activities as a deduction from income
D. In operating activities as an addition to income

AICPA.090666.FAR.III

63. Baker Co. began its operations during the current year. The following is Baker's Balance Sheet at December 31:

Baker Co. Balance Sheet	
Assets	
Cash	$192,000
Accounts receivable	82,000
Total Assets	$274,000
Liabilities and stockholders' equity	
Accounts payable	$24,000
Common stock	200,000
Retained earnings	50,000
Total liabilities and stockholders' equity	$274,000

Baker's net income for the current year was $78,000, and dividends of $28,000 were declared and paid. Common stock was issued for $200,000. What amount should Baker report as cash provided by operating activities in its Statement of Cash Flows for the current year?

A. $20,000
B. $50,000
C. $192,000
D. $250,000

Notes to Financial Statements

Notes to Financial Statements

AICPA.061201FAR

64. Which of the following should be disclosed in a summary of significant accounting policies?

A. Basis of profit recognition on long-term construction contracts.
B. Future minimum lease payments in the aggregate and for each of the five succeeding fiscal years.
C. Depreciation expense.
D. Composition of sales by segment.

AICPA.061215FAR

65. Which of the following must be included in the notes to the financial statements in a company's summary of significant accounting policies?

   A. Description of current year equity transactions.
   B. Summary of long-term debt outstanding.
   C. Schedule of fixed assets.
   D. Revenue recognition policies.

AICPA.101078FAR

66. Neely Co. disclosed in the notes to its financial statements that a significant number of its unsecured trade account receivables are with companies that operate in the same industry. This disclosure is required to inform financial statement users of the existence of

   A. Concentration of credit risk.
   B. Concentration of market risk.
   C. Risk of measurement uncertainty.
   D. Off-balance sheet risk of accounting loss.

Risks and Uncertainties

AICPA.101112FAR

67. Which of the following is not a source of risk and uncertainty for which disclosures are required by GAAP?

   A. Nature of a firm's operations
   B. Effect of changes in government regulations
   C. Use of estimates in financial statements
   D. Vulnerability to significant concentrations

AICPA.101113FAR

68. Which of the following is not an aspect of a firm's operations necessitating disclosure of risks and uncertainties?

   A. Principal markets
   B. Products and services
   C. Pension plan
   D. Geographical location

AICPA.101116FAR

69. Under what conditions is disclosure about risks and uncertainty pertaining to concentrations required?

   A. If the firm has any of the concentrations for which disclosures are required by GAAP
   B. If events affecting the firm negatively have already occurred, with respect to a concentration
   C. If the firm is vulnerable to a severe impact in the near term because of a concentration,

and it is at least reasonably possible that the impact will occur
   D. If the Board of Directors has taken a direct action serving to reduce risk and uncertainty within a given concentration

Subsequent Events

AICPA.100886FAR-SIM

70. Welnet Inc. was sued in October of 20x8 for breach of contract. Based on the advice of counsel, Welnet recognized a $2 million estimated lawsuit loss and liability at December 31, 20x8. The lawsuit was settled in February, 20x9 in the amount of $2.2 million, before Welnet's 20x8 financial statements were available to be issued. What is the appropriate accounting procedure for the 20x8 statements?

   A. Welnet recognizes $0.2 million of lawsuit loss in its 20x9 statements.
   B. Welnet recognizes the entire $2.2 million loss in its 20x8 statements.
   C. Welnet reports the $0.2 million amount as a retrospective adjustment to its 20x8 statements.
   D. Welnet recognizes the entire $2.2 million loss in its 20x9 statements.

AICPA.120632FAR

71. On March 21, year 2, a company with a calendar year end issued its year 1 financial statements. On February 28, year 2, the company's only manufacturing plant was severely damaged by a storm and had to be shut down. Total property losses were $10 million and determined to be material. The amount of business disruption losses is unknown. How should the impact of the storm be reflected in the company's year 1 financial statements?

   A. Provide NO information related to the storm losses in the financial statements until losses and expenses become fully known.
   B. Accrue and disclose the property loss with NO accrual or disclosure of the business disruption loss.
   C. Do NOT accrue the property loss or the business disruption loss, but disclose them in the notes to the financial statements.
   D. Accrue and disclose the property loss and additional business disruption losses in the financial statements.

Exit or Disposal Activities

AICPA.081295FAR-SIM

72. In 20x5, a firm decided to discontinue a segment with a book value of $200 million and a fair value of $250 million. The cost to dispose of the segment in 20x6 is estimated to be $10 million. In the 20x5 income statement, what amount of disposal gain or loss will be reported in the discontinued operations section?

   A. $-0-
   B. $50 million loss.
   C. $50 million gain.
   D. $40 million gain.

AICPA.110578FAR

73. A company decided to sell an unprofitable division of its business. The company can sell the entire operation for $800,000, and the buyer will assume all assets and liabilities of the operations. The tax rate is 30%. The assets and liabilities of the discontinued operation are as follows:

Buildings	$5,000,000
Accumulated depreciation	3,000,000
Mortgage on buildings	1,100,000
Inventory	500,000
Accounts payable	600,000
Accounts receivable	200,000

What is the after-tax net loss on the disposal of the division?

   A. $140,000
   B. $200,000
   C. $1,540,000
   D. $2,200,000

Evaluating Financial Statements

Ratios—Liquidity/Solvency and Operational

AICPA.082117FAR-I.C

74. TGR Enterprises provided the following information from its statement of financial position for the year ended December 31, Year 1:

	January 1	December 31
Cash	$10,000	$50,000
Accounts receivable	120,000	100,000
Inventories	200,000	160,000
Prepaid expenses	20,000	10,000
Accounts payable	175,000	120,000
Accrued liabilities	25,000	30,000

TGR's sales and cost of sales for Year 1 were $1,400,000 and $840,000, respectively. What is the accounts receivable turnover, in days?

   A. 26.1
   B. 28.7
   C. 31.3
   D. 41.7

AICPA.082118FAR-I.C

75. Redwood Co.'s financial statements had the following information at year end:

Cash	$60,000
Accounts receivable	180,000
Allowance for uncollectible accounts	8,000
Inventory	240,000
Short-term marketable securities	90,000
Prepaid rent	18,000
Current liabilities	400,000
Long-term debt	220,000

What was Redwood's quick ratio?

   A. 0.81 to 1
   B. 0.83 to 1
   C. 0.94 to 1
   D. 1.46 to 1

AICPA.082119FAR-I.C

76. The following information was taken from Baxter Department Store's financial statements:

Inventory on January 1	$100,000
Inventory on December 31	300,000
Net sales	2,000,000
Net purchases	700,000

What was Baxter's inventory turnover for the year ending December 31?

   A. 2.5
   B. 3.5
   C. 5
   D. 10

Ratios—Profitability and Equity

AICPA.051166FAR-FA

77. The following financial ratios and calculations were based on information from Kohl Co.'s financial statements for the current year.

   Accounts receivable turnover

   Ten times during the year

   Total assets turnover

Two times during the year

Average receivables during the year

$200,000

What were Kohl's average total assets for the year?

A. $2,000,000
B. $1,000,000
C. $400,000
D. $200,000

AICPA.070776FAR

78. Stent Co. had total assets of $760,000, capital stock of $150,000, and retained earnings of $215,000. What was Stent's debt-to-equity ratio?

A. 2.63
B. 1.08
C. 0.52
D. 0.48

AICPA.951160FAR-FA

79. The following data pertain to Cowl, Inc., for the year ended December 31, 2004:

Net sales	$600,000
Net income	150,000
Total assets, January 1, 2004	2,000,000
Total assets, December 31, 2004	3,000,000

What was Cowl's rate of return on assets for 2004?

A. 5%
B. 6%
C. 20%
D. 24%

Consolidated Financial Statements

Introduction to Consolidated Financial Statements

aicpa.aq.intro.consld.fin.001_17

80. For the purpose of consolidating financial interests, a majority voting interest is deemed to be

A. 50% of the directly or indirectly owned outstanding voting shares of another entity.
B. 50% of the directly or indirectly owned outstanding voting shares and at least 50% of the directly or indirectly owned outstanding nonvoting shares of another entity.
C. Greater than 50% of the directly or indirectly owned outstanding voting shares of another.

D. Greater than 50% of the directly or indirectly owned outstanding voting shares and at least 50% of the directly or indirectly owned outstanding nonvoting shares of another entity.

AICPA.070729FAR-P1-FA

81. The preparation of consolidated statements likely will require the following information about the subsidiary's assets and liabilities at the date of acquisition:

	Book Value	Fair Value
A.	Yes	No
B.	No	Yes
C.	Yes	Yes
D.	No	No

AICPA.090441FAR-SIM

82. Following a business combination accomplished through a legal acquisition, transactions between the affiliated entities can originate with the/a:

	Parent Company	Subsidiary Company
A.	Yes	Yes
B.	Yes	No
C.	No	Yes
D.	No	No

Consolidating Process

Consolidation at Acquisition

AICPA.071011FAR

83. A subsidiary, acquired for cash in a business combination, owned inventories with a market value different from the book value as of the date of combination. A consolidated balance sheet prepared immediately after the acquisition would include this difference as part of:

A. Deferred Credits
B. Goodwill
C. Inventories
D. Retained Earnings

AICPA.083794FAR-SIM

84. Which one of the following would be of concern in preparing consolidated financial statements at the end of the operating period following a business combination that would not be a concern in preparing financial statements immediately following a combination?

A. Whether or not there are intercompany accounts receivable/accounts payable.

B. Whether or not goodwill resulted from the business combination.

C. Whether the parent carries its investment in the subsidiary using the cost method or the equity method.

D. Whether or not there is a noncontrolling interest in the subsidiary.

AICPA.090111FAR-SIM

85. Under which of the following methods of carrying a subsidiary on its books, if any, will the carrying value of the investment normally change following a combination?

	Cost Method	Equity Method
A.	Yes	Yes
B.	Yes	No
C.	No	Yes
D.	No	No

Consolidation Subsequent to Acquisition

AICPA.071015FAR

86. On January 1, 20X1, Prim, Inc. acquired all the outstanding common shares of Scarp, Inc. for cash equal to the book value of the stock. The carrying amount of Scarp's assets and liabilities approximated their fair values, except that the carrying amount of its building was more than fair value. In preparing Prim's 20X1 consolidated income statement, which of the following adjustments would be made?

A. Depreciation expense would be decreased, and goodwill would be recognized.

B. Depreciation expense would be increased, and goodwill would be recognized.

C. Depreciation expense would be decreased, and no goodwill would be recognized.

D. Depreciation expense would be increased, and no goodwill would be recognized.

AICPA.090442FAR-SIM

87. When a parent company uses the cost method on its books to carry its investment in a subsidiary, which one of the following will be recorded by the parent on its books?

A. Parent's share of subsidiary's net income/net loss.

B. Parent's amortization of goodwill resulting from excess investment cost over fair value of subsidiary's net assets.

C. Parent's share of subsidiary's cash dividends declared.

D. Parent's depreciation of excess investment cost over book values of subsidiary's net assets.

AICPA.090444FAR-SIM

88. On October 1, 2008, Potato Company acquired 100% of the voting stock of Spud Company in a legal acquisition. Potato chose to account for its investment in Spud on its books using the cost method. Spud had the following incomes and dividends for the periods shown:

	10/1 – 12/31/08	1/1 – 12/31/09
Net Income	$3,000	$15,000
Dividends Declared/Paid	1,000	3,000

In its December 31, 2009, consolidating process, which one of the following is the amount of the reciprocity entry Potato will make on the consolidating worksheet?

A. $2,000

B. $3,000

C. $14,000

D. $18,000

Consolidation Less than 100% Ownership

aicpa.aq.consld.less.001_17

89. Thyme, Inc. owns 16,000 of Sage Co.'s 20,000 outstanding common shares. The carrying value of Sage's equity is $500,000. Sage subsequently issues an additional 5,000 previously unissued shares for $200,000 to an outside party that is unrelated to either Thyme or Sage. What is the total noncontrolling interest after the additional shares are issued?

A. $140,000

B. $172,000

C. $252,000

D. $300,000

aicpa.aq.consld.less.002_18

90. Parent Co. owns 90% of the 10,000 outstanding shares of Subsidiary Co.'s common stock on December 31, Year 1. On that date, the stockholders' equity of Subsidiary was $150,000, consisting of $100,000 of no-par common stock and $50,000 of retained earnings. On January 2, Year 2, Subsidiary issued 2,000 previously unissued shares for $24,000 to various outside investors. As a consequence of this transaction, Parent's ownership share was reduced to 75%. Which of the following correctly reports this transaction?

A. Parent's investment in Subsidiary is reduced by $4,500.

B. Parent's investment in Subsidiary is increased by $3,000.

C. The consolidated income statement reports a loss of $7,500.

D. The consolidated income statement reports a gain of $4,000.

AICPA.090113FAR-SIM

91. If a parent uses the equity method on its books to carry its investment in a subsidiary, which one of the following current year entries (made by the parent) must be reversed on the consolidating worksheet?

	Income from Subsidiary	Dividends from Subsidiary
A.	Yes	Yes
B.	Yes	No
C.	No	Yes
D.	No	No

AICPA.090764.FAR-SIM

92. On January 1, 20x1 Ritt Corp. purchased 80% of Shaw Corp.'s $10 par common stock for $975,000. Ritt's cost reflects an appropriate fair value measure for all of Shaw's outstanding common stock. The original cost to the noncontrolling investors for the 20% of Shaw's common stock not acquired by Ritt was $200,000. At the date of Ritt's purchase, the carrying amount of Shaw's net assets was $1,000,000. The fair values of Shaw's identifiable assets and liabilities were the same as their carrying amounts except for plant assets (net) which were $100,000 in excess of the carrying amount. Which one of the following is the amount of noncontrolling interest that should be reported in a consolidated balance sheet prepared immediately following the business combination?

A. $125,000
B. $200,000
C. $220,000
D. $243,750

Intercompany (I/C) Transactions and Balances

Intercompany I/C Transactions and Balances— Introduction

AICPA.090445FAR-SIM

93. Parco sells goods to its subsidiary, Subco, which in turn sells the goods to Noco, an unaffiliated firm. Which of these transactions, if any, should be eliminated in the consolidating process?

	Parco to Subco	Subco to Noco
A.	Yes	Yes
B.	Yes	No
C.	No	Yes
D.	No	No

AICPA.090447FAR-SIM

94. Which of the following kinds of transactions should be eliminated in the consolidating process?

	Parent to Subsidiary	Subsidiary to Parent	Subsidiary 1 Subsidiary 2
A.	Yes	Yes	Yes
B.	Yes	Yes	No
C.	Yes	No	No
D.	No	Yes	Yes

Intercompany (I/C) Inventory Transactions

AICPA.090448FAR-SIM

95. Which one of the following will occur on consolidated financial statements if an intercompany inventory transaction is not eliminated?

A. An understatement of sales.
B. An overstatement of sales.
C. An understatement of purchases.
D. An overstatement of accounts receivable.

AICPA.090449FAR-SIM

96. Pine Company acquired goods for resale from its manufacturing subsidiary, Strawco, at Strawco's cost to manufacture of $12,000. Pine subsequently resold the goods to a nonaffiliate for $18,000. Which one of the following is the amount of the elimination that will be needed as a result of the intercompany inventory transaction?

A. $-0-
B. $6,000
C. $12,000
D. $18,000

assess.AICPA.FAR.ic.ivntry-0012

97. Tulip Co. owns 100% of Daisy Co.'s outstanding common stock. Tulip's cost of goods sold for the year totals $600,000, and Daisy's cost of goods sold totals $400,000. During the year, Tulip sold inventory costing $60,000 to Daisy for $100,000. By the end of the year, all transferred inventory was sold to third parties. What amount should be reported as cost of goods sold in the consolidated statement of income?

A. $900,000
B. $940,000
C. $960,000
D. $1,000,000

Intercompany (I/C) Fixed Asset Transactions

AICPA.070794FAR

98. Zest Co. owns 100% of Cinn, Inc. On January 2, 1999, Zest sold equipment with an original cost of $80,000 and a carrying amount of $48,000 to Cinn for $72,000. Zest had been depreciating the equipment over a five-year period using straight-line depreciation with no residual value. Cinn is using straight-line depreciation over three years with no residual value. In Zest's December 31, 1999, consolidating worksheet, by what amount should depreciation expense be decreased?

   A. $0
   B. $8,000
   C. $16,000
   D. $24,000

AICPA.071026FAR

99. For consolidated purposes, what effect will the intercompany sale of a fixed asset at a profit or at a loss have on depreciation expense recognized by the buying affiliate?

	At a Profit	At a Loss
A.	Overstate	Overstate
B.	Overstate	Understate
C.	Understate	Overstate
D.	Understate	Understate

Intercompany (I/C) Bond Transactions

AICPA.090462FAR-SIM

100. Which one of the following is not a characteristic of intercompany bonds?

   A. Intercompany bonds may occur on the date of a business combination or subsequent to a business combination.
   B. When bonds become intercompany, it is as though the bonds have been retired for consolidated purposes.
   C. Intercompany bonds can result in the recognition of a gain or a loss for consolidating purposes.
   D. When bonds become intercompany, they are written off of the books of the issuing affiliate and the investing affiliate.

AICPA.090463FAR-SIM

101. On December 31, 2008, Pico acquired $250,000 par value of the outstanding $1,000,000 bonds of its subsidiary, Sico, in the market for $200,000. On that date, Sico had a $100,000 premium on its total bond liability.

Which one of the following is the amount of premium or discount on Pico's investment in Sico's bonds?

   A. $250,000 premium
   B. $100,000 premium
   C. $50,000 premium
   D. $50,000 discount

IFRS—Consolidations

AICPA.100978FAR-SIM

102. Which of the following statements about the differences between U.S. GAAP and IFRS in determining whether or not to consolidate an entity is/are correct?

   I. IFRS guidelines for determining the eligibility of an entity to be consolidated are more principles-based than are U.S. GAAP guidelines.
   II. In assessing an investor's level of ownership of an investee, both U.S. GAAP and IFRS consider outstanding securities that are exercisable or convertible into voting shares.
   III. Under both U.S. GAAP and IFRS, there are circumstances under which a majority-owned subsidiary does not have to be consolidated.

   A. I only.
   B. I and II only.
   C. I and III only.
   D. I, II, and III.

BCC-0068B

103. Under IFRS the asset goodwill may be recognized

   A. When it is acquired by purchase.
   B. When it is internally generated or acquired by purchase.
   C. When it is clear that it exists and has value.
   D. When it has future economic benefits.

BCC-0043

104. Under IFRS, a parent may exclude a subsidiary from consolidation if all of the following conditions exist, **except**:

   A. It is wholly or partially owned and its other owners do not object to nonconsolidation.
   B. It reports only one class of stock in its balance sheet.
   C. Its parent prepares consolidated financial statements that comply with IFRS.
   D. It does not have any debt or equity instruments publicly traded.

Combined Financial Statements

AICPA.082078FAR-I.A

105. Mr. Allen owns all of the common stock of Astro Company and 80% of the common stock of Bio Company. Astro owns the remaining 20% interest in Bio's common stock, for which it paid $8,000, and which it carries at cost, because there is no ready market for Bio's stock. The condensed balance sheets for Astro and Bio as of December 31, 2007, were:

	Astro	Bio
Assets	$300,000	120,000
Liabilities	$100,000	$60,000
Common Stock	50,000	40,000
Retained Earnings	150,000	20,000
Total	$300,000	120,000

What amount should be reported as total owner's equity in a combined balance sheet for Astro and Bio as of December 31, 2007?

A. $260,000
B. $252,000
C. $212,000
D. $200,000

AICPA.082082FAR-I.A

106. The following information pertains to shipments of merchandise from Home Office to Branch during 2007:

Home Office's cost of merchandise	$160,000
Intracompany billing	200,000
Sales by Branch	250,000
Unsold merchandise at Branch on December 31, 2007	20,000

In the combined income statement of Home Office and Branch for the year ended December 31, 2007, what amount of the above transactions should be included in sales?

A. $250,000
B. $230,000
C. $200,000
D. $180,000

Variable Interest Entities (VIEs)

AICPA.081267FAR-SIM

107. Which of the following legal forms of business combination will result in the need to prepare consolidated financial statements?

	Merger	Acquisition	Consolidation
A.	Yes	Yes	Yes
B.	Yes	Yes	No
C.	No	No	Yes
D.	No	Yes	No

AICPA.081268FAR-SIM

108. In which one of the following cases is the subsidiary *most likely* to be reported as an unconsolidated subsidiary?

A. The subsidiary is in an industry unrelated to the parent.
B. The subsidiary has a fiscal year-end that is one month different from the parent's year-end.
C. The subsidiary is in legal bankruptcy.
D. The subsidiary has a controlling interest in another entity.

AICPA.081269FAR-SIM

109. Parco has the following three subsidiaries: Finco, Serco, and Euroco. Finco is a 100% owned finance subsidiary. Serco is an 80% owned service company. Euroco is a 100% owned foreign subsidiary that conducts operations in Western Europe. Which one of the following is the *most likely* number of entities, including Parco, to be included in Parco's consolidated financial statements?

A. One.
B. Two.
C. Three.
D. Four.

Public Company Reporting Topics (SEC, EPS, Interim, and Segment)

U.S. Securities and Exchange Commission (SEC)

SEC—Role and Standard-Setting Process

AICPA.101191FAR-SIM

110. The SEC is comprised of five commissioners, appointed by the President of the United States, and five divisions. Which of the following divisions is responsible for overseeing compliance with the securities acts?

A. Division of Corporate Finance.
B. Division of Enforcement.
C. Division of Trading and Markets.
D. Division of Investment Management.

AICPA.101193FAR-SIM

111. Even though the SEC delegates the creation of accounting standards to the private sector, the SEC frequently comments on accounting and auditing issues. The main pronouncements published by the SEC are:

A. Federal Reporting Updates (FRU).
B. Financial Reporting Releases (FRR).
C. Staff Auditing Bulletins (SAB).
D. Accounting Principles Opinions (APO).

SEC Reporting Requirements

aicpa.aq.sec.report.001_17

112. Which of the following is the annual report that is filed with the United States Securities and Exchange Commission (SEC)?

A. Form 8-K.
B. Form 10-K.
C. Form S-1.
D. Form 10-Q.

aicpa.aq.sec.report.002_0818

113. A nonaccelerated filer, as established by the U.S. Securities and Exchange Commission, includes companies with less than exactly what amount in public equity float?

A. $75 million
B. $100 million
C. $125 million
D. $150 million

aicpa.aq.sec.report.003_18

114. Which of the following reports would a company file to meet the U.S. Securities and Exchange Commission's requirements for unaudited, interim financial statements reviewed by an independent accountant?

A. Form 10-Q
B. Form 10-K
C. 14A Proxy Statement
D. Form S-1

AICPA.101179FAR

115. Which of the following is not a required component of the 10-K filing?

A. Product market share.
B. Description of the business.
C. Market price of common stock.
D. Executive compensation.

assess.AICPA.FAR.sec.report-0028

116. U.S. Securities and Exchange Commission (SEC) regulations for the financial statement presentation and disclosure requirements of SEC filings can be found in

A. Regulation S-B.
B. Regulation S-K.
C. Regulation S-T.
D. Regulation S-X.

Earnings per Share

Introduction to Earnings per Share

AICPA.051183FAR-FA

117. During the current year, Comma Co. had outstanding: 25,000 shares of common stock, 8,000 shares of $20 par, 10% cumulative preferred stock, and 3,000 bonds that are $1,000 par and 9% convertible. The bonds were originally issued at par, and each bond was convertible into 30 shares of common stock. During the year, net income was $200,000, no dividends were declared, and the tax rate was 30%.

What amount was Comma's basic earnings per share for the current year?

A. $3.38
B. $7.36
C. $7.55
D. $8.00

AICPA.070766FAR

118. Jen Co. had 200,000 shares of common stock and 20,000 shares of 10%, $100 par value cumulative preferred stock. No dividends on common stock were declared during the year. Net income was $2,000,000. What was Jen's basic earnings per share?

A. $9.00
B. $9.09
C. $10.00
D. $11.11

AICPA.120638FAR

119. Wood Co.'s dividends on noncumulative preferred stock have been declared but not paid. Wood has not declared or paid dividends on its cumulative preferred stock in the current or the prior year and has reported a net loss in the current year. For the purpose of computing basic earnings per share, how should the income available to common stockholders be calculated?

   A. The current-year dividends and the dividends in arrears on the cumulative preferred stock should be added to the net loss, but the dividends on the noncumulative preferred stock should NOT be included in the calculation.
   B. The dividends on the noncumulative preferred stock should be added to the net loss, but the current-year dividends and the dividends in arrears on the cumulative preferred stock should NOT be included in the calculation.
   C. The dividends on the noncumulative preferred stock and the current-year dividends on the cumulative preferred stock should be added to the net loss.
   D. Neither the dividends on the noncumulative preferred stock nor the current-year dividends and the dividends in arrears on cumulative preferred stock should be included in the calculation.

Basic Earnings per Share

AICPA.120633FAR

120. Balm Co. had 100,000 shares of common stock outstanding as of January 1. The following events occurred during the year:

4/1	Issued 30,000 shares of common stock.
6/1	Issued 36,000 shares of common stock.
7/1	Declared a 5% stock dividend.
9/1	Purchased as treasury stock 35,000 shares of its common stock. Balm used the cost method to account for the treasury stock.

What is Balm's weighted average of common stock outstanding at December 31?

   A. 131,000
   B. 139,008
   C. 150,675
   D. 162,342

assess.AICPA.FAR.basic.eps-0020

121. A company had 400,000 shares of common stock issued and outstanding on January 1, year 1, and had the following equity transactions for year 1:

Transactions	Date
Issued 200,000 new shares for cash	April 1
Issued new shares as a result of a 3-for-1 stock split	July 1
Purchased 300,000 shares treasury stock for cash	October 1

What should the company use as the denominator for the calculation of basic earnings per share for year ended December 31, year 1?

   A. 1,650,000
   B. 1,575,000
   C. 1,325,000
   D. 1,075,000

Diluted Earnings per Share

AICPA.070789FAR

122. The following information pertains to Ceil Co., a company whose common stock trades in a public market:

Shares outstanding at 1/1	100,000
Stock dividend at 3/31	24,000
Stock issuance at 6/30	5,000

What is the weighted average number of shares Ceil should use to calculate its basic earnings per share for the year ended December 31?

   A. 120,500
   B. 123,000
   C. 126,500
   D. 129,000

AICPA.083700FAR-SIM

123. The treasury stock method of entering stock options into the calculation of diluted EPS:

   A. Is used only for dilutive treasury stock.
   B. Computes the increase in common shares outstanding from assumed exercise of options to be the number of shares under option.
   C. Is called the treasury stock method because the proceeds from assumed exercise are assumed to be used to purchase treasury stock.
   D. Assumes the treasury shares are purchased at year-end.

Earnings per Share and IFRS

AICPA.101221FAR-SIM

124. If everything else is held constant, earnings per share is increased by:

   A. Purchase of treasury stock.
   B. Issuance of new shares of common stock.
   C. Payment of a cash dividend to common stockholders.
   D. Payment of a cash dividend to both preferred and common stockholders.

AICPA.101222FAR-SIM

125. AB Company reported earnings per share of $10.50 on income before discontinued operations, ($2.00) on income (loss) attributed to discontinued operations, and $8.50 on net income. Which EPS figure is more relevant to a potential investor?

   A. ($2.00)
   B. $7.50
   C. $8.50
   D. $10.50

AICPA.101223FAR-SIM

126. LM Company has net income of $130,000, weighted average shares of common stock outstanding of 50,000, and preferred dividends for the period of $20,000. What is LM's earnings per share of common stock?

   A. $2.60
   B. $2.50
   C. $2.20
   D. $0.40

Segment Reporting

aicpa.aq.seg.report.001_17

127. A public entity sells steel for use in construction. One of its customer's accounts for 43% of sales, and another customer accounts for 40% of sales. What should the entity disclose in its annual financial statements about these two customers?

   A. The payment terms of accounts receivable due from each of the two customers.
   B. The amount of the entity's revenue from each of the two customers.
   C. The names of the two customers.
   D. The financial condition of the two customers.

AICPA.070783FAR

128. Which of the following types of entities are required to report on business segments?

   A. Nonpublic business enterprises
   B. Publicly traded enterprises
   C. Not-for-profit enterprises
   D. Joint ventures

Interim Financial Reporting

Interim Reporting Principles

aicpa.aq.interim.rep.prin.001_17

129. Yellow Co. received a large worker's compensation claim of $90,000 in the third quarter for an injury occurring in the third quarter. How should Yellow account for the transaction in its interim financial report?

   A. Recognize $30,000 for each of the first three quarters.
   B. Recognize $90,000 in the third quarter.
   C. Recognize $22,500 ratably over the four quarters of the year.
   D. Disclose the $90,000 in the third quarter and recognize it at year end.

AICPA.101138FAR

130. Bard Co., a calendar-year corporation, reported income before income tax expense of $10,000 and income tax expense of $1,500 in its interim income statement for the first quarter of the year. Bard had income before income tax expense of $20,000 for the second quarter and an estimated effective annual rate of 25%. What amount should Bard report as income tax expense in its interim income statement for the second quarter?

   A. $3,500
   B. $5,000
   C. $6,000
   D. $7,500

AICPA.950503FAR-FA

131. ASC 270, Interim Reporting, concluded that interim financial reporting should be viewed primarily in which of the following ways?

   A. As useful only if activity is spread evenly throughout the year.
   B. As if the interim period were an annual accounting period.
   C. As reporting for an integral part of an annual period.
   D. As reporting under a comprehensive basis of accounting other than GAAP.

Special Purpose Frameworks

Cash, Modified Cash, Income Tax

AICPA.100911FAR-OCB-SIM

132. Which one of the following is not an other comprehensive basis of accounting?

    A. Pure cash basis.
    B. Modified cash basis.
    C. Pure accrual basis.
    D. Income tax basis.

AICPA.100912FAR-OCB-SIM

133. When a set of financial statements is prepared using the cash basis or the modified cash basis of accounting, which one of the following is *least likely* to be an appropriate financial statement title?

    A. Statement of Cash Receipts and Cash Disbursements.
    B. Balance Sheet.
    C. Income Statement.
    D. Statement of Financial Position.

AICPA.100916FAR-OCB-SIM

134. Which of the following items would be recognized in financial statements prepared using an income tax basis of accounting relating to permanent differences?

	Nontaxable Income	Nondeductible Expenses
A.	Yes	Yes
B.	Yes	No
C.	No	Yes
D.	No	No

Private Company Council

aicpa.aq.private.com.002_18

135. If a company that is **not** a public business entity wants to apply the simplified hedge accounting approach to a cash flow hedge of a variable rate borrowing with a receive-variable, pay-fixed interest rate swap, which of the following is a condition that must be met?

    A. The notional value of the swap is greater than the principal of the hedged borrowing.
    B. The fair value of the interest rate swap executed has a value equivalent to the hedged borrowing.
    C. The variable interest rate on the interest rate swap is capped at 250 basis points above the cap on the hedged borrowing.
    D. The variable interest rate on the interest rate swap and the variable interest rate on the hedged borrowing are linked to the same index.

AICPA.140400FAR-SIM

136. The Private Company Council has issued modified accounting for private companies for what aspect of Goodwill?

    A. Goodwill impairment testing.
    B. Goodwill amortization.
    C. Goodwill measurement.
    D. Goodwill reporting.

Select Financial Statement Accounts

Cash and Cash Equivalents

Cash

AICPA.051178FAR-FA

137. The following are held by Smite Co.:

Cash in checking account	$20,000
Cash in bond sinking fund account	30,000
Postdated check from customer dated one month from balance sheet date	250
Petty cash	200
Commercial paper (matures in two months)	7,000
Certificate of deposit (matures in six months)	5,000

What amount should be reported as cash and cash equivalents on Smite's balance sheet?

A. $57,200
B. $32,200
C. $27,450
D. $27,200

AICPA.930510FAR-P1-FA

138. Cook Co. had the following balances on December 31, 20X4:

Cash in checking account	$350,000
Cash in money market account	250,000
U.S. Treasury bill, purchased 12/1/X4, maturing 2/28/X5	800,000
U.S. Treasury bond, purchased 3/1/X4, maturing 2/28/X5	500,000

Cook's policy is to treat as cash equivalents all highly liquid investments with a maturity of three months or less when purchased. What amount should Cook report as cash and cash equivalents in its December 31, 20X4, balance sheet?

A. $600,000
B. $1,150,000
C. $1,400,000
D. $1,900,000

AICPA.940512FAR-FA

139. The following information pertains to Grey Co. on December 31, 20X3:

Checkbook balance	$12,000
Bank statement balance	16,000
Check drawn on Grey's account, payable to a vendor, dated and recorded 12/31/X3 but not mailed until 1/10/X4	1,800

On Grey's December 31, 20X3 balance sheet, what amount should be reported as cash?

A. $12,000
B. $13,800
C. $14,200
D. $16,000

Bank Reconciliations

aicpa.aq.bank.rec.001_17

140. Alton Co. had a cash balance of $32,300 recorded in its general ledger at the end of the month, prior to receiving its bank statement. Reconciliation of the bank statement reveals the following information:

Bank service charge: $15

Check deposited and returned for insufficient funds check: $120

Deposit recorded in the general ledger as $258 but should be $285

Checks outstanding: $1,800

After reconciling its bank statement, what amount should Alton report as its cash account balance?

A. $30,338
B. $30,392
C. $32,138
D. $32,192

AICPA.083703FAR-SIM

141. A bank reconciliation with the headings "Balance per Books" and "Balance per Bank" lists three adjustments under the former and four adjustments under the latter. The company makes separate adjusting entries for each item in the reconciliation that requires an adjustment. How many adjusting entries are recorded?

A. 3
B. 4
C. 7
D. 0

AICPA.110568FAR

142. Hilltop Co.'s monthly bank statement shows a balance of $54,200. Reconciliation of the statement with company books reveals the following information:

Bank service charge	$10
Insufficient funds check	650
Checks outstanding	1,500
Deposits in transit	350
Check deposited by Hilltop and cleared by the bank for $125 but improperly recorded by Hilltop as $152	

What is the net cash balance after the reconciliation?

A. $52,363
B. $53,023
C. $53,050
D. $53,077

Receivables

Accounts Receivable—Accounting and Reporting

AICPA.900510FAR-P1-FA

143. On June 1, 2005, Pitt Corp. sold merchandise with a list price of $5,000 to Burr on account. Pitt allowed trade discounts of 30% and 20%. Credit terms were 2/15, n/40 and the sale was made FOB shipping point. Pitt prepaid $200 of delivery costs for Burr as an accommodation.

On June 12, 2005, Pitt received from Burr a remittance in full payment amounting to

A. $2,744
B. $2,940
C. $2,944
D. $3,140

CACL-0011

144. Steven Corporation began operations in year 1. For the year ended December 31, year 1, Steven made available the following information:

Total merchandise purchases for the year	$350,000
Merchandise inventory at December 31, year 1	70,000
Collections from customers	200,000

All merchandise was marked to sell at 40% above cost. Assuming that all sales are on a credit basis and all receivables are collectible, what should be the balance in accounts receivable at December 31, year 1?

A. $50,000
B. $192,000
C. $250,000
D. $290,000

CACL-0018

145. When the allowance method of recognizing bad debt expense is used, the entries at the time of collection of a small account previously written off would

A. Increase net income.
B. Decrease the allowance for doubtful accounts.
C. Have no effect on the allowance for doubtful accounts.
D. Increase the allowance for doubtful accounts.

Uncollectible—Direct Write-Off and Allowance

AICPA.120626FAR

146. During the year, Hauser Co. wrote off a customer's account receivable. Hauser used the allowance method for uncollectable accounts. What impact would the write-off have on net income and total assets?

	Net income	Total assets
A.	Decrease	Decrease
B.	Decrease	No effect
C.	No effect	Decrease
D.	No effect	No effect

AICPA.930517FAR-P1-FA

147. The following information pertains to Tara Co.'s accounts receivable on December 31, Year 4:

Days outstanding	Amount	Estimated % uncollectible
0-60	$120,000	1%
61-120	90,000	2%
Over 120	100,000	6%
	$310,000	

During 2004, Tara wrote off $7,000 in receivables and recovered $4,000 that had been written off in prior years. Tara's December 31, 2003, allowance for uncollectible accounts was $22,000. Under the aging method, what amount of allowance for uncollectible accounts should Tara report on December 31, 2004?

A. $9,000
B. $10,000
C. $13,000
D. $19,000

Allowance—Income Statement and Balance Sheet Approach

AICPA.110576FAR

148. Marr Co. had the following sales and accounts receivable balances, prior to any adjustments at year end:

Credit sales	$10,000,000
Accounts receivable	3,000,000
Allowance for uncollectible accounts (debit balance)	50,000

Marr uses 3% of accounts receivable to determine its allowance for uncollectible accounts at year end. By what amount should Marr adjust its allowance for uncollectible accounts at year end?

A. $0
B. $40,000
C. $90,000
D. $140,000

AICPA.941145FAR-FA

149. Inge Co. determined that the net value of its accounts receivable on December 31, 2005, based on an aging of the receivables, was $325,000. Additional information is as follows:

Allowance for uncollectible accounts – 1/1/05	$30,000
Uncollectible accounts written off during 2005	18,000
Uncollectible accounts recovered during 2005	2,000
Accounts receivable at 12/31/05	350,000

For 2005, what would be Inge's uncollectible accounts expense?

A. $5,000
B. $11,000
C. $15,000
D. $21,000

Notes Receivable

AICPA.070791FAR

150. On December 31, 1999, Key Co. received two $10,000 noninterest-bearing notes from customers in exchange for services rendered. The note from Alpha Co., which is due in nine months, was made under customary trade terms, but the note from Omega Co., which is due in two years, was not. The market interest rate for both notes at the date of issuance is 8%. The present value of $1 due in nine months at 8% is .944. The present value of $1 due in two years at 8% is .857. At what amounts should these two notes receivable be reported in Key's December 31, 1999, balance sheet?

	Alpha	Omega
A.	$9,440	$8,570
B.	$10,000	$8,570
C.	$9,440	$10,000
D.	$10,000	$10,000

AICPA.941138FAR-FA

151. Leaf Co. purchased from Oak Co. a $20,000, 8%, 5-year note that required five equal annual year-end payments of $5,009. The note was discounted to yield a 9% rate to Leaf. At the date of purchase, Leaf recorded the note at its present value of $19,485.

What should be the total interest revenue earned by Leaf over the life of this note?

A. $5,045
B. $5,560
C. $8,000
D. $9,000

AICPA.950508FAR-FA

152. On December 30, 2005, Chang Co. sold a machine to Door Co. in exchange for a noninterest-bearing note requiring ten annual payments of $10,000. Door made the first payment on December 30, 2005. The market interest rate for similar notes at the date of issuance was 8%. Information on present value factors is as follows:

Period	Present value of $1 at 8%	Present value of ordinary annuity of $1 at 8%
9	0.50	6.25
10	0.46	6.71

In its December 31, 2005, balance sheet, what amount should Chang report as note receivable?

A. $45,000
B. $46,000
C. $62,500
D. $67,100

Criteria for Sale of Receivables

AICPA.920541FAR-P1-FA

153. Ace Co. sold King Co. a $20,000, 8%, 5-year note that required five equal annual year-end payments. This note was discounted to yield a 9% rate to King. The present value factors of an ordinary annuity of $1 for five periods are as follows:

8%	3.992
9%	3.890

What should be the total interest revenue earned by King on this note?

A. $9,000
B. $8,000
C. $5,560
D. $5,050

AICPA.931115FAR-P1-FA

154. Roth, Inc. received from a customer a one-year, $500,000 note bearing annual interest of 8%. After holding the note for six months, Roth discounted the note at Regional Bank at an effective interest rate of 10%. What amount of cash did Roth receive from the bank?

A. $540,000
B. $523,810
C. $513,000
D. $495,238

Factoring, Assignment, and Pledging

AICPA.101058FAR

155. Milton Co. pledged some of its accounts receivable to Good Neighbor Financing Corporation in return for a loan. Which of the following statements is correct?

A. Good Neighbor Financing cannot take title to the receivables if Milton does not repay the loan. Title can only be taken if the receivables are factored.
B. Good Neighbor Financing will assume the responsibility of collecting the receivables.
C. Milton will retain control of the receivables.
D. Good Neighbor Financing will take title to the receivables, and will return title to Milton after the loan is paid.

AICPA.101059FAR

156. On April 1, Aloe, Inc. factored $80,000 of its accounts receivable without recourse. The factor retained 10% of the accounts receivable as an allowance for sales returns and charged a 5% commission on the gross amount of the factored receivables. What amount of cash did Aloe receive from the factored receivables?

A. $68,000
B. $68,400
C. $72,000
D. $76,000

AICPA.931141FAR-P1-FA

157. On November 1, 2004, Davis Co. discounted with recourse at 10%, a one-year, noninterest-bearing, $20,500 note receivable maturing on January 31, 2005.

What amount of contingent liability for this note must Davis disclose in its financial statements for the year ended December 31, 2004?

A. $0
B. $20,000
C. $20,333
D. $20,500

Notes Receivable—Impairment

AICPA.082108FAR-II.B

158. Choose the correct accounting by the creditor for a loan impairment. Column (1): recognize a loss or expense upon recognizing the impairment. Column (2): rate of interest to use

in computing the revised book value of the receivable after the impairment.

	1	2
A.	Yes	Original effective rate
B.	Yes	New implied effective rate
C.	No	Original effective rate
D.	No	New implied effective rate

AICPA.083708FAR-SIM

159. A creditor's note receivable has a carrying value of $60,000 at the end of Year 1. Based on information about the debtor, the creditor believes the note is impaired and establishes the new carrying value of the note to be $25,000 at the end of Year 1. During Years 2 and 3, the debtor pays $14,000 on the note each year (total payments, $28,000). For Year 3, under which method of the two indicated is interest revenue recognized?

	Interest Method	Cost Recovery Method
A.	Yes	Yes
B.	No	No
C.	Yes	No
D.	No	Yes

AICPA.110603FAR-SIM

160. Under IFRS, a cash generating unit (CGU) is:

A. The smallest business segment.
B. Any grouping of assets that generates cash flows.
C. Any group of assets that are reported separately to management.
D. The smallest group of assets that generates independent cash flows from continuing use.

Inventory

Introduction to Inventory

aicpa.aq.intro.invent.001_17

161. During a reporting period, a computer manufacturing company used raw materials of $50,000, had direct labor costs of $75,000, and factory overhead of $30,000. Other expenses were for advertising of $5,000, staff salaries of $10,000, and bad debt of $3,000. The company did not have a beginning balance in any inventory account. All goods manufactured during the period were sold during the period. What amount was the company's cost of goods sold during the reporting period?

A. $155,000
B. $160,000

C. $170,000
D. $173,000

aicpa.aq.intro.invent.002_17

162. On June 1, Year 2, Archer, Inc. issued a purchase order to Cotton Co. for a new copier machine. The machine requires one month to produce and is shipped f.o.b. destination on July 1, Year 2, and is received by Archer on July 15, Year 2. Cotton issues a sales invoice dated July 2, Year 2, for the machine. As of what date should Archer record a liability for the machine?

A. June 1, Year 2
B. July 1, Year 2
C. July 2, Year 2
D. July 15, Year 2

AICPA.941113FAR-FA

163. Herc Co.'s inventory on December 31, 2005 was $1,500,000, based on a physical count priced at cost, and before any necessary adjustment for the following:

Merchandise costing $90,000, shipped FOB shipping point from a vendor on December 30, 2005, was received and recorded on January 5, 2006.

Goods in the shipping area were excluded from inventory although shipment was not made until January 4, 2006. The goods, billed to the customer FOB shipping point on December 30, 2005, had a cost of $120,000.

What amount should Herc report as inventory in its December 31, 2005, balance sheet?

A. $1,500,000
B. $1,590,000
C. $1,620,000
D. $1,710,000

Periodic Inventory System and Cost-Flow Assumption

AICPA.930548FAR-P1-FA

164. The following information pertains to Deal Corp.'s 2004 cost of goods sold:

Inventory, 12/31/03	$90,000
2004 purchases	124,000
2004 write-off of obsolete inventory	34,000
Inventory, 12/31/04	30,000

The inventory written off became obsolete due to an unexpected and unusual technological advance by a competitor. In its 2004 income statement, what amount should Deal report as cost of goods sold?

A. $218,000
B. $184,000
C. $150,000
D. $124,000

AICPA.990511FAR-FA

165. The following information pertained to Azur Co. for the year:

Purchases	$102,800
Purchase discounts	10,280
Freight-in	15,420
Freight-out	5,140
Beginning inventory	30,840
Ending inventory	20,560

What amount should Azur report as cost of goods sold for the year?

A. $102,800
B. $118,220
C. $123,360
D. $128,500

Perpetual Inventory System and Cost-Flow Assumption

aicpa.aq.perpetual.cost.001_18

166. Beck Co.'s inventory of trees is as follows:

Beginning I((nventory		10 trees @ $50
March 4	purchased	6 trees @ 55
March 12	sold	8 trees @ 100
March 20	purchased	9 trees @ 60
March 27	sold	7 trees @ 105
March 30	purchased	4 trees @ 65

What was Beck's cost of goods sold using the last in, first out (LIFO) perpetual method?

A. $910
B. $850
C. $808
D. $775

AICPA.020507FAR-FA

167. During periods of inflation, a perpetual inventory system would result in the same dollar amount of ending inventory as a periodic inventory system under which of the following inventory valuation methods?

	FIFO	LIFO
A.	Yes	No
B.	Yes	Yes
C.	No	Yes
D.	No	No

AICPA051165FAR-TI

168. Which of the following statements regarding inventory accounting systems is true?

A. A disadvantage of the perpetual inventory system is that the inventory dollar amounts used for interim reporting purposes are estimated amounts.
B. A disadvantage of the periodic inventory system is that the cost of goods sold amount used for financial reporting purposes includes both the cost of inventory sold and inventory shortages.
C. An advantage of the perpetual inventory system is that the record keeping required to maintain the system is relatively simple.
D. An advantage of the periodic inventory system is that it provides a continuous record of the inventory balance.

Comparison: FIFO, LIFO, and Weighted Average

AICPA.0821122FAR-II.C

169. Which inventory costing method would a company that wishes to maximize profits in a period of rising prices use?

A. FIFO
B. Dollar-value LIFO.
C. Weighted average.
D. Moving average.

AICPA.920524FAR-TH-FA

170. When the FIFO inventory method is used during periods of rising prices, a perpetual inventory system results in an ending inventory cost that is

A. The same as in a periodic inventory system.
B. Higher than in a periodic inventory system.
C. Lower than in a periodic inventory system.
D. Higher or lower than in a periodic inventory system, depending on whether physical quantities have increased or decreased.

AICPA.951109FAR-FA

171. A company decided to change its inventory valuation method from FIFO to LIFO in a period of rising prices. What was the result of the change on ending inventory and net income in the year of the change?

	Ending inventory	Net income
A.	Increase	Increase
B.	Increase	Decrease
C.	Decrease	Decrease
D.	Decrease	Increase

Dollar-Value LIFO

AICPA.010501FAR-FA

172. Bach Co. adopted the dollar-value LIFO inventory method as of January 1, 2006. A single inventory pool and an internally computed price index are used to compute Bach's LIFO inventory layers. Information about Bach's dollar-value inventory follows:

	Inventory	
Date	At base-year cost	At current-year cost
1/1/06	$90,000	$90,000
2006 layer	20,000	30,000
2007 layer	40,000	80,000

What was the price index used to compute Bach's 2007 dollar-value LIFO inventory layer?

A. 1.09
B. 1.25
C. 1.33
D. 2.00

AICPA.110564FAR

173. In January, Stitch, Inc. adopted the dollar-value LIFO method of inventory valuation. At adoption, inventory was valued at $50,000. During the year, inventory increased $30,000 using base-year prices, and prices increased 10%. The designated market value of Stitch's inventory exceeded its cost at year-end. What amount of inventory should Stitch report in its year-end balance sheet?

A. $80,000
B. $83,000
C. $85,000
D. $88,000

Gross Margin and Relative Sales Value Method

aicpa.aq.gross.marg.001_18

174. Lyon Co. estimated its ending inventory using a method based on the financial statements of prior periods in order to prepare its quarterly interim financial statements. What type of inventory system and method of estimating ending inventory is Lyon using?

	Inventory system	Method of estimating ending inventory
A.	Perpetual	Retail method
B.	Perpetual	Gross profit method
C.	Periodic	Sales method
D.	Periodic	Gross profit method

AICPA.061203FAR

175. A flash flood swept through Hat, Inc.'s warehouse on May 1. After the flood, Hat's accounting records showed the following:

Inventory, January 1	$35,000
Purchases, January 1 through May 1	200,000
Sales, January 1 through May 1	250,000
Inventory not damaged by flood	30,000
Gross profit percentage on sales	40%

What amount of inventory was lost in the flood?

A. $55,000
B. $85,000
C. $120,000
D. $150,000

AICPA.083710FAR-SIM

176. The following two inventory items were purchased as a group in a liquidation sale for $1,000.

Item	Replacement Cost	Carrying Value on Seller's Books
A	$400	$390
B	700	755

The firm purchasing the inventory records item A at what amount?

A. $341
B. $390
C. $364
D. $500

Retail Inventory Method

AICPA.083713FAR-SIM

177. How does the retail inventory method establish the lower-of-cost-or-market valuation for ending inventory?

    A. The procedure is applied on a cost basis at the unit level.
    B. By excluding net markups from the cost-to-retail ratio.
    C. By excluding beginning inventory from the cost-to-retail ratio.
    D. By excluding net markdowns from the cost-to-retail ratio.

AICPA.901116FAR-TH-FA

178. The retail inventory method includes which of the following in the calculation of both cost and retail amounts of goods available for sale?

    A. Purchase returns.
    B. Sales returns.
    C. Net markups.
    D. Freight in.

Dollar-Value LIFO Retail

AICPA.082111FAR-II.C

179. A firm uses the dollar value LIFO retail method and has $2,000 in beginning inventory at retail at the beginning of the current year. The base year equivalent of this amount is $1,600. The base year index is 1.00. The beginning inventory reported in the Balance Sheet is $800. During the current year, the firm purchased $12,000 of inventory at cost and marked that up to $40,000. Sales for the year were $28,000. The relevant ending price index is 1.60. What amount does this firm report as inventory in its Balance Sheet at the end of the current year?

    A. $4,286
    B. $13,440
    C. $4,232
    D. $4,200

AICPA.083716FAR-SIM

180. Information for a firm using the dollar value (DV) LIFO retail method follows. The cost to retail (C/R) is provided along with price level indices. The data reflects the use of the method through year one.

Layer	Retail Base	Retail Index	Retail Current	DV LIFO C/R	DV LIFO Cost
Base	$200	1.00	$200	.40	$80
year one	80	1.10	88	.34	$30

For year two, ending inventory at retail (by count) totaled $450. The ending price-level index for the year was 1.15. The cost-to-retail ratio was .42. What is the ending inventory for financial reporting purposes for this firm?

    A. $164
    B. $54
    C. $189
    D. $177

Subsequent Measurement of Inventory

AICPA.110573FAR

181. The replacement cost of an inventory item is below the net realizable value and above the net realizable value less a normal profit margin. The inventory item's original cost is above the net realizable value. Under the lower of cost or market method, the inventory item should be valued at

    A. Original cost.
    B. Replacement cost.
    C. Net realizable value.
    D. Net realizable value less normal profit margin.

AICPA.120627FAR

182. The original cost of an inventory item is above the replacement cost. The inventory item's replacement cost is above the net realizable value. Under the lower of cost or market method, the inventory item should be valued at

    A. Original cost.
    B. Replacement cost.
    C. Net realizable value.
    D. Net realizable value LESS normal profit margin.

Inventory Errors

AICPA.083718FAR-SIM

183. If ending inventory for 20x5 is understated because certain items were missed in the count, then:

    A. Net income for 20x5 will be overstated.
    B. CGS for 20x5 will be understated.
    C. Net income for 20x5 will be understated, but net income for 20x6 will be unaffected.
    D. Net income for 20x5 will be understated and CGS for 20x6 will be understated.

AICPA.083719FAR-SIM

184. When an inventory overstatement in year one counterbalances in year two, this means:

   A. There are no reporting errors, even if the overstatement is never discovered.
   B. A prior period adjustment is recorded if the error is discovered in year three.
   C. The year one Balance Sheet does not need to be restated if the error is discovered in year three.
   D. A prior period adjustment is recorded if the error is discovered in year two.

Losses on Purchase Commitments

AICPA.083721FAR-SIM

185. Losses on purchase commitments are recorded at the end of the current year when:

   A. The current cost of the inventory is less than the inventory cost in the purchase contract.
   B. The purchase contract is irrevocable.
   C. The contractual cost of the inventory in an irrevocable purchase contract exceeds the current cost.
   D. The buyer purchased a quantity of inventory that was not sufficient to avoid a LIFO liquidation.

Inventory and IFRS

aicpa.aq.invent.ifrs.001_17

186. As of December 31, Year 2, a company has an inventory item that was originally purchased for $80 in Year 1. The inventory item was written down to its net realizable value of $60 as of December 31, Year 1. As of December 31, Year 2, the inventory item had a net realizable value of $75 and a replacement cost of $65. Normal profit margins for this company are 20%. Under IFRS, what is the carrying amount of the inventory item as of December 31, Year 2?

   A. $60
   B. $65
   C. $75
   D. $80

assess.AICPA.FAR.invent.ifrs-0014

187. At the end of year 1, a company reduced its inventory cost from $100 to its net realizable value of $80. As of the end of year 2, the inventory was still on hand, and its net realizable value increased to $150. Under IFRS, what journal entry should the company record for year 2 to properly report the inventory value?

   A. Debit inventory for $20 and credit expense for $20.
   B. Debit inventory for $70 and credit expense for $70.
   C. Debit inventory for $70, credit retained earnings for $50, and credit expense for $20.
   D. Debit inventory for $20, debit expense for $30, and credit retained earnings for $50.

assess.AICPA.FAR.invent.ifrs-0030

188. The following information relates to a company's year-end inventory:

Inventory cost	$910
Selling price of inventory	$1,000
Normal profit margin	10% of selling price
Current replacement cost	$740
Cost of completion and disposal	$100

Under IFRS, what is the company's year-end inventory balance?

   A. $740
   B. $800
   C. $900
   D. $910

Property, Plant, and Equipment

Categories and Presentation

aicpa.aq.cat.pres.001_17

189. A company issued a purchase order on December 15, Year 1, for a piece of capital equipment that costs $100,000. The capital equipment was shipped from the vendor on December 31, Year 1, and received by the company on January 5, Year 2. The equipment was installed and placed in service on February 1, Year 2. On what date should the depreciation expense begin?

   A. December 15, Year 1
   B. December 31, Year 1
   C. January 5, Year 2
   D. February 1, Year 2

AICPA.101216FAR-SIM

190. Which of the following is not requirement for an asset to be categorized as a plant asset?

    A. Have physical substance.
    B. Have a useful life of at least three years.
    C. Currently used in operations.
    D. Not held for investment purposes.

AICPA.130723FAR

191. A company recently moved to a new building. The old building is being actively marketed for sale, and the company expects to complete the sale in four months. Each of the following statements is correct regarding the old building, **except**:

    A. It will be reclassified as an asset held for sale.
    B. It will be classified as a current asset.
    C. It will **no** longer be depreciated.
    D. It will be valued at historical cost.

Capitalized Costs

aicpa.aq.ppe.ifrs.001_18

192. A corporation issued debt to purchase 10 acres of land for development purposes. Expenditures related to this purchase are as follows:

Description	Amount
Purchase price	$1,000,000
Real estate taxes in arrears	15,000
Debt issuance costs	2,000
Attorney fee—title search on land	5,000

The company should record its acquisition of the land in its financial statements at a value of

    A. $1,000,000.
    B. $1,015,000.
    C. $1,020,000.
    D. $1,022,000.

AICPA.101048FAR

193. Newt Co. sold a warehouse and used the proceeds to acquire a new warehouse. The excess of the proceeds over the carrying amount of the warehouse sold should be reported as a(an):

    A. Reduction of the cost of the new warehouse.
    B. Gain from discontinued operations, net of income taxes.
    C. Part of continuing operations.
    D. Extraordinary gain, net of taxes.

AICPA.101049FAR

194. Talton Co. installed new assembly line production equipment at a cost of $185,000. Talton had to rearrange the assembly line and remove a wall to install the equipment. The rearrangement cost was $12,000 and the wall removal cost was $3,000. The rearrangement did not increase the life of the assembly line but it did make it more efficient. What amount of these costs should be capitalized by Talton?

    A. $185,000
    B. $188,000
    C. $197,000
    D. $200,000

Valuation

AICPA.070770FAR

195. Oak Co., a newly formed corporation, incurred the following expenditures related to land and building:

County assessment for sewer lines	$2,500
Title search fees	625
Cash paid for land with a building to be demolished	135,000
Excavation for construction of basement	21,000
Removal of old building $21,000 less salvage of $5,000	16,000

At what amount should Oak record the land?

    A. $138,125
    B. $153,500
    C. $154,125
    D. $175,625

AICPA.083724FAR-SIM

196. A plant asset under construction by a firm for its own use was completed at the end of the current year. The following costs were incurred:

Materials	$60,000
Labor	30,000
Incremental overhead	10,000
Capitalized interest	20,000

The asset has a service life of 10 years, estimated residual value of $10,000, and will be depreciated under the double declining balance method. At completion, the asset was worth $105,000 at fair value. What amount of depreciation will be recognized on the asset in total over its service life?

A. $105,000
B. $120,000
C. $95,000
D. $90,000

AICPA.08211246FAR-II.C

197. A corporation entered into a purchase commitment to buy inventory. At the end of the accounting period, the current market value of the inventory was less than the fixed purchase price, by a material amount. Which of the following accounting treatments is most appropriate?

A. Describe the nature of the contract in a note to the financial statements, recognize a loss in the Income Statement, and recognize a liability for the accrued loss.
B. Describe the nature of the contract and the estimated amount of the loss in a note to the financial statements, but do not recognize a loss in the Income Statement.
C. Describe the nature of the contract in a note to the financial statements, recognize a loss in the Income Statement, and recognize a reduction in inventory equal to the amount of the loss by use of a valuation account.
D. Neither describe the purchase obligation nor recognize a loss on the Income Statement or Balance Sheet.

Interest Capitalization Basics

AICPA.083732FAR-SIM

198. A firm is constructing a warehouse for its own use and purchased the land for the site immediately before beginning construction. Interest is capitalized on which of the following:

	Warehouse	Land
A.	Yes	Yes
B.	Yes	No
C.	No	Yes
D.	No	No

AICPA.101068FAR

199. Sun Co. was constructing fixed assets that qualified for interest capitalization. Sun had the following outstanding debt issuances during the entire year of construction:

$6,000,000 face value, 8% interest.

$8,000,000 face value, 9% interest.

None of the borrowings were specified for the construction of the qualified fixed asset.

Average expenditures for the year were $1,000,000. What interest rate should Sun use to calculate capitalized interest on the construction?

A. 8.00%
B. 8.50%
C. 8.57%
D. 9.00%

Interest Capitalization LImits

assess.AICPA.FAR.int.cap2-0015

200. A company with a June 30 fiscal year-end entered into a $3,000,000 construction project on April 1 to be completed on September 30. The cumulative construction-in-progress balances at April 30, May 31, and June 30 were $500,000, $800,000, and $1,500,000, respectively. The interest rate on company debt used to finance the construction project was 5% from April 1 through June 30 and 6% from July 1 through September 30. Assuming that the asset is placed into service on October 1, what amount of interest should be capitalized to the project on June 30?

A. $11,666
B. $18,750
C. $75,000
D. $90,000

Post-Acquisition Expenditures

AICPA.083734FAR-SIM

201. Many years after constructing a plant asset, management spent a significant sum on the asset. Which of the following types of expenditures should be capitalized in this instance:

(1) an expenditure for routine maintenance that increases the useful life compared with deferring the maintenance,

(2) an expenditure that increases the useful life of the asset compared with the original estimate assuming normal maintenance at the required intervals,

(3) an expenditure that increases the utility of the asset.

	(1)	(2)	(3)
A.	Yes	Yes	Yes
B.	No	Yes	Yes
C.	No	No	Yes
D.	No	Yes	No

AICPA.930526FAR-TH-FA

202. A building suffered uninsured fire damage. The damaged portion of the building was refurbished with higher quality materials. The cost and related accumulated depreciation of the damaged portion are identifiable. To account for these events, the owner should:

A. Reduce accumulated depreciation equal to the cost of refurbishing.
B. Record a loss in the current period equal to the sum of the cost of refurbishing and the carrying amount of the damaged portion of the building.
C. Capitalize the cost of refurbishing, and record a loss in the current period equal to the carrying amount of the damaged portion of the building.
D. Capitalize the cost of refurbishing by adding the cost to the carrying amount of the building.

Non-Accelerated Depreciation Methods

aicpa.aq.nonacc.dm.001_17

203. Ott Co. purchased a machine at an original cost of $90,000 on January 2, Year 1. The estimated useful life of the machine is 10 years, and the machine has no salvage value. Ott uses the straight-line method to calculate depreciation. On July 1, Year 10, Ott sold the machine for $5,000. What is the amount of gain or loss on the disposal of the machine?

A. $500 loss
B. $500 gain
C. $4,500 loss
D. $4,500 gain

AICPA.08211231FAR-II.D

204. In year 6, Spirit, Inc. determined that the 12-year estimated useful life of a machine purchased for $48,000 in January year 1 should be extended by three years. The machine is being depreciated using the straight-line method and has no salvage value. What amount of depreciation expense should Spirit report in its financial statements for the year ending December 31, year 6?

A. $2,800
B. $3,200
C. $43,200
D. $4,800

AICPA.970510FAR-FA

205. Ichor Co. reported equipment with an original cost of $379,000 and $344,000 and accumulated depreciation of $153,000 and $128,000, respectively, in its comparative financial statements for the years ended December 31, 20X5 and 20X4. During 20X5, Ichor purchased equipment costing $50,000 and sold equipment with a carrying value of $9,000.

What amount should Ichor report as depreciation expense for 20X5?

A. $19,000
B. $25,000
C. $31,000
D. $34,000

Accelerated Depreciation Methods

AICPA.08211232FAR-II.D

206. A depreciable asset has an estimated 15% salvage value. Under which of the following methods, properly applied, would the accumulated depreciation equal the original cost at the end of the asset's estimated useful life?

	Straight-line	Double-declining balance
A.	Yes	Yes
B.	Yes	No
C.	No	Yes
D.	No	No

AICPA.990507FAR-FA

207. Spiro Corp. uses the sum-of-the-years' digits method to depreciate equipment purchased in January 20X3 for $20,000. The estimated salvage value of the equipment is $2,000, and the estimated useful life is four years.

What should Spiro report as the asset's carrying amount as of December 31, 20X5?

A. $1,800
B. $2,000
C. $3,800
D. $4,500

Natural Resources

AICPA.083735FAR-SIM

208. Choose the best association of terms in the natural resources accounting area with the conceptual framework.

A. Successful efforts method-matching.
B. Full costing method-definition of asset.
C. Depletion-fair value accounting.
D. Successful efforts method-definition of asset.

AICPA.083736FAR-SIM

209. A firm began a mineral exploitation venture during the current year by spending (1) $40 million for the mineral rights; (2) $100 million exploring for the minerals, one-fourth of which were successful; and (3) $60 million to develop the site. Management estimated that 20 million tons of ore would ultimately be removed from the property. Wages and other extraction costs for the current year amounted to $10 million. In total, 2 million tons of ore were removed from the deposit in the current year. The entire production for the period was sold. What amount of depletion is recognized during the current year under the full costing method?

    A. $20 million
    B. $12.5 million
    C. $10 million
    D. $21 million

AICPA.083737FAR-SIM

210. A firm began a mineral exploitation venture during the current year by spending (1) $40 million for the mineral rights; (2) $100 million exploring for the minerals, one-fourth of which were successful; and (3) $60 million to develop the site. Management estimated that 20 million tons of ore would ultimately be removed from the property. Wages and other extraction costs for the current year amounted to $10 million. In total, 2 million tons of ore were removed from the deposit in the current year. The entire production for the period was sold. Compute cost of goods sold under the successful efforts method.

    A. $30 million
    B. $12.5 million
    C. $10 million
    D. $22.5 million

PPE: Impairment—Assets for Use and Held-for-Sale

AICPA.061212FAR

211. Which of the following conditions must exist in order for an impairment loss to be recognized?

    I.   The carrying amount of the long-lived asset is less than its fair value.
    II. The carrying amount of the long-lived asset is not recoverable.

    A. I only.
    B. II only.
    C. Both I and II.
    D. Neither I nor II.

AICPA.101074FAR

212. Last year, Katt Co. reduced the carrying amount of its long-lived assets used in operations from $120,000 to $100,000 in connection with its annual impairment review. During the current year, Katt determined that the fair value of the same assets had increased to $130,000. What amount should Katt record as restoration of previously recognized impairment loss in the current year's financial statements?

    A. $0
    B. $10,000
    C. $20,000
    D. $30,000

AICPA.110579FAR

213. Four years ago on January 2, Randall Co. purchased a long-lived asset. The purchase price of the asset was $250,000, with no salvage value. The estimated useful life of the asset was 10 years. Randall used the straight-line method to calculate depreciation expense. An impairment loss on the asset of $30,000 was recognized on December 31 of the current year. The estimated useful life of the asset at December 31 of the current year did not change. What amount should Randall report as depreciation expense in its income statement for the next year?

    A. $20,000.
    B. $22,000.
    C. $25,000.
    D. $30,000.

assess.AICPA.FAR.impair.assets-0033

214. An asset group is being evaluated for an impairment loss. The following financial information is available for the asset group:

Carrying value	$100,000,000
Sum of the undiscounted cash flows	95,000,000
Fair value	80,000,000

What amount of impairment loss, if any, should be recognized?

    A. $0
    B. $5,000,000
    C. $15,000,000
    D. $20,000,000

Impairment and IFRS

AICPA.120205FAR-SIM

215. Restoration of the carrying value of a long-lived asset is permitted under IFRS if the asset's fair value increases subsequent to recording an impairment loss for which of the following?

	Held for use	Held for disposal
A.	Yes	Yes
B.	Yes	No
C.	No	Yes
D.	No	No

AICPA.120206FAR-SIM

216. Under IFRS the test for asset impairment is to compare the carrying value of the asset to its recoverable amount. Which of the following is the recoverable amount according to IFRS?

   A. The greater of future undiscounted cash flows or future discounted cash flows.
   B. The greater of future discounted cash flows or fair value.
   C. The greater of fair value less cost to sell or value in use.
   D. The greater of fair value or value in use.

AICPA.101065FAR

217. Under IFRS, when an entity chooses the revaluation model as its accounting policy for measuring property, plant, and equipment, which of the following statements is correct?

   A. When an asset is revalued, the entire class of property, plant, and equipment to which that asset belongs must be revalued.
   B. When an asset is revalued, individual assets within a class of property, plant, and equipment to which that asset belongs can be revalued.
   C. Revaluations of property, plant and equipment must be made at least every three years.
   D. Increases in an asset's carry value as a result of the first revaluation must be recognized as a component of profit and loss.

PPE and IFRS

AICPA.130725FAR

218. A company has a parcel of land to be used for a future production facility. The company applies the revaluation model under IFRS to this class of assets. In year 1, the company acquired the land for $100,000. At the end of year 1, the carrying amount was reduced to $90,000, which represented the fair value at that date. At the end of year 2, the land was revalued, and the fair value increased to $105,000. How should the company account for the year 2 change in fair value?

   A. By recognizing $10,000 in other comprehensive income.
   B. By recognizing $15,000 in other comprehensive income.
   C. By recognizing $15,000 in profit or loss.
   D. By recognizing $10,000 in profit or loss and $5,000 in other comprehensive income.

assess.AICPA.FAR.ppe.ifrs-0031

219. A transportation company purchased a passenger bus for $100,000 on January 1, year 1. The company expects the bus to be used for 20 years if it follows a maintenance schedule of replacing the engine after 10 years and replacing the seats every 8 years. It estimates that the current cost to replace the engine is $25,000 and the current cost to replace the seats is $10,000. The company uses straight-line depreciation, and the bus has no residual value. The company considers any component equal to or greater than 10% of the overall cost to be significant. Under IFRS, how much depreciation expense should the company recognize for the bus for the year ended December 31, year 1?

   A. $5,000
   B. $7,000
   C. $7,250
   D. $8,500

Nonmonetary Exchange

Commercial Substance

AICPA.110571FAR

220. Which of the following statements correctly describes the proper accounting for nonmonetary exchanges that are deemed to have commercial substance?

   A. It defers any gains and losses.
   B. It defers losses to the extent of any gains.
   C. It recognizes gains and losses immediately.
   D. It defers gains and recognizes losses immediately.

AICPA.130737FAR

221. A company exchanged land with an appraised value of $50,000 and an original cost of $20,000 for machinery with a fair value of $55,000. Assuming that the transaction has commercial substance, what is the gain on the exchange?

    A. $0
    B. $5,000
    C. $30,000
    D. $35,000

No Commercial Substance

AICPA.110572FAR

222. Campbell Corp. exchanged delivery trucks with Highway, Inc. Campbell's truck originally cost $23,000, its accumulated depreciation was $20,000, and its fair value was $5,000. Highway's truck originally cost $23,500, its accumulated depreciation was $19,900, and its fair value was $5,700. Campbell also paid Highway $700 in cash as part of the transaction. The transaction lacks commercial substance. What amount is the new book value for the truck Campbell received?

    A. $5,700
    B. $5,000
    C. $3,700
    D. $3,000

aicpa.aq.no.comm.sub.001_18

223. Charm Co. owns a delivery truck with an original cost of $10,000 and accumulated depreciation of $7,000. Charm acquired a new truck by exchanging the old truck and paying $2,000 in cash. The new truck has a fair value of $5,000 at the time of the exchange. What amount of gain or loss should Charm recognize?

    A. $0
    B. $2,000 gain
    C. $2,000 loss
    D. $3,000 loss

AICPA.950530FAR-FA

224. Slate Co. and Talse Co. exchanged similar plots of land with fair values in excess of carrying amounts. In addition, Slate received cash from Talse to compensate for the difference in land values. The exchange lacks commercial substance.

    As a result of the exchange, Slate should recognize

    A. A gain equal to the difference between the fair value and the carrying amount of the land given up.
    B. A gain in an amount determined by the ratio of cash received to total consideration.

    C. A loss in an amount determined by the ratio of cash received to total consideration.
    D. Neither a gain nor a loss.

Nonmonetary Exchanges and IFRS

AICPA.101237FAR-SIM

225. In a barter transaction where advertising services provided are exchanged for advertising services received, under which of the following situations can the advertising provider recognize revenue for the services performed? Assume the accounting is under IFRS guidelines.

    A. When the advertising services in the exchange are similar
    B. When the fair value of the advertising services received can be reliably measured
    C. When there is a nonbarter transaction for similar advertising services that can be reliably measured with the same counterparty
    D. When there is a nonbarter transaction for similar advertising services that can be reliably measured with a different counterparty

Investments

Introduction—Investments in Equity and Debt Securities

AICPA.081218FAR-SIM

226. Which one of the following is *least likely* to be a factor in determining how an investment in debt or equity securities is accounted for and reported in financial statements?

    A. The nature of the investment
    B. The method of payment used to acquire the investment
    C. The extent or proportion of the investment securities acquired
    D. The purpose for which the investment was made

AICPA.081219FAR-SIM

227. Which of the following statements is true concerning the correct accounting for equity investments?

   I. An investor must account for (measure) all equity investments using fair value.

   II. An investor may elect to account for (measure) some equity investments at fair value.

   A. I only.
   B. II only.
   C. Both I and II.
   D. Neither I nor II.

AICPA.081220FAR-SIM

228. In the absence of other relevant factors, what minimum level of voting ownership is considered to give an investor significant influence over an investee?

   A. 10%
   B. 20%
   C. 50%
   D. 100%

Investments in Equity Securities

Equity Investments at Fair Value

aq.eq.invest.fv.001_17

229. Paxton Corporation purchased 100 shares of Swedberg Company's common stock. The purchase is for $40 per share plus brokerage fees of $280. Paxton's entry to record the investment would include

	Debit	Credit
A.	Cash $4,000	Investment Swedberg $4,000
B.	Investment Swedberg $4,280	Cash $4,280
C.	Investment Swedberg $4,000 Brokerage Fee Expense 280	Cash $4,280
D.	Investment Swedberg $4,000	Cash $4,000

aq.eq.invest.fv.002_17

230. On March 14, Apple Corporation purchased 6,000 shares of Pear Inc. for $25 per share plus a $340 brokerage fee. On June 30, when the shares were trading at $27, Apple prepared an adjustment to fair value and recorded the annual dividend of $0.40 per share. On August 14, Apple sold 4,000 shares of Pear for $29 per share less a brokerage fee of $225. The journal entry at the date of sale would include

   A. a debit to cash for $115,775.
   B. a debit to cash for $108,000.
   C. a credit to investments for $100,000.
   D. a credit to gain on the sale of investments for $8,000.

aq.eq.invest.fv.006_17

231. When an investor does not exert influence over the investee and accounts for an equity investment at fair value, cash dividends received by the investor from the investee should normally be recorded as

   A. Dividend income.
   B. An addition to the investor's share of the investee's profit.
   C. A deduction from the investor's share of the investee's profit.
   D. A deduction from the investment account.

Equity Investments at Cost

aq.eq.invest.cost.001_17

232. Assume an entity is holding an equity security where there is not a readily determinable fair value. Which of the following is **not** a factor to consider in the evaluation of potential impairment?

   A. A significant deterioration in the earnings performance, credit rating, asset quality, or business outlook of the investee
   B. A significant adverse change in the regulatory, economic, or technological environment of the investee
   C. The costs associated with gathering data on similar investments, researching valuation methodologies, and the cost to hire a valuation consultant
   D. A significant adverse change in the general market condition of either the geographical area or the industry in which the investee operates

aq.eq.invest.cost.005_17

233. On December 31, Ott Co. had investments in equity securities as follows:

% Owned	Investment	Cost	Fair value 12/31
3%	Man Co.	$10,000	$11,000
19%	Kemo, Inc.	9,000	Not readily available
5%	Fenn Corp.	11,000	7,000

Ott's December 31 balance sheet should report the equity securities as

A. $30,000.
B. $26,000.
C. $27,000.
D. $21,000.

Equity Investments using Equity Method Accounting

AICPA.081231FAR-SIM

234. Which of the following kinds of investments can result in the investor obtaining significant influence over an investee?

	Equity investments	Debt investments
A.	Yes	Yes
B.	Yes	No
C.	No	Yes
D.	No	No

AICPA.081235FAR-SIM

235. On October 1, 200X, Catco acquired 12% of the common stock of Dexco. The firms had no other relationships or transactions. On January 1, 200Y, Catco acquired an additional 18% of Dexco's common stock. There were no other transactions or relationships between the firms during 200Y. What method(s) of accounting would Catco have used for the investment during each of the following periods?

	October 1–December 31, 200X	January 1–December 31, 200Y
A.	Fair value	Fair value
B.	Fair value	Equity method
C.	Equity method	Fair value
D.	Equity method	Equity method

AICPA.130712FAR

236. A company has a 22% investment in another company that it accounts for using the equity method. Which of the following disclosures should be included in the company's annual financial statements?

A. The names and ownership percentages of the other stockholders in the investee company
B. The reason for the company's decision to invest in the investee company
C. The company's accounting policy for the investment
D. Whether the investee company is involved in any litigation

Investments in Debt Securities

Debt Investments at Fair Value

aicpa.aq.debt.invest.fv.001_17

237. In year 1, a company reported in other comprehensive income an unrealized holding loss on a debt investment classified as available-for-sale. During Year 2, these securities were sold at a loss equal to the unrealized loss previously recognized. The reclassification adjustment should include which of the following?

A. The unrealized loss should be credited to the investment account.
B. The unrealized loss should be credited to the other comprehensive income account.
C. The unrealized loss should be debited to the other comprehensive income account.
D. The unrealized loss should be credited to beginning retained earnings.

aicpa.aq.debt.invest.fv.005_17

238. For a debt securities portfolio classified as available-for-sale, which of the following amounts should be included in the period's net income?

I. Unrealized temporary losses during the period
II. Realized gains during the period
III. Changes in the valuation allowance during the period

A. III only
B. II only
C. I and II
D. I, II, and III

aicpa.aq.debt.invest.fv.007_17

239. Which of the following is true with respect to impairment of available-for-sale securities?

A. If the decline in fair value is considered to be other-than-temporary, the unrealized losses in OCI are reclassified to earnings.
B. If the decline in fair value is considered to be other-than-temporary, the unrealized losses are recorded in OCI.
C. If the decline in fair value is not considered to be other-than-temporary, the unrealized gains in OCI are reclassified to earnings.
D. If the decline in fair value is not considered to be other-than-temporary, the unrealized gains are recorded in OCI.

aicpa.aq.debt.invest.fv.009_17

240. Beach Co. determined that the decline in the fair value (FV) of an investment was below the amortized cost and permanent in nature (other-than-temporary). The investment was classified as available-for-sale on Beach's books. Beach Co. does not elect the fair value option to account for these securities. The controller would properly record the decrease in FV by including it in which of the following?

   A. Other comprehensive income section of the income statement only
   B. Earnings section of the income statement
   C. Extraordinary items section of the income statement
   D. Accumulated other comprehensive income section of the balance sheet only

Debt Investments at Amortized Cost

aicpa.aq.debt.invest.amort.003_17

241. On October 1, 2014, Park Co. purchased 200 of the $1,000-face-value, 10% bonds of Ott, Inc., for $220,000, including accrued interest of $5,000. The bonds, which mature on January 1, 2021, pay interest semiannually on January 1 and July 1. Park used the straight-line method of amortization and appropriately recorded the bonds as held-to-maturity.

   On Park's December 31, 2015, balance sheet, the bonds should be reported at

   A. $215,000.
   B. $214,400.
   C. $214,200.
   D. $212,000.

aicpa.aq.debt.invest.amort.004_17

242. An investor purchased a bond classified as a held-to-maturity investment between interest dates at a discount. At the purchase date, the carrying amount of the bond is more than the:

	Cash paid to seller	Face amount of bond
A.	No	Yes
B.	No	No
C.	Yes	No
D.	Yes	Yes

aicpa.aq.debt.invest.amort.008_17

243. Zinc Company does not elect to use the fair value option for reporting financial assets. An unrealized gain, net of tax, on Zinc's held-to-maturity portfolio of marketable debt securities should be reflected in the current financial statements as

   A. An extraordinary item shown as a direct increase to retained earnings.
   B. A current gain resulting from holding marketable debt securities.
   C. A footnote or parenthetical disclosure only.
   D. A valuation allowance and included in the equity section of the statement of financial position.

AICPA.081217FAR-SIM

244. On April 1, North Company issued bonds in the market. Upon issue, South Company acquired 10% of North Company's issue. On November 30, South sold the North Company bonds in the market; the bonds were acquired by East Company. On December 31, which, if any, of the following companies is an investee?

	North	South	East
A.	Yes	Yes	No
B.	Yes	No	No
C.	No	Yes	Yes
D.	No	No	Yes

Investor Stock Dividends, Splits, and Rights

AICPA.010505FAR-FA

245. Plack Co. purchased 10,000 shares (2% ownership) of Ty Corp. on February 14. Plack received a stock dividend of 2,000 shares on April 30 when the market value per share was $35. Ty paid a cash dividend of $2 per share on December 15.

   In its Income Statement, what amount should Plack report as dividend income?

   A. $20,000
   B. $24,000
   C. $90,000
   D. $94,000

AICPA.941139FAR-FA

246. Stock dividends on common stock should be recorded at their fair value by the investor when the related investment is accounted for under which of the following methods?

	Cost	Equity
A.	Yes	Yes
B.	Yes	No
C.	No	Yes
D.	No	No

AICPA.990508FAR-FA

247. Band Co. uses the equity method to account for its investment in Guard, Inc. common stock. How should Band record a 2% stock dividend received from Guard?

A. As dividend revenue at Guard's carrying value of the stock
B. As dividend revenue at the market value of the stock
C. As a reduction in the total cost of Guard stock owned
D. As a memorandum entry, reducing the unit cost of all Guard stock owned

Comparison and Transfers of Investments

aq.cost.meth.001_17

248. Clarion had the following investments in its portfolio that were purchased during year 2.

Investment	Classification	Cost	Fair Value 12-31-Y2
Common stock of Company X	Fair value	$100,000	$121,000
Bond of Company Y	Available-for-sale	$96,000	$101,000
Bond of Company Z	Held-to-maturity	$64,000	$63,000

On December 31, Year 2, the amortized cost of Bond Y was $97,000, and the amortized cost of Bond Z was $63,500. Clarion does not elect the fair value option for reporting financial assets. What amount should Clarion record as an unrealized gain in its Year 2 income statement?

A. $21,000
B. $25,000
C. $26,000
D. $0

aq.cost.meth.003_17

249. On December 31, Year 1, Ott Co. had investments in marketable debt securities as follows:

	Cost	Market value
Mann Co.	$10,000	$8,000
Kemo, Inc.	9,000	10,000
Fenn Corp.	11,000	9,000
	$30,000	$27,000

The Mann investment is classified as held-to-maturity, while the remaining securities are classified as available-for-sale. Ott does not elect the fair value option for reporting financial assets. Ott's December 31, Year 1, balance sheet should report total marketable debt securities as

A. $26,000.
B. $28,000
C. $29,000
D. $30,000

AICPA.081228FAR-SIM

250. Which, if any, of the following transfers between classifications of debt investments are possible?

	Held-to-maturity to held-for-trading	Held-for-trading to held-to-maturity
A.	Yes	Yes
B.	Yes	No
C.	No	Yes
D.	No	No

AICPA.081230FAR-SIM

251. The method of accounting for debt investments is based on the investor's intent for holding the investment. When investor intent changes, the classification of and accounting for the debt investment changes. When debt investments are transferred between classifications, which one of the following valuation baseis is *most likely* to be used when recording the investment in the new classification?

A. Historic cost
B. Amortized cost
C. Prior carrying value
D. Fair value

IFRS—Investments in Equity and Debt Securities

AICPA.100943FAR-NSI-SIM

252. Which, if any, of the following characteristics concerning the categories of investments under IFRS No. 9 is/are correct?

I. There is a single category for debt investments and a single category for equity investments.
II. The business model test used in evaluating debt instruments for classification purposes is concerned with the investor's intent.

A. I only
B. II only
C. Both I and II
D. Neither I nor II

AICPA.100944FAR-NSI-SIM

253. Inco, Inc., a U.S. entity, has elected to prepare financial statements in accordance with IFRS to provide to its foreign suppliers. Inco has the following information concerning an investment in the bonds of Tryco, Inc., as of December 31

Par value	$100,000
Original cost	108,000
Current premium	3,500
Fair value	105,000

Inco's business model is to regularly invest in debt to receive the cash flow provided by interest and the repayment of principal on maturity. The bonds are not associated with any other asset or liability. Which one of the following is the amount at which Inco should report its investment in Tryco in its December 31 IFRS-based Statement of Financial Position?

A. $100,000
B. $103,500
C. $105,000
D. $108,000

AICPA.100948FAR-NSI-SIM

254. Which of the following are possible ways that gains or losses on changes in the fair value of investments in equity securities may be reported under IFRS requirements?

	In Profit/ Loss (Income Statement)	In Other Comprehensive Income
A.	Yes	Yes
B.	Yes	No
C.	No	Yes
D.	No	No

Intangible Assets—Goodwill and Other

Introduction to Intangible Assets

aicpa.aq.intro.intang.asset.001_17

255. Which of the following types of assets would typically be reported on a company's balance sheet as an intangible asset?

A. Derivative securities
B. Cost of research and development
C. Leasehold improvements
D. Cost of patent registrations

aicpa.aq.intro.intang.asset.003_17

256. West Co. paid $50,000 for an intangible asset other than goodwill. Fair value of the asset is $55,000. West signed a contract to sell the asset for $10,000 in 10 years. What amount of amortization expense should West record each year?

A. $4,000
B. $4,500
C. $5,000
D. $5,500

AICPA.110577FAR

257. Grayson Co. incurred significant costs in defending its patent rights. Which of the following is the appropriate treatment of the related litigation costs?

A. Litigation costs would be capitalized regardless of the outcome of the litigation.
B. Litigation costs would be expensed regardless of the outcome of the litigation.
C. Litigation costs would be capitalized if the patent right is successfully defended.
D. Litigation costs would be capitalized only if the patent was purchased rather than internally developed.

Goodwill

aicpa.aq.goodwill.001_17

258. A company has experienced operating losses from its appliances division for the past five years. The division is the lowest level of identifiable cash flows. Having determined the division is the lowest level of identifiable cash flows, the company's next step in performing its impairment test is to

A. Perform a recoverability test on the carrying amount of the division's assets.
B. Reduce the carrying amount of the division's assets to the amount of expected divisional cash flows.
C. Adjust the carrying amount of the division's assets to fair value.
D. Adjust the carrying amount of the division's assets to replacement value.

aicpa.aq.goodwill.002_18

259. For a public business entity, the goodwill impairment test is required to be performed

A. Only at the end of the fiscal year.
B. Only at the beginning of the fiscal year.
C. Any time during the last quarter of the fiscal year.
D. Any time during the fiscal year, provided that it is performed at the same time every year.

AICPA.110601FAR-SIM

260. Which of the following is **not** one of the qualitative factors considered to determine if it is *more likely* than not that the reporting unit is less than its carrying value?

A. Industry and market conditions, such as deterioration in the industry environment, increased competition, decline in market-dependent multiples, change in the market for the entity's products or services, or a regulatory or political development.

B. Cost factors, such as increases in raw materials, labor or other costs that have a negative effect on earnings and cash flows.

C. Decline in the implied goodwill by using a discounted cash flow model.

D. Overall financial performance, such as negative cash flows or actual or projected declines in revenues, earnings or cash flows

assess.AICPA.FAR.goodwill-0024

261. Which of the following is an intangible asset that is subject to the recoverability test when testing for impairment?

A. A patent.
B. Goodwill.
C. R&D costs for a patent.
D. A trademark with indefinite useful life.

AICPA.130729FAR

262. A company is completing its annual impairment analysis of the goodwill included in one of its cash generating units (CGUs). The recoverable amount of the CGU is $32,000. The company noted the following related to the CGU:

	Good-will	Patents	Other assets	Total
Historical cost	$15,000	$10,000	$35,000	$60,000
Depreciation and amortization	0	3,333	11,667	15,000
Carrying amount, December 31	$15,000	$6,667	$23,333	$45,000

Under IFRS, which of the following adjustments should be recognized in the company's consolidated financial statements?

A. Decrease goodwill by $13,000.
B. Decrease goodwill by $15,000.
C. Decrease goodwill by $3,250; patents by $2,167; and other assets by $7,583.
D. Decrease goodwill by $4,333; patents by $1,926; and other assets by $6,741.

Research and Development Costs

aicpa.aq.rd.costs.002_17

263. Which of the following should a company classify as a research and development expense?

A. Periodic design changes to existing products.
B. Routine design of tools, jigs, molds, and dies.
C. Redesign of a product prerelease.
D. Legal work on patent applications.

AICPA.130731FAR

264. Which of the following is the proper treatment of the cost of equipment used in research and development activities that will have alternative future uses?

A. Expensed in the year in which the research and development project started.
B. Capitalized and depreciated over the term of the research and development project.
C. Capitalized and depreciated over its estimated useful life.
D. Either capitalized or expensed, but **not** both, depending on the term of the research and development project

AICPA.130738FAR

265. During the current year ended December 31, Metal, Inc. incurred the following costs:

Laboratory research aimed at discovery of new knowledge	$75,000
Design of tools, jigs, molds, and dies involving new technology	22,000
Quality control during commercial production, including routine testing	35,000
Equipment acquired two years ago, having an estimated useful life of five years with no salvage value, used in various R&D projects	150,000
Research and development services performed by Stone Co. for Metal, Inc.	23,000
Research and development services performed by Metal, Inc. for Clay Co.	32,000

What amount of research and development expenses should Metal report in its current-year income statement?

A. $120,000
B. $150,000
C. $187,000
D. $217,000

Software Costs

aicpa.aq.rd.costs.001_17

266. On January 1, Year 1, a company with a calendar year end began developing a software program that it intends to market and sell to its customers. The software coding was completed on March 31, Year 1, at a cost of $200,000, and the software testing was completed on June 30, Year 1, at a cost of $100,000. The company achieved technological feasibility on July 31, Year 1, at which time the company began producing product masters at a cost of $125,000. What amount should the company report for the total research and development expense for the year ended December 31, Year 1?

    A. $100,000
    B. $200,000
    C. $300,000
    D. $425,000

AICPA.150415FAR-SIM

267. Which of the following is an indication that a cloud computing arrangement includes a software license?

    I. The customer has contractual right to take possession of the software at any time during the hosting period without significant penalty.
    II. The cloud computing arrangement has an indefinite life because the contract is renewable indefinitely.
    III. It is feasible for the customer to either run the software on its own hardware or contract with another party unrelated to the vendor to host the software.

    A. I., II., and III.
    B. I. and II.
    C. I. and III.
    D. II. and III.

AICPA.061211FAR

268. Standard Co. spent $10,000,000 on its new software package that is to be used only for internal use. The amount spent is for costs after the application development stage. The economic life of the product is expected to be three years. The equipment on which the package is to be used is being depreciated over five years.

    What amount of expense should Standard report on its income statement for the first full year?

    A. $0
    B. $2,000,000
    C. $3,333,333
    D. $10,000,000

Intangibles and IFRS

AICPA.120201FAR-SIM

269. Under IFRS, the test for asset impairment is to compare the carrying value of the intangible asset to its recoverable amount. Which of the following is the recoverable amount according to IFRS?

    A. The greater of future undiscounted cash flows or future discounted cash flows.
    B. The greater of future discounted cash flows or fair value.
    C. The greater of fair value less cost to sell or value in use.
    D. The greater of fair value or value in use.

AICPA.120202FAR-SIM

270. After an impairment loss is recognized, the adjusted carrying amount of the intangible asset shall be its new accounting basis. Under IFRS, which of the following statements about subsequent reversal of a previously recognized impairment loss is correct?

    A. It is prohibited.
    B. It is allowed when events and circumstances change.
    C. It is allowed only if the intangible asset is recorded at fair value.
    D. The recovery amount can exceed the carrying value at the time of the initial impairment.

Payables and Accrued Liabilities

Introduction to Current Liabilities

AICPA.130718FAR

271. As of December 1, year 2 a company obtained a $1,000,000 line of credit maturing in one year on which it has drawn $250,000, a $750,000 secured note due in five annual installments, and a $300,000 three-year balloon note. The company has no other liabilities. How should the company's debt be presented in its classified balance sheet on December 31, year 2 if **no** debt repayments were made in December?

    A. Current liabilities of $1,000,000; long-term liabilities of $1,050,000.
    B. Current liabilities of $500,000; long-term liabilities of $1,550,000.

C. Current liabilities of $400,000; long-term liabilities of $900,000.

D. Current liabilities of $500,000; long-term liabilities of $800,000.

AICPA.130724FAR

272. Hemple Co. maintains escrow accounts for various mortgage companies. Hemple collects the receipts and pays the bills on behalf of the customers. Hemple holds the escrow monies in interest-bearing accounts. They charge a 10% maintenance fee to the customers based on interest earned. Hemple reported the following account data:

Escrow liability beginning of year	$500,000
Escrow receipts during the year	1,200,000
Real estate taxes paid during the year	1,450,000
Interest earned during the year	40,000

What amount represents the escrow liability balance on Hemple's books?

A. $290,000
B. $286,000
C. $214,000
D. $210,000

Specific Current Liabilities

AICPA.051158FAR-FA

273. As of December 15, Year 1, Aviator had dividends in arrears of $200,000 on its cumulative preferred stock. Dividends for Year 1 of $100,000 have not yet been declared. The Board of Directors plans to declare cash dividends on its preferred and common stock on January 16, Year 2. Aviator paid an annual bonus to its CEO based on the company's annual profits. The bonus for Year 1 was $50,000, which will be paid on February 10, Year 2. What amount should Aviator report as current liabilities on its balance sheet at December 31, Year 1?

A. $50,000
B. $150,000
C. $200,000
D. $350,000

assess.AICPA.130715FAR

274. On January 1, year 1, Alpha Co. signed an annual maintenance agreement with a software provider for $15,000 and the maintenance period begins on March 1, year 1. Alpha also incurred $5,000 of costs on January 1, year 1, related to software modification requests that will increase the functionality of the software. Alpha depreciates and amortizes its computer and software assets over five years using the straight-line method. What amount is the total expense that Alpha should recognize related to the maintenance agreement and the software modifications for the year ended December 31, year 1?

A. $5,000
B. $13,500
C. $16,000
D. $20,000

Payroll and Compensated Absences

AICPA.931128FAR-TH-FA

275. If the payment of employees' compensation for future absences is probable, the amount can be reasonably estimated, and the obligation relates to rights that accumulate, the compensation should be

A. Accrued if attributable to employees' services not already rendered.
B. Accrued if attributable to employees' services already rendered.
C. Accrued if attributable to employees' services, whether already rendered or not.
D. Recognized when paid.

AICPA.940522FAR-FA

276. Under state law, Acme may pay 3% of eligible gross wages or it may reimburse the state directly for actual unemployment claims.

Acme believes that actual unemployment claims will be 2% of eligible gross wages and has chosen to reimburse the state. Eligible gross wages are defined as the first $10,000 of gross wages paid to each employee. Acme had five employees each of whom earned $20,000 during 20X4.

In its December 31, 20X4 balance sheet, what amount should Acme report as accrued liability for unemployment claims?

A. $1,000
B. $1,500
C. $2,000
D. $3,000

Contingencies, Commitments, and Guarantees (Provisions)

Contingent Liability Principles

aicpa.aq.conting.liab.001_17

277. Which of the following methods should a company use to account for a contingent liability when the loss is probable but **not** reasonably estimated?

   A. The liability should not be reported.
   B. The liability should be reported as a short-term liability.
   C. The liability should be reported as a long-term liability.
   D. The liability should only be disclosed in the notes to the financial statements.

aicpa.aq.conting.liab.002_17

278. Hill Corp. began production of a new product. During the first calendar year, 1,000 units of the product were sold for $1,200 per unit. Each unit had a two-year warranty. Based on warranty costs for similar products, Hill estimates that warranty costs will average $100 per unit. Hill incurred $12,000 in warranty costs during the first year and $22,000 in warranty costs during the second year. The company uses the expense warranty accrual method. What should be the balance in the estimated liability under warranties account at the end of the first calendar year?

   A. $66,000
   B. $88,000
   C. $100,000
   D. $112,000

AICPA.120631FAR

279. Hudson Corp. operates several factories that manufacture medical equipment. The factories have a historical cost of $200 million. Near the end of the company's fiscal year, a change in business climate related to a competitor's innovative products indicated to Hudson's management that the $170 million carrying amount of the assets of one of Hudson's factories may not be recoverable. Management identified cash flows from this factory and estimated that the undiscounted future cash flows over the remaining useful life of the factory would be $150 million. The fair value of the factory's assets is reliably estimated to be $135 million. The change in business climate requires investigation of possible impairment.

Which of the following amounts is the impairment loss?

   A. $15 million
   B. $20 million
   C. $35 million
   D. $65 million

Examples of Contingent Liabilities and Additional Aspects

AICPA.940557FAR-FA

280. During 2005, Smith Co. filed suit against West, Inc. seeking damages for patent infringement.

At December 31, 2005, Smith's legal counsel believed that it was probable that Smith would be successful against West for an estimated amount in the range of $75,000 to $150,000, with all amounts in the range considered equally likely. In March 2006, Smith was awarded $100,000 and received full payment thereof.

In its 2005 financial statements, issued in February 2006, how should this award be reported?

   A. As a receivable and revenue of $100,000.
   B. As a receivable and deferred revenue of $100,000.
   C. As a disclosure of a contingent gain of $100,000.
   D. As a disclosure of a contingent gain of an undetermined amount in the range of $75,000 to $150,000.

AICPA.951117FAR-FA

281. Eagle Co. has cosigned the mortgage note on the home of its president, guaranteeing the indebtedness in the event that the president should default. Eagle considers the likelihood of default to be remote.

How should the guarantee be treated in Eagle's financial statements?

   A. Disclosed only.
   B. Accrued only.
   C. Accrued and disclosed.
   D. Neither accrued nor disclosed.

IFRS—Contingencies

AICPA.101107FAR

282. Choose the correct statement about international accounting standards as they relate to contingent liabilities and similar items.

A. A provision that has a reasonably possible chance of requiring the outflow of benefits is treated as a contingent liability.
B. Provisions are recognized only when there is greater than a 90% probability of an outflow of benefits occurring.
C. A recognized provision is a contingent liability.
D. A provision for which it is probable that an outflow of benefits will be required is recognized, even if it is not of estimable amount.

AICPA.101111FAR

283. Which of the following is not a contingent liability under international accounting standards?

A. A provision with a 60% chance of requiring an outflow of benefits, amount is estimable.
B. A provision with a 40% chance of requiring an outflow of benefits, amount is estimable.
C. A provision with a 90% chance of requiring an outflow of benefits, amount not estimable.
D. A possible obligation.

Long-Term Debt (Financial Liabilities)

Notes Payable

aicpa.aq.notes.pay.001_17

284. Pane Co. had the following borrowings on its books at the end of the current year:

$100,000, 12% interest rate, borrowed five years ago on September 30; interest payable March 31 and September 30.

$75,000, 10% interest rate, borrowed two years ago on July 1; interest paid April 1, July 1, October 1, and January 1.

$200,000, noninterest bearing note, borrowed July 1 of current year, due January 2 of next year; proceeds of $178,000.

What amount should Pane report as interest payable in its December 31 balance sheet?

A. $4,875
B. $6,750
C. $26,875
D. $41,500

AICPA.101132FAR

285. On September 30, World Co. borrowed $1,000,000 on a 9% note payable. World paid the first of four quarterly payments of $264,200

when due on December 30. In its December 31, balance sheet, what amount should World report as note payable?

A. $735,800
B. $750,000
C. $758,300
D. $825,800

AICPA.951116FAR-FA

286. On March 1, 20X4, Fine Co. borrowed $10,000 and signed a two-year note bearing interest at 12% per annum compounded annually. Interest is payable in full at maturity on February 28, 20X6.

What amount should Fine report as a liability for accrued interest at December 31, 20X5?

A. $0
B. $1,000
C. $1,200
D. $2,320

Bonds Payable

Bond Accounting Principles

AICPA.090662.FAR.II

287. A company issued a bond with a stated rate of interest that is less than the effective interest rate on the date of issuance. The bond was issued on one of the interest payment dates. What should the company report on the first interest payment date?

A. An interest expense that is less than the cash payment made to bondholders.
B. An interest expense that is greater than the cash payment made to bondholders.
C. A debit to the unamortized bond discount
D. A debit to the unamortized bond premium

AICPA.120601FAR

288. On January 2, Vole Co. issued bonds with a face value of $480,000 at a discount to yield 10%. The bonds pay interest semiannually. On June 30, Vole paid bond interest of $14,400. After Vole recorded amortization of the bond discount of $3,600, the bonds had a carrying amount of $363,600. What amount did Vole receive upon issuing the bonds?

A. $360,000
B. $367,200
C. $476,400
D. $480,000

Bond Complications

AICPA.910546FAR-P1-FA

289. On December 31, 20X5. Cobb issued 2,000 of its 10%, $1,000 bonds at 99. The issuance price established a bond discount of $20,000. In connection with the sale of these bonds. Cobb paid the following expenses:

Legal and accounting fees	$45,000
Printing of the prospectus	55,000
Underwriting fees	85,000

In Cobb's December 31, 20X5, balance sheet, bond issue costs total

A. $120,000.
B. $130,000.
C. $160,000.
D. $185,000.

AICPA.950519FAR-FA

290. On July 1, Year 5, Eagle Corp. issued 600 of its 10%, $1,000 bonds at 99 plus accrued interest. The bonds are dated April 1, Year 5 and mature on April 1, Year 5. Interest is payable semiannually on April 1 and October 1.

What amount did Eagle receive from the bond issuance?

A. $579,000
B. $594,000
C. $600,000
D. $609,000

Bond Fair Value Option, International

AICPA.070779FAR

291. Foley Co. is preparing the electronic spreadsheet below to amortize the discount on its 10-year, 6%, $100,000 bonds payable. Bonds were issued on December 31 to yield 8%. Interest is paid annually. Foley uses the effective interest method to amortize bond discounts.

	A	B	C	D	E
1	Year	Cash paid	Interest expense	Discount amortization	Carrying amount
2	1				$86,580
3	2	$6,000			

Which formula should Foley use in cell E3 to calculate the carrying amount of the bonds at the end of Year 2?

A. E2+D3
B. E2-D3
C. E2+C3
D. E2-C3

PVB-0022B

292. On February 1, year 1, Blake Corporation issued bonds with a fair value of $1,000,000. Blake prepares its financial statements in accordance with IFRS. What methods may Blake use to report the bonds on its December 31, year 1 statement of financial position?

I. Amortized cost.
II. Fair value method.
III. Fair value through profit or loss.

A. I only.
B. II only.
C. I and III only.
D. III only.

Modification and Debt Retirement

Refinancing Short-Term Obligations

AICPA.090646FAR-II-G

293. Willem Co. reported the following liabilities at December 31, 20x1:

Accounts payable-trade	$750,000
Short-term borrowings	400,000
Mortgage payable, current portion $100,000	3,500,000
Other bank loan, matures June 30, 20x2	1,000,000

The $1,000,000 bank loan was refinanced with a 20-year loan on January 15, 20x2, with the first principal payment due January 15, 20x3. Willem's audited financial statements were issued February 28, 20x2. What amount should Willem report as current liabilities at December 31, 2001?

A. $850,000
B. $1,150,000
C. $1,250,000
D. $2,250,000

AICPA.090659.FAR.II.G

294. A company has the following liabilities at year end:

Mortgage note payable; $16,000 due within 12 months	$355,000
Short-term debt that the company is refinancing with long-term debt	175,000
Deferred tax liability arising from depreciation	25,000

What amount should the company include in the current liability section of the balance sheet?

A. $0
B. $16,000
C. $41,000
D. $191,000

Debt Retirement

AICPA.931140FAR-P1-FA

295. On June 2, year 1, Tory, Inc. issued $500,000 of 10%, 15-year bonds at par. Interest is payable semiannually on June 1 and December 1. Bond issue costs were $6,000. On June 2, year 6, Tory retired half of the bonds at 98.

     What is the net amount that Tory should use in computing the gain or loss on the retirement of debt?

     A. $249,000
     B. $248,500
     C. $248,000
     D. $247,000

AICPA.941142FAR-FA

296. On July 31, year 1, Dome Co. issued $1,000,000 of 10%, 15-year bonds at par and used a portion of the proceeds to call its 600 outstanding 11%, $1,000 face-value bonds, due on July 31, year 15, at 102. On that date, the unamortized bond premium relating to the 11% bonds was $65,000.

     In its year 1 income statement, what amount should Dome report as a gain or loss, before income taxes, from the retirement of the bonds?

     A. $53,000 gain
     B. $0
     C. $(65,000) loss
     D. $(77,000) loss

Troubled Debt

AICPA.010509FAR-FA

297. For a troubled debt restructuring involving only a modification of terms, which of the following items specified by the new terms would be compared to the carrying amount of the debt to determine if the debtor should report a gain on restructuring?

     A. The total future cash payments
     B. The present value of the debt at the original interest rate

C. The present value of the debt at the modified interest rate
D. The amount of future cash payments designated as principal repayments

AICPA.101086FAR

298. Choose the correct statement regarding the accounting treatment of troubled debt restructures (TDRs) under international accounting standards (IAS).

     A. Settlements are treated the same way as under U.S. standards.
     B. Modification of terms TDRs are treated the same way as under U.S. standards.
     C. A significant modification of terms for IAS is treated as a modification of terms type II under U.S. standards.
     D. A non-significant modification of terms for IAS is treated as a modification of terms type I under U.S. standards.

Debt Covenant Compliance

AICPA.101087FAR

299. A firm is required by its creditors to maintain a 2.00 (or greater) current ratio in order to maintain compliance with a debt covenant. The current ratio of the firm is currently at the minimum before any of the transactions are listed. Which of the following actions would cause the firm to fall out of compliance?

     A. Sell a used plant asset at book value.
     B. Pay an account payable.
     C. Declare cash dividends.
     D. Pay cash dividends previously declared.

AICPA.101091FAR

300. Choose the correct statement concerning the classification of a liability when a firm is subject to a debt covenant.

     A. All liabilities callable on demand are classified as current in all circumstances.
     B. If the liability is callable on demand, the covenant is violated, and the covenant is violated, then the liability is classified as current if the violation is waived by the creditor.
     C. If the covenant includes a subjective acceleration clause and there is only a remote chance that debt will be called, then the liability is classified as noncurrent.
     D. If a covenant grants a grace period during which it is possible that the violation will be cured, then the liability is classified as noncurrent.

Distinguishing Liabilities from Equity

AICPA.101117FAR

301. Allam, Inc. contracted for services to be provided over a period of time with full payment in Allam's $2 par common stock when the service is completed. At the time of the agreement, Allam stock was trading at $20 per share. The agreed-upon total value of the contract is $20,000. When the service was completed, Allam's stock price was $25 per share. Therefore, Allam

   A. Recognizes $25,000 of expense.
   B. Increases the common stock account $1,600.
   C. Increases contributed capital in excess of par $23,000.
   D. Debits a liability for $25,000.

AICPA.101121FAR

302. Early in 20x3, Shifter, Inc. wrote put options for 1,000 shares of its common stock. Purchasers of the options can sell Shifter stock back to Shifter for $20 per share on 12/31/x3. The estimated fair value of each option is $2 at the time of sale. At 12/31/x3, the share price is $15 and the options are exercised. As a result, Shifter

   A. Recognizes a $3,000 loss.
   B. Recognizes a $5,000 loss.
   C. Increases the treasury stock account $20,000 upon purchase.
   D. Decreases contributed capital $3,000.

Equity

Owners' Equity Basics

AICPA.120605FAR

303. Jones Co. had 50,000 shares of $5 par value common stock outstanding at January 1. On August 1, Jones declared a 5% stock dividend followed by a two-for-one stock split on September 1. What amount should Jones report as common shares outstanding at December 31?

   A. 105,000
   B. 100,000
   C. 52,500
   D. 50,000

AICPA.130743FAR

304. An entity authorized 500,000 shares of common stock. At January 1, year 2, the entity had 110,000 shares of common stock issued and 100,000 shares of common stock outstanding. The entity had the following transactions in year 2:

March 1	Issued 15,000 shares of common stock
June 1	Resold 2,500 shares of treasury stock
September 1	Completed a 2-for-1 common stock split

What is the total number of shares of common stock that the entity has outstanding at the end of year 2?

   A. 117,500
   B. 230,000
   C. 235,000
   D. 250,000

AICPA.951118FAR-FA

305. Nest Co. issued 100,000 shares of common stock. Of these, 5,000 were held as treasury stock at December 31, 20X4. During 20X5, transactions involving Nest's common stock were as follows:

May 3	1,000 shares of treasury stock were sold.
August 6	10,000 shares of previously unissued stock were sold.
November 18	A 2-for-1 stock split took effect.

Laws in Nest's state of incorporation protect treasury stock from dilution. At December 31, 20X5, how many shares of Nest's common stock were issued and outstanding?

	Shares Issued	Shares Outstanding
A.	220,000	212,000
B.	220,000	216,000
C.	222,000	214,000
D.	222,000	218,000

Stock Issuance

AICPA.083744FAR-SIM

306. An individual contracts for the purchase of 200 shares of $10 par common stock at a subscription price of $15. After making payments totaling $1,200, the subscriber defaults. Shares are issued in proportion to the amount of cash paid by the investor. The

summary journal entry to record the net effect of these two transactions includes:

A. Debit share purchase contract receivable $1,800.
B. Credit common stock $2,000
C. Credit paid in capital in excess of par on common, $400
D. Credit share purchase contract receivable $600

AICPA.930506FAR-P1-FA

307. On April 1, 20X4, Hyde Corp., a newly formed company, had the following stock issued and outstanding:

- Common stock, no par, $1 stated value, 20,000 shares originally issued for $30 per share.
- Preferred stock, $10 par value, 6,000 shares originally issued for $50 per share.

Hyde's April 1, 20X4 statement of stockholders' equity should report

	Common stock	Preferred stock	Additional paid-in capital
A.	$20,000	$60,000	$820,000
B.	$20,000	$300,000	$580,000
C.	$600,000	$300,000	$0
D.	$600,000	$60,000	$240,000

Preferred Stock

AICPA.083748FAR-SIM

308. When preferred stock is called and retired, which account or aggregate category of accounts can be increased?

	Total Owners' Equity	Retained Earnings
A.	Yes	Yes
B.	No	No
C.	Yes	No
D.	No	Yes

AICPA.083749FAR-SIM

309. 500 shares of 6%, $100 par callable preferred stock are called at $101. The shares were issued at $103 per share. The journal entry to record the retirement includes which of the following?

A. Cr. paid in capital from retirement of preferred stock, $1,000.
B. Dr. paid in capital from retirement of preferred stock $1,500.
C. Cr. retained earnings $1,000
D. Dr. preferred stock $51,500

Treasury Stock

AICPA.090640FAR-II-K

310. During the current year, Onal Co. purchased 10,000 shares of its own stock at $7 per share. The stock was originally issued at $6. The firm sold 5,000 of the treasury shares for $10 per share. The firm uses the cost method to account for treasury stock. What amount should Onal report in its income statement for these transactions?

A. $0
B. $5,000 gain.
C. $10,000 loss.
D. $15,000 gain

AICPA.930511FAR-P1-FA

311. On December 1, 20X4, Line Corp. received a donation of 2,000 shares of its $5 par value common stock from a stockholder. On that date, the stock's market value was $35 per share. The stock was originally issued for $25 per share.

By what amount would this donation cause total stockholders' equity to decrease?

A. $70,000
B. $50,000
C. $20,000
D. $0

Dividends

AICPA.061210FAR

312. Godart Co. issued $4.5mn notes payable as a scrip dividend that matured in five years. At maturity, each shareholder of Godart's 3mn shares will receive payment of the note principal, plus interest. The annual interest rate was 10%.

What amount should be paid to the stockholders at the end of the fifth year?

A. $450,000
B. $2.25m
C. $4.5mn
D. $6.75mn

AICPA.941130FAR-FA

313. When a company declares a cash dividend, retained earnings is decreased by the amount of the dividend on the date of

A. Declaration.
B. Record.
C. Payment.
D. Declaration or record, whichever is earlier.

Stock Dividends and Splits

AICPA.130747FAR

314. A company whose stock is trading at $10 per share has 1,000 shares of $1 par common stock outstanding when the board of directors declares a 30% common stock dividend. Which of the following adjustments should be made when recording the stock dividend?

A. Treasury stock is debited for $300.
B. Additional paid-in capital is credited for $2,700.
C. Retained earnings is debited for $300.
D. Common stock is debited for $3,000.

AICPA.950529FAR-FA

315. Wood Co. owns 2,000 shares of Arlo, Inc.'s 20,000 shares of $100 par, 6% cumulative, non-participating preferred stock and 1,000 shares (2%) of Arlo's common stock.

During 20X5, Arlo declared and paid dividends of $240,000 on preferred stock. No dividends had been declared or paid during 20X4. In addition, Wood received a 5% common stock dividend from Arlo when the quoted market price of Arlo's common stock was $10 per share.

What amount should Wood report as dividend income in its 20X5 income statement?

A. $12,000
B. $12,500
C. $24,000
D. $24,500

Dividend Allocation

AICPA.083745FAR-SIM

316. The owners' equity section of a firm includes (1) $10,000 of 8%, $100 par cumulative preferred stock, and (2) $40,000 of $5 par common stock. There is additional paid-in capital on both issues. The preferred participates up to an additional 4% and there are two years of dividends in arrears as of the beginning of the current year. If the firm pays $30,000 in dividends, what amount is allocated to common?

A. $27,600
B. $28,800
C. $27,200
D. $24,000

AICPA.083746FAR-SIM

317. The owners' equity section of a firm includes (1) $10,000 of 8%, $100 par cumulative preferred stock, and (2) $40,000 of $5 par common stock. There is additional paid-in capital on both issues. The preferred participates up to an additional 4% and there are two years of dividends in arrears as of the beginning of the current year. If the firm pays $7,100 in dividends, what amount is allocated to common?

A. $4,400
B. $3,200
C. $4,700
D. $6,000

AICPA.083747FAR-SIM

318. The owners' equity section of a firm includes (1) $10,000 of 8%, $100 par cumulative preferred stock, and (2) $40,000 of $5 par common stock. There is additional paid-in capital on both issues. The preferred is fully participating and there are two years of dividends in arrears as of the beginning of the current year. If the firm pays $30,000 in dividends, what amount is allocated to common?

A. $23,360
B. $22,720
C. $22,080
D. $24,320

Stock Rights, Retained Earnings

AICPA.931115FAR-TH-FA

319. On November 2, 20X3, Finsbury, Inc. issued warrants to its stockholders, giving them the right to purchase additional $20 par value common shares at a price of $30.

The stockholders exercised all warrants on March 1, 20X4. The shares had market prices of $33, $35, and $40 on November 2, 20X3, December 31, 20X3, and March 1, 20X4, respectively.

What were the effects of the warrants on Finsbury's additional paid-in capital and net income?

	Additional paid-in capital	Net income
A.	Increased in 20X4	No effect
B.	Increased in 20X3	No effect
C.	Increased in 20X4	Decreased in 20X3 and 20X4
D.	Increased in 20X3	Decreased in 20X3 and 20X4

AICPA.941109FAR-FA

320. The following trial balance of Trey Co. at December 31, 20X5 has been adjusted, except for income tax expense.

	Dr.	Cr.
Cash	$550,000	
Accounts receivable, net	1,650,000	
Prepaid taxes	300,000	
Accounts payable		$120,000
Common stock		500,000
Additional paid-in capital		680,000
Retained earnings		630,000
Foreign currency translation adjustment	430,000	
Revenues		3.6mn
Expenses	2.6mn	
	$5.53mn	$5.53mn

Additional information:

- During 20X5, estimated tax payments of $300,000 were charged to prepaid taxes. Trey has not yet recorded income tax expense. There were no differences between financial statement and income tax income, and Trey's tax rate is 30%.
- Included in accounts receivable is $500,000 due from a customer. Special terms granted to this customer require payment in equal semi-annual installments of $125,000 every April 1 and October 1.

In Trey's December 31, 20X5 balance sheet, what amount should be reported as total retained earnings?

A. $1.029mn
B. $1.2mn
C. $1.33mn
D. $1.63mn

AICPA.951122FAR-FA

321. In September Year 1, West Corp. made a dividend distribution of one right for each of its 120,000 shares of outstanding common stock.

Each right was exercisable for the purchase of one-hundredth of a share of West's $50 variable-rate preferred stock at an exercise price of $80 per share. On March 20, Year 5, none of the rights

had been exercised, and West redeemed them by paying each stockholder $0.10 per right.

As a result of this redemption, West's stockholders' equity was reduced by

A. $120
B. $2,400
C. $12,000
D. $36,000

Book Value per Share

AICPA.921143FAR-P2-FA

322. Boe Corp.'s stockholders' equity at December 31, 20X4 was as follows:

6% non-cumulative preferred stock, $100 par (liquidation value $105 per share)	$100,000
Common stock, $10 par	300,000
Retained earnings	95,000

At December 31, 20X4, Boe's book value per common share was

A. $13.17
B. $13.00
C. $12.97
D. $12.80

AICPA.951125FAR-FA

323. The stockholders' equity section of Brown Co.'s December 31, 20X5 balance sheet consisted of the following:

Common stock, $30 par, 10,000 shares authorized and outstanding	$300,000
Additional paid-in capital	150,000
Retained earnings (deficit)	(210,000)

On January 2, 20X6, Brown put into effect a stockholder-approved quasi-reorganization by reducing the par value of the stock to $5 and eliminating the deficit against additional paid-in capital. Immediately after the quasi-reorganization, what amount should Brown report as additional paid-in capital?

A. $(60,000)
B. $150,000
C. $190,000
D. $400,000

Select Transactions

Revenue Recognition

Five Steps of Revenue Recognition

aq.revrecog.5steps.001_10_17

324. A CPA has been asked by a client to describe revenue. Which of the following statements would be best for the CPA to use in his/her description?

 A. Revenue is equal to the cash received from a customer for goods.
 B. Revenue is equal to the difference between the amount charged to the customer and the cost of the goods sold that results from an enhancement of assets.
 C. Revenue is the inflows of assets or settlements of liabilities from the sale of assets such as property, plant, and equipment or long-term investments.
 D. Revenue is the inflows or other enhancements of assets of an entity or settlements of its liabilities from delivering or producing goods, rendering services, or other activities that constitute the entity's ongoing major or central operations.

aq.revrecog.5steps.003_10_17

325. The following information is available about a signed agreement between two entities:

 - The entities have agreed to specific performance obligations.
 - The entities have agreed on a price related to the performance obligations.
 - No work has begun on the performance obligations, and the contract is cancelable without payment of penalty or other consideration.
 - It is probable that the company completing the work will collect the agreed-upon consideration.

 Does a contract exist between the entities to which the revenue recognition criteria may be applied?

 A. A contract to which the revenue recognition criteria applies exists because it identifies specific performance obligations and collectibility of the consideration is probable.
 B. A contract to which the revenue recognition criteria applies exists because the contract includes important terms, such as the agreed-upon price and specific performance obligations.
 C. A contract to which the revenue recognition criteria applies does not exist because the transaction price has not yet been allocated to the specific performance obligations.
 D. A contract to which the revenue recognition criteria applies does not exist because it is cancelable without penalty and no work on the performance obligations has begun.

Determining Transaction Price

aq.revrecog.det.trans.001_10_17

326. Holt Company enters into a contract to build a new plant facility for Segal Company for $2,500,000. In the contract, Segal will pay a performance bonus of $100,000 if Holt is able to complete the facility by October 1, 20X6. The performance bonus is reduced by 50% for each of the first two weeks after October 1, 20X6. If the completion is delayed more than two weeks, then Holt forfeits the entire performance bonus. Holt's prior experience with performance bonuses on similar contracts indicates the following probabilities of completion outcomes:

Completed by	Probability
October 1, 20X6	80%
October 8, 20X6	10%
October 15, 20X6	5%
After October 15, 20X6	5%

How much should Holt record as the transaction price of the contract and why?

 A. $2,500,000 because the performance bonus is not guaranteed
 B. $2,600,000 because the *most likely* outcome is that Holt will deliver the facility by October 1, 20X6
 C. $2,461,250 because Holt should use the expected cost method
 D. $2,586,250 because Holt should use the expected value method

aq.revrecog.det.trans.002_10_17

327. What method does a company use to determine the transaction price for a contract that includes variable consideration when the company has numerous other contracts with similar characteristics and there are more than two possible results?

   A. Expected outcome method
   B. Expected value method
   C. *Most likely* value method
   D. *Most likely* amount method

Allocating Transaction Price

aq.revrecog.alloc.trans.001_10_17

328. Wolf Company produces large pieces of machinery for use in the manufacturing industry. Blue Jay Manufacturing Company purchases a large piece of machinery from Wolf for use in Blue Jay's new production plant. Although Blue Jay could install the equipment on its own, management decides to include installation of the machinery in its contract with Wolf. Blue Jay agrees to a total contract price of $850,000 for both the equipment and the installation. Wolf does not offer a discount on the machinery if it completes the installation. The fair value of the equipment is $850,000, and its cost is $760,000. The fair value of the installation is $50,000, and the cost of the labor to Wolf is $40,000. How much of the contract price should Wolf allocate to the equipment and installation respectively? If a proportion is necessary, round to the nearest one hundredth of a percent (e.g..####) and round all answers to the nearest dollar.

	Equipment	Installation
A.	$850,000	$0
B.	$800,000	$50,000
C.	$807,500	$42,500
D.	$802,740	$47,260

aq.revrecog.alloc.trans.005_10_17

329. For a contract that contains multiple performance obligations, revenue is allocated to each performance obligation by

   A. Calculating the proportion of total cost of goods sold represented by each performance obligation and multiplying the proportion for each performance obligation by the total transaction price.
   B. Assigning the transaction price based on covering cost of goods sold first, then allocating the profit portion of the transaction price evenly between the performance obligations.
   C. Allocating the total contract transaction price evenly to the performance obligations to support representational fairness.
   D. Calculating the proportion of the total stand-alone price represented by each performance obligation and multiplying the proportion by the total transaction price to allocate the transaction price to the separate performance obligations.

Special Issues in Revenue Recognition

aq.recrecog.spec.iss.001_10_17

330. On January 1, 20X2, Dot Company sold a three-year, service-type extended warranty to Matrix Company for $36,000. The warranty took effect on the date of purchase (January 1, 20X2). What amount of Unearned Warranty Revenue should be reported on Dot's December 31, 20X3, Balance Sheet?

   A. $36,000
   B. $24,000
   C. $12,000
   D. $6,000

aq.recrecog.spec.iss.003_10_17

331. A shoe retailer allows customers to return shoes within 90 days of purchase. The company estimates that 5% of sales will be returned within the 90-day period. During the month, the company has sales of $200,000 and returns of sales made in prior months of $5,000. What amount should the company record as net sales revenue for new sales made during the month?

   A. $185,000
   B. $190,000
   C. $195,000
   D. $200,000

Contract Modifications and Other Considerations

AICPA.aq.recrecog.contra.mod.003_90

332. On January 1, 20X5, Wren Co. leased a building to Brill under an operating lease for 10 years at $50,000 per year, payable the first day of each lease year. Wren paid $15,000 to a real estate broker as a finder's fee. The building is depreciating $12,000 per year.

   For 20X5, Wren incurred insurance and property tax expenses totaling $9,000. Wren's net rental income for 20X5 should be

   A. $27,500.
   B. 9,000
   C. $35,000
   D. $36,500

aq.recrecog.contra.mod.001_10_17

333. A new separate contract is created when:

    I. The additional products included in the contract modification are distinct from the products in the original contract.
    II. The blended price of the original and additional products is appropriately reflected in the recognition of revenue after the modification.
    III. The consideration for the additional products reflects an appropriate standalone selling price.

    A. I, II, and III.
    B. I and II.
    C. I and III.
    D. II and III.

Accounting for Construction Contracts

AICPA.101093FAR

334. Choose the correct statement regarding accounting methods for revenue recognition on long-term contracts, for international and US accounting standards.

    A. Only US standards require recognition of an overall loss in the year it becomes known.
    B. Both sets of standards allow the completed contract method when the percentage of completion method is not appropriate.
    C. International standards require the cost recovery method when the percentage of completion method is not appropriate.
    D. The percentage of completion method is allowed only under US standards.

AICPA.110554FAR

335. Frame construction company's contract requires the construction of a bridge in three years. The expected total cost of the bridge is $2mn, and Frame will receive $2.5mn for the project. The actual costs incurred to complete the project were $500,000, $900,000, and $600,000, respectively, during each of the three years. Progress payments received by Frame were $600,000, $1.2mn, and $700,000 in each year, respectively. Assuming that the percentage-of-completion method is used, what amount of gross profit should Frame report during the last year of the project?

    A. $120,000
    B. $125,000
    C. $140,000
    D. $150,000

Employee/Retiree Benefit Plans

Pension Principles, Reporting

aq.pen.princ.0001_1801

336. Multiple components comprise Net Periodic Pension Cost. The component reported as part of compensation expense and included in the subtotal for income from operations is

    A. Interest cost
    B. Amortization of prior service cost
    C. Corridor amortization
    D. Service cost

Pension Expense Basics

AICPA.101137FAR

337. An entity sponsors a defined-benefit pension plan that is underfunded by $800,000. A $500,000 increase in the fair value of plan assets would have which of the following effects on the financial statements of the entity?

    A. An increase in the assets of the entity.
    B. An increase in accumulated other comprehensive income of the entity for the full amount of the increase in the value of the assets.
    C. A decrease in accumulated other comprehensive income of the entity for the full amount of the increase in the value of the assets.
    D. A decrease in the liabilities of the entity.

Pension Expense, Delayed Recognition

aicpa.aq.pen.exp.recog.005_17

338. At year end, a company has a defined benefit pension plan with a projected benefit obligation of $350,000; a net gain of $140,000 that was not previously recognized in net periodic pension cost; and prior service cost of $210,000 that was not previously recognized in net periodic pension cost. What amount should be reported in accumulated other comprehensive income related to the company's defined benefit pension plan at year end?

    A. A credit balance of $420,000.
    B. A debit balance of $420,000.
    C. A credit balance of $70,000.
    D. A debit balance of $70,000.

AICPA.101097FAR

339. Choose the correct statement regarding the treatment of prior service cost (PSC) for defined benefit plans under international accounting.

A. Firms have an option to record PSC directly into other comprehensive income or in earnings.

B. The entire PSC amount, at present value, is recognized immediately in pension expense.

C. The entire PSC amount, at present value, is recognized immediately in other comprehensive income, as per U.S. standards.

D. The estimated nominal increase in benefits is recognized immediately in pension expense.

Pension Plan Reporting, International

AICPA.101099FAR

340. A firm is applying international accounting standards to its defined-benefit pension plan and has pension gains and losses. As a result,

A. The gains and losses are gradually recognized in defined benefit obligation.

B. The gains and losses are never recognized in defined benefit obligation.

C. The firm's earnings will not be affected.

D. The gain and losses will be amortized gradually in pension expense.

AICPA.140411FAR-SIM

341. A firm is applying international accounting standards to its defined-benefit pension plan. At the end of the current year, the actuary informs the firm that the plan has experienced an actuarial gain of $2mn. The average remaining service period of plan participants is ten years. Therefore,

A. Defined-benefit obligation does not reflect the decrease of $2mn immediately.

B. Pension expense will be reduced by $200,000 the following year.

C. Other comprehensive income is immediately increased.

D. The unrecognized net gain or loss account is immediately debited.

Postretirement Benefits

AICPA.083755FAR-SIM

342. An employee covered by a post-retirement healthcare plan just completed her 18th year of service for a firm. Each year of employment to full eligibility provides credit for post-retirement healthcare benefits for this firm. She must work an additional seven years from today to be eligible for 75% healthcare coverage during retirement. She is expected to work ten more years from today. If this employee worked 15 more years from today, the firm would pay all her healthcare costs during retirement. Choose the correct statement.

A. The employee's full eligibility date is reached when she has worked 33 years in total.

B. Accumulated post-retirement benefit obligation equals expected post-retirement benefit obligation for the employee, as of today.

C. Service cost will not be computed for the employee during her last three years of service to the firm.

D. Expected post-retirement benefit obligation reflects only 18 years of service, as of today, for the employee.

AICPA.130746FAR

343. An overfunded single-employer defined benefit postretirement plan should be recognized in a classified statement of financial position as a

A. Noncurrent liability.

B. Current liability.

C. Noncurrent asset.

D. Current asset.

Share-Based Payments

Stock Options

aicpa.aq.stock.opt.001_17

344. A company granted its employees 100,000 stock options on January 1, Year 1. The stock options had a grant date fair value of $15 per option and a three-year vesting period. On January 1, Year 2, the company estimated the fair value of the stock options to be $18 per option. Assuming that the company did **not** grant any additional options or modify the terms of any existing option grants during Year 2, what amount of share-based compensation expense should the company report for the year ended December 31, Year 2?

A. $500,000

B. $600,000

C. $700,000

D. $800,000

assess.AICPA.FAR.stock.comp-0046

345. On January 1, year 1, the board of directors of a corporation granted 10,000 stock options to the CEO. Each option permits the purchase of one share of stock at $25 per share, the current market price of the stock. The options are exercisable on December 31, year 4, as long as the CEO is still employed. The options expire on December 31, year 5. The grant date fair value of each option is $5. The corporation must recognize

   A. $50,000 of compensation expense when the options are exercised.
   B. $50,000 of compensation expense in year 1.
   C. $12,500 of compensation expense per year for four years.
   D. $10,000 of compensation expense per year for five years.

Stock Awards

AICPA.061264FAR-P1-FA

346. A restricted stock award was granted at the beginning of 20X5 calling for 3,000 shares of stock to be awarded to executives at the beginning of 20X9. The fair value of one option was $20 at grant date. During 20X7, 100 shares were forfeited because an executive left the firm.

What amount of compensation expense is recognized for 20X7?

   A. $14,000
   B. $15,000
   C. $14,500
   D. $13,500

AICPA.130748FAR

347. On January 1, year 1, a company issued its employees 10,000 shares of restricted stock. On January 1, year 2, the company issued to its employees an additional 20,000 shares of restricted stock. Additional information about the company's stock is as follows:

Date	Fair Value of Stock (per share)
January 1, year 1	$20
December 31, year 1	22
January 1, year 2	25
December 31, year 2	30

The shares vest at the end of a four-year period. There are no forfeitures. What amount should be recorded as compensation expense for the 12-month period ended December 31, year 2?

   A. $175,000
   B. $205,000
   C. $225,000
   D. $500,000

Stock Appreciation Rights

AICPA.083751FAR-SIM

348. Select the correct statement about executive compensation plans involving stock.

   A. The total amount of compensation expense for a restricted stock award plan is recognized when the stock is issued.
   B. The total amount of compensation expense for a restricted stock award plan is determined at the grant date.
   C. For stock-appreciation rights plans payable in cash, compensation expense is recognized only during the service period.
   D. For stock-appreciation rights plans payable in cash, compensation expense recognized in any given reporting period cannot be negative.

Income Taxes

Income Tax Basics

aicpa.aq.income.tax.bas.001_17

349. Which of the following statements is a primary objective of accounting for income taxes?

   A. To compare an enterprise's federal tax liability to its state tax liability.
   B. To identify all of the permanent and temporary differences of an enterprise.
   C. To estimate the effect of the tax consequences of future events.
   D. To recognize the amount of deferred tax liabilities and deferred tax assets reported for future tax consequences.

aq.income.tax.bas.002_0318

350. A company has two temporary differences resulting in deferred tax consequences. One difference results in a deferred tax asset; the other difference results in a deferred tax liability. The deferred tax asset is greater than the deferred tax liability. How should the company report the deferred tax consequences of the temporary differences on the balance sheet?

   A. Report the deferred tax asset in the noncurrent assets portion of the balance sheet and report the deferred tax liability in the noncurrent liabilities portion of the balance sheet.

B. Report a net noncurrent deferred tax asset in the noncurrent assets section of the balance sheet.

C. Report a net current deferred tax asset in the noncurrent assets section of the balance sheet.

D. Report a net noncurrent deferred tax liability in the noncurrent liability section of the balance sheet.

Permanent Differences

AICPA.910541FAR-P1-FA

351. On June 30, 20X4, Ank Corp. pre-paid a $19,000 premium on an annual insurance policy. The premium payment was a tax-deductible expense in Ank's 20X4 cash-basis tax return. The accrual-basis income statement will report a $9,500 insurance expense in 20X4 and 20X5.

Ank elected early application of FASB Statement No. 109, Accounting for Income Taxes. Ank's income tax rate is 30% in 20X4 and 25% thereafter. In Ank's December 31, 20X4 balance sheet, what amount related to the insurance should be reported as a deferred income tax liability?

A. $5,700
B. $4,750
C. $2,850
D. $2,375

Temporary Differences

AICPA.911132FAR-P1-FA

352. Lake Corp., a newly organized company, reported pre-tax financial income of $100,000 for Year 1. Among the items reported in Lake's Year 1 income statement are the following:

Premium on officer's life insurance with Lake as owner and beneficiary	$15,000
Interest received on municipal bonds	20,000

The enacted tax rate for Year 1 is 30% and 25% thereafter. In its December 31, Year 1 balance sheet, Lake should report a deferred income tax liability of

A. $28,500
B. $4,500
C. $3,750
D. $0

AICPA.101127FAR

353. When accounting for income taxes, a temporary difference occurs in which of the following scenarios?

A. An item is included in the calculation of net income, but is neither taxable nor deductible.

B. An item is included in the calculation of net income in one year and in taxable income in a different year.

C. An item is no longer taxable, owing to a change in the tax law.

D. The accrual method of accounting is used.

AICPA.921127FAR-P1-FA

354. For the year ended December 31, 20X4, Mont Co.'s books showed income of $600,000 before provision for income tax expense. To compute taxable income for federal income tax purposes, the following items should be noted:

Income from exempt municipal bonds	$60,000
Depreciation deducted for tax purposes in excess of depreciation recorded on the books	$120,000
Proceeds received from life insurance on death of officer	$100,000
Estimated tax payments	0
Enacted corporate tax rate	30%

Ignoring the alternative minimum tax provisions, what amount should Mont report at December 31, 20X4 as its current federal income tax liability?

A. $96,000
B. $114,000
C. $150,000
D. $162,000

Tax Accrual Entry

AICPA.110560FAR

355. Fern Co. has net income, before taxes, of $200,000, including $20,000 interest revenue from municipal bonds and $10,000 paid for officers' life insurance premiums where the company is the beneficiary. The tax rate for the current year is 30%. What is Fern's effective tax rate?

A. 27.0%
B. 28.5%
C. 30.0%
D. 31.5%

AICPA.941151FAR-FA

356. In its 20X5 income statement, Cere Co. reported income before income taxes of $300,000.

    Cere estimated that, because of permanent differences, taxable income for 20X5 would be $280,000. During 20X5, Cere made estimated tax payments of $50,000, which were debited to income tax expense. Cere is subject to a 30% tax rate.

    What amount should Cere report as income tax expense?

    A. $34,000
    B. $50,000
    C. $84,000
    D. $90,000

Interperiod Tax Allocation Process

AICPA.051155FAR-FA

357. Miro Co. began business on January 2, 20X0. Miro uses the double-declining balance method of depreciation for financial statement purposes for its building, and the straight-line method for income taxes.

    On January 16, 20X2 Miro elected to switch to the straight-line method for both financial statement and tax purposes. The building cost $240,000 in 20X0, which has an estimated useful life of 15 years and no salvage value.

    Data related to the building are as follows:

Year	Double-Declining Depreciation	Straight-Line Depreciation
20X0	$30,000	$16,000
20X1	$20,000	$16,000

    Miro's tax rate is 40%

    A. There should be no reduction in Miro's deferred tax liabilities or deferred tax assets in 2002.
    B. Miro's deferred tax liability should be reduced by $7,200 in 20X2.
    C. Miro's deferred tax asset should be reduced by $7,200 in 20X2.
    D. Miro's deferred tax asset should be increased by $7,200 in 20X2.

assess.AICPA.FAR.inter.tax.pro-0008

358. A company reported the following financial information:

Taxable income for current year	$120,000
Deferred income tax liability, beginning of year	50,000
Deferred income tax liability, end of year	55,000
Deferred income tax asset, beginning of year	10,000
Deferred income tax asset, end of year	16,000
Current and future years' tax rate	35%

    The current-year's income tax expense is what amount?

    A. $41,000
    B. $42,000
    C. $43,000
    D. $53,000

Valuation Allowance for Deferred Tax Assets

AICPA.951136FAR-FA

359. On its December 31, 20X5 balance sheet, Shin Co. has income tax payable of $13,000 and a current deferred tax asset of $20,000, before determining the need for a valuation account.

    Shin had reported a deferred tax asset of $15,000 at December 31, 20X4. No estimated tax payments are made during 20X5. At December 31, 20X5, Shin determines that it is *more likely* than not that 10% of the deferred tax asset would not be realized.

    In its 20X5 income statement, what amount should Shin report as total income tax expense?

    A. $8,000
    B. $8,500
    C. $10,000
    D. $13,000

Uncertain Tax Positions

AICPA.090876FAR

360. At the end of the current year, Swen Inc. prepares its tax return, which reflects an uncertain amount, reducing the firm's tax liability by $40,000. Swen estimates that, upon audit by the IRS, there is a 20% chance that the full $40,000 benefit will be upheld, and

a 40% chance that the benefit will be only $25,000. As a result of the required recognition and measurement principles for uncertain tax positions, current-year income tax expense is reduced by what amount?

A. $18,000
B. $25,000
C. $40,000
D. $15,000

AICPA.090877FAR

361. Two years ago, Aggre Inc. recognized the tax benefit of an uncertain tax position. income tax expense in that year was reduced by $20,000 as a result. In addition, Aggre recorded a $5,000 tax liability for unrecognized benefits for the same tax position. During the current year, the uncertainty is resolved and a benefit of $22,000 is upheld. By what amount is current-year income tax expense affected by the resolution of the prior uncertainty?

A. $2,000 decrease.
B. $22,000 decrease.
C. $5,000 decrease.
D. There is no effect.

Net Operating Losses

AICPA.061213FAR

362. Which of the following should be disclosed in a company's financial statements related to deferred taxes?

I. The types and amounts of existing temporary differences.
II. The types and amounts of existing permanent differences.
III. The nature and amount of each type of operating loss and tax credit carry-forward.

A. I and II only.
B. I and III only.
C. II and III only.
D. I, II, and III.

AICPA.083752FAR-SIM

363. At the end of the previous year, a firm reported a $6,000 deferred tax asset from a net-operating-loss carry-forward that can be carried forward several years into the future. The tax rate is 30%. For the current year, the firm records estimated warranty expense of $30,000 for the year and incurred $10,000 of warranty-claims costs. Taxable income for the current year is

$12,000. Compute income tax expense (benefit) for the current year.

A. ($5,400)
B. ($2,400)
C. $3,600
D. Neither expense nor benefit.

Accounting Changes and Error Corrections

Types of Changes and Accounting Approaches

AICPA.090665.FAR.III

364. How should a company report its decision to change from a cash-basis to an accrual-basis of accounting?

A. As a change in accounting principle, requiring the cumulative effect of the change (net of tax) to be reported in the income statement.
B. Prospectively, with no amounts restated and no cumulative adjustment.
C. As an extraordinary item (net of tax).
D. As a Prior period adjustment (net of tax), by adjusting the beginning balance of retained earnings.

AICPA.951143FAR-FA

365. Lore Co. changed from the cash basis to the accrual basis of accounting during 2005. The cumulative effect of this change should be reported in Lore's 2005 financial statements as a

A. Prior period adjustment resulting from the correction of an error.
B. Prior period adjustment resulting from the change in accounting principle.
C. Adjustment to retained earnings for an accounting principle change.
D. Component of income after extraordinary item.

Retrospective Application

AICPA.950545FAR-FA

366. During 2005, Orca Corp. decided to change from the FIFO method of inventory valuation to the weighted-average method. Inventory balances under each method were as follows:

	FIFO	Weighted-Average
January 1, 2005	$71,000	$77,000
December 31, 2005	$79,000	$83,000

Orca's income tax rate is 30%.

In its 2005 financial statements, what amount should Orca report as the cumulative effect of this accounting change?

- A. $2,800
- B. $4,000
- C. $4,200
- D. $6,000

Prospective Application

AICPA.130727FAR

367. Which of the following statements is correct as it relates to changes in accounting estimates?

- A. Most changes in accounting estimates are accounted for retrospectively.
- B. Whenever it is impossible to determine whether a change in an estimate or a change in accounting principle occurred, the change should be considered a change in principle.
- C. Whenever it is impossible to determine whether a change in accounting estimate or a change in accounting principle has occurred, the change should be considered a change in estimate.
- D. It is easier to differentiate between a change in accounting estimate and a change in accounting principle than it is to differentiate between a change in accounting estimate and a correction of an error.

Accounting Errors—Restatement

AICPA.101125FAR

368. The senior accountant for Carlton Co., a public company with a complex capital structure, has just finished preparing Carlton's income statement for the current fiscal year. While reviewing the income statement, Carlton's finance director noticed that the earnings-per-share data have been omitted. What changes will have to be made to Carlton's income statement as a result of the omission of the earnings-per-share data?

- A. No changes will have to be made to Carlton 's income statement. The income statement is complete without the earnings-per-share data.
- B. Carlton's income statement will have to be revised to include the earnings-per-share data.
- C. Carlton's income statement will only have to be revised to include the earnings-per-share

data if Carlton's market capitalization is greater than $5mn.
- D. Carlton's income statement will only have to be revised to include the earnings-per-share data if Carlton's net income for the past two years is greater than $5mn.

AICPA.130732FAR

369. Cuthbert Industrials, Inc. prepares three-year comparative financial statements. In year 3, Cuthbert discovered an error in the previously issued financial statements for year 1. The error affects the financial statements that were issued in years 1 and 2. How should the company report the error?

- A. The financial statements for years 1 and 2 should be restated; an offsetting adjustment to the cumulative effect of the error should be made to the comprehensive income in the year 3 financial statements.
- B. The financial statements for years 1 and 2 should **not** be restated; financial statements for year 3 should disclose the fact that the error was made in prior years.
- C. The financial statements for years 1 and 2 should **not** be restated; the cumulative effect of the error on years 1 and 2 should be reflected in the carrying amounts of assets and liabilities as of the beginning of year 3.
- D. The financial statements for years 1 and 2 should be restated; the cumulative effect of the error on years 1 and 2 should be reflected in the carrying amounts of assets and liabilities as of the beginning of year 3.

Business Combinations

Introduction to Business Combinations

AICPA.081240FAR-SIM

370. Topco owns 60% of the voting common stock of Midco and 40% of the voting common stock of Botco. Topco wishes to gain control of Botco by having Midco buy shares of Botco's voting stock. Which one of the following minimum levels of ownership of Botco must Midco additionally need to obtain in order for Topco to have controlling interest of Botco's voting stock?

- A. 11%
- B. 17%
- C. 26%
- D. 50+%

Acquisition Method of Accounting

Introduction to Acquisition Method of Accounting

AICPA.090670.FAR.III.A-SIM

371. The requirements of ASC 805, *Business Combinations*, apply to all of the following business combinations **except** for which one?

   A. Combination between financial institutions
   B. The acquisition of a foreign entity by a U.S. entity
   C. Combination between not-for-profit organizations
   D. The acquisition of a group of assets that constitutes a business

AICPA.090806.FAR.III.A-SIM

372. Which of the following is/are acceptable methods to account for a business combination?

	Purchase Method	Acquisition Method	Pooling of Interests Method
A.	Yes	Yes	Yes
B.	Yes	Yes	No
C.	Yes	No	No
D.	No	Yes	No

Determining the Cost of the Business Acquired

aicpa.aq.cost.bus.acq.001_17

373. A company acquires another company for $3,000,000 in cash, $10,000,000 in stock, and the following contingent consideration:

   - $1,000,000 after Year 1, $1,000,000 after Year 2, and $500,000 after year 3, if earnings of the subsidiary exceed $10,000,000 in each of the three years.

   The fair value of the contingent -based consideration portion is $2,100,000. What is the total consideration transferred for this business combination?

   A. $15,500,000
   B. $15,100,000
   C. $13,000,000
   D. $5,100,000

AICPA.130734FAR

374. Bale Co. incurred $100,000 of acquisition costs related to the purchase of the net assets of Dixon Co. The $100,000 should be

   A. Allocated on a pro rata basis to the nonmonetary assets acquired.
   B. Capitalized as part of goodwill and tested annually for impairment.
   C. Capitalized as an other asset and amortized over five years.
   D. Expensed as incurred in the current period.

Recognizing/Measuring Assets, Liabilities, and Noncontrolling Interest

aicpa.aq.recog.assets.001_17

375. On December 31, Year 1, Andover Co. acquired Barrelman, Inc. Before the acquisition, a product lawsuit seeking $10 million in damages was filed against Barrelman. As of the acquisition date, Andover believed that it was probable that a liability existed and that the fair value of the liability was $5 million. What amount should Andover record as a liability as of December 31, Year 1?

   A. $0
   B. $5,000,000
   C. $7,500,000
   D. $10,000,000

AICPA.090709.FAR.III.A-SIM

376. Which of the following statements, if any, concerning a noncontrolling interest in an acquiree is/are correct?

   I. The value assigned to a noncontrolling interest in an acquiree should be based on the proportional share of that interest in the net assets of the acquiree.
   II. The fair value per share of the noncontrolling interest in an acquiree must be the same as the fair value per share of the controlling (acquirer) interest.

   A. Both I and II.
   B. I only.
   C. II only.
   D. Neither I nor II.

Recognizing/Measuring Goodwill or Bargain Purchase Amount

AICPA.090712.FAR.III.A-SIM

377. Windco, Inc. acquired 100% of the voting common stock of Trace, Inc. by transferring the following consideration to Trace's shareholders:

Cash	$100,000
5,000 new shares of Windco's $10 par common stock (which is less than 1% of Windco's outstanding stock)	$50,000 (par)

In addition, Windco paid $12,000 direct cost of carrying out the combination.

At the date of the acquisition, Windco's common stock was selling in an active market for $18 per share. Also, at the date of the acquisition, Trace had the following assets and liabilities with the book values and fair values shown:

	Book Value	Market Value
Accounts Receivable	$20,000	$20,000
Property and Equipment	80,000	100,000
Land	60,000	80,000
Other Assets	40,000	40,000
Total Assets	$200,000	$240,000
Accounts Payable	$15,000	$15,000
Other Short-term Debt	10,000	10,000
Long-term Debt	35,000	35,000
Total Liabilities	$60,000	$60,000

Which one of the following is the fair value of Trace's net assets at the date of the business combination?

A. $140,000
B. $180,000
C. $192,000
D. $240,000

AICPA.110546FAR

378. Damon Co. purchased 100% of the outstanding common stock of Smith Co. in an acquisition by issuing 20,000 shares of its $1 par common stock that had a fair value of $10 per share and providing contingent consideration that had a fair value of $10,000 on the acquisition date. Damon also incurred $15,000 in direct acquisition costs. On the acquisition date, Smith had assets with a book value of $200,000, a fair value of $350,000, and related liabilities with a book and fair value of $70,000. What amount of gain should Damon report related to this transaction?

A. $55,000
B. $70,000
C. $80,000
D. $250,000

Post-Acquisition Issues

AICPA.090722.FAR.III.A-SIM

379. Which one of the following assets recognized in a business combination will require that the amount recognized be amortized over future periods?

A. An asset arising from a contingency
B. A reacquired right asset
C. An indemnification asset
D. A contingent consideration asset

AICPA.130733FAR

380. How should the acquirer recognize a bargain purchase in a business acquisition?

A. As negative goodwill in the statement of financial position
B. As goodwill in the statement of financial position
C. As a gain in earnings at the acquisition date
D. As a deferred gain that is amortized into earnings over the estimated future periods benefited

Disclosure Requirements—Acquisition Method

AICPA.090728.FAR.III.A-SIM

381. An entity must disclose information about a business combination it carries out if the acquisition date occurs:

	During the Reporting Period	After the Reporting Period but Before Statements are Released
A.	Yes	Yes
B.	Yes	No
C.	No	Yes
D.	No	No

AICPA.090733.FAR.III.A-SIM

382. When a bargain purchase occurs in a business combination, which of the following types of information must be disclosed in the period of the combination?

I. The amount of gain recognized.
II. The income statement line item that includes the gain.
III. A description of the basis for the bargain purchase amount.

A. I only.
B. I and II only.
C. I and III only.
D. I, II, and III.

Recording Business Combinations

AICPA.081257FAR-SIM

383. Pine Company acquired all of the assets and liabilities of Straw Company for cash in a legal merger. Which one of the following would not be recognized by Pine on its books in recording the business combination?

   A. Accounts receivable.
   B. Investment in Straw.
   C. Intangible asset—Patent.
   D. Accounts payable.

AICPA.090736.FAR.III.A-SIM

384. Sayon Co. issues 200,000 shares of $5 par value common stock to acquire Trask Co. in an acquisition-business combination. The market value of Sayon's common stock is $12 per share. Legal and consulting fees incurred in relation to the acquisition are $110,000 paid in cash. Registration and issuance costs for the common stock are $35,000. What should be recorded in Sayon's additional paid-in capital account for this business combination?

   A. $1,545,000
   B. $1,400,000
   C. $1,365,000
   D. $1,255,000

IFRS—Business Combinations

aq.ifrs.bus.001_17

385. Under IFRS, the asset goodwill may be recognized

   A. When it is acquired in a business combination.
   B. When it is internally generated or acquired by purchase.
   C. When it is clear that it exists and has value.
   D. When it has future economic benefits.

AICPA.121101FAR-SIM

386. Under IFRS, which of the following would not be recognized as part of a business combination?

   A. Contingent asset
   B. Contingent liability
   C. Goodwill
   D. Fair value of the consideration transferred

Financial Instruments

Financial Instruments Introduction

AICPA.090150FAR-SIM

387. Which one of the following is not a characteristic of financial instruments?

   A. Financial instruments include derivative instruments.
   B. Certain disclosure requirements apply to all financial instruments.
   C. Financial instruments can be used for hedging purposes.
   D. All financial instruments have the same accounting requirements.

IFRS—Financial Instruments

AICPA.101234FAR-SIM

388. Which of the following is the correct accounting measurement and treatment under IFRS for assets classified as "Loans and Receivables"?

   A. Amortized cost, with interest and amortization recognized in current income.
   B. Amortized cost, with interest and amortization recognized in other comprehensive income.
   C. Fair value, with changes in fair value recognized in current income.
   D. Fair value, with changes in fair value recognized in other comprehensive income.

Financial Instruments Disclosures

AICPA.070731FAR

389. If it is not practicable for an entity to estimate the fair value of a financial instrument, which of the following should be disclosed?

   I. Information pertinent to estimating the fair value of the instrument.
   II. The reasons it is not practicable to estimate fair value.

   A. I only.
   B. II only.
   C. Both I and II.
   D. Neither I nor II.

AICPA.090319FAR-SIM

390. Disclosure of information about significant concentrations of credit risk is required for:

   A. All financial instruments.
   B. Financial instruments with off-balance-sheet credit risk only.

Multiple Choice Questions

C. Financial instruments with off-balance-sheet market risk only.
D. Financial instruments with off-balance-sheet risk of accounting loss only.

Derivatives and Hedging

Derivatives Introduction

AICPA.101197FAR
391. A derivative financial instrument is best described as:

   A. Evidence of an ownership interest in an entity such as shares of common stock.
   B. A contract that has its settlement value tied to an underlying notional amount.
   C. A contract that conveys to a second entity a right to receive cash from a first entity.
   D. A contract that conveys to a second entity a right to future collections on accounts receivable from a first entity.

AICPA.130736FAR
392. Smythe Co. invested $200 in a call option for 100 shares of Gin Co. $.50 par common stock, when the market price was $10 per share. The option expired in three months and had an exercise price of $9 per share. What was the intrinsic value of the call option at the time of initial investment?

   A. $50
   B. $100
   C. $200
   D. $900

Hedging Introduction

AICPA.101226FAR-SIM
393. Which of the following statements, if either, concerning accounting for derivative financial instruments is/are correct?

   I. Derivative instruments can be used only for hedging purposes.
   II. Derivative instruments can be used only to hedge fair value.

   A. I only.
   B. II only.
   C. Both I and II.
   D. Neither I nor II.

Fair Value Hedges

AICPA.090328FAR-SIM
394. On October 1, 2008, Buyco entered into a legally enforceable contract to acquire raw material inventory in 180 days for $20,000. In order to mitigate the risk of a change in the value of the raw materials, Buyco also entered into a qualified 180-day forward contract to hedge the fair value of the raw materials. At December 31, 2008, the value of the raw materials had decreased by $500, and the fair value of the futures contract had increased by $480. On March 29, 2009, the date the raw materials were delivered to Buyco, they had a fair value of $19,300, and the forward contract had a fair value of $700. Which one of the following is the amount by which the derivative is ineffective as a fair value hedge for 2008?

   A. $980
   B. $500
   C. $480
   D. $20

AICPA.090332FAR-SIM
395. Which one of the following is *least likely* to be a characteristic of a firm commitment?

   A. It is evidenced by a contractual obligation.
   B. It can be the hedged item in a fair value hedge.
   C. It has been recorded as an asset or liability.
   D. It is subject to the risk of change in fair value.

Cash-Flow Hedges

AICPA.090333FAR-SIM
396. Which one of the following is not a characteristic of a cash flow hedge?

   A. Can be used to hedge the risk of variability in cash flow of a forecasted transaction.
   B. Measures the hedged item using the present value of expected cash flows.
   C. The derivative used as the hedging instrument is measured at fair value.
   D. All differences between the change in value of the hedged item and the change in value of the hedging instrument is recognized in current income.

AICPA Release Questions are Copyright 2019 American Institute of CPAs. All rights reserved. Used with permission.

66

assess.AICPA.FAR.cash.flow.hedg-0026

397. Which of the following items is included in accumulated other comprehensive income or loss?

   A. Unrealized gains and losses from the ineffective portion of a derivative properly designated as a cash flow hedge
   B. Unrealized holding gains or losses on securities classified as trading securities
   C. A reduction of shareholders' equity related to employee stock ownership plans
   D. Prior service costs not previously recognized as a component of net periodic pension costs

Foreign Currency Hedges

AICPA.090357FAR-SIM

398. Which one of the following is not a characteristic of a foreign currency hedge?

   A. Hedges the risk due to change in foreign currency exchange rates.
   B. Can hedge net investments in a foreign entity.
   C. Are all treated as fair value hedges.
   D. Can be used to hedge forecasted intercompany transactions.

AICPA.090360FAR-SIM

399. Which of the following statements concerning derivatives used as foreign currency hedges is/are correct?

   I. Can be used to hedge the risk of exchange rate changes on planned transactions.
   II. Can be used to hedge the risk of exchange rate changes on available-for-sale investments.
   III. Can be used to hedge the risk of exchange rate changes on accounts receivable and accounts payable.

   A. I only.
   B. I and II only.
   C. II and III only.
   D. I, II, and III.

Effectiveness and Disclosure

AICPA.090361FAR-SIM_0818

400. Specific disclosures are required for entities that:

	Issue Derivatives	Hold Derivatives
A.	Yes	Yes
B.	Yes	No
C.	No	Yes
D.	No	No

IFRS—Hedging

AICPA.121102FAR-SIM

401. Which of the following concepts is not part of the definition of a derivative under IFRS?

   A. The instrument has one or more underlyings.
   B. The instrument requires little or no initial net investment.
   C. The instrument permits net settlement.
   D. The instrument has a notional amount.

Foreign Currency Denominated Transactions

Introduction and Definitions

AICPA.090171FAR-SIM

402. If a foreign currency exchange gain results from the effects of a change in exchange rates on an account receivable, where will the exchange gain be reported in the financial statements?

   A. As other comprehensive income.
   B. As an extraordinary gain.
   C. As an item of income from continuing operations.
   D. As a deferred gain.

Import Transactions

AICPA.090173FAR-SIM

403. Can a gain or loss on a foreign currency import transaction be recognized if the transaction is initiated in one fiscal period and settled:

	In the Same Fiscal Period	In a Later Fiscal Period
A.	Yes	Yes
B.	Yes	No
C.	No	Yes
D.	No	No

AICPA.090179FAR-SIM

404. Fogg Co., a U.S. company, contracted to purchase foreign goods. Payment in foreign currency was due one month after the goods were received at Fogg's warehouse. Between the receipt of goods and the time of payment, the exchange rates changed in Fogg's favor.

The resulting gain should be included in Fogg's financial statements as a(an):

A. Component of income from continuing operations.
B. Extraordinary item.
C. Deferred credit.
D. Component of comprehensive income.

Export Transactions

AICPA.090180FAR-SIM

405. A sale of goods, denominated in a currency other than the entity's functional currency, resulted in a receivable that was fixed in terms of the amount of foreign currency that would be received. Exchange rates between the functional currency and the currency in which the transaction was denominated changed. The resulting gain should be included as a:

A. Translation gain reported as a component of comprehensive income.
B. Translation gain reported as a component of income from continuing operations.
C. Transaction gain reported as a component of comprehensive income.
D. Transaction gain reported as a component of income from continuing operations.

AICPA.120622FAR

406. On June 19, Don Co., a U.S. company, sold and delivered merchandise on a 30-day account to Cologne GmbH, a German corporation, for 200,000 euros. On July 19, Cologne paid Don in full. Relevant currency exchange rates were:

	June 19	July 19
Spot rate	$.988	$.995
30-day forward rate	.990	1.000

What amount should Don record on June 19 as an account receivable for its sale to Cologne?

A. $197,600
B. $198,000
C. $199,000
D. $200,000

Foreign Currency Hedges

Introduction to Forward and Option Contracts

AICPA.090197FAR-SIM

407. When used for speculative purposes, which of the following contracts is likely to result in a foreign currency loss to the contract holder who initiated the contract?

	Foreign Currency Forward Exchange Contract	Foreign Currency Option Contract
A.	Yes	Yes
B.	Yes	No
C.	No	Yes
D.	No	No

Natural (Economic) Hedge

AICPA.090120FAR-SIM

408. Which one of the following is not a characteristic of hedging?

A. Typically involves offsetting transactions or positions.
B. Assures no gain or loss on the item being hedged.
C. Is a strategy for managing risks.
D. Can be used for obligations to be satisfied in a foreign currency.

AICPA.09024FAR-SIM

409. The net effect of a change in value of a hedged item and its related hedging instrument may be:

I. A gain.
II. A loss.
III. Neither a gain nor a loss.

A. I only.
B. II only.
C. III only.
D. I, II, and III.

Hedging Forecasted Transactions and Firm Commitment

AICPA.090207FAR-SIM

410. A hedge to offset the risk of exchange rate changes on converting the financial statements of a foreign subsidiary to the domestic (functional) currency would be the hedge of:

A. A forecasted transaction.
B. A recognized asset.
C. A net investment in a foreign operation.
D. An available-for-sale investment.

AICPA.090219FAR-SIM

411. If a firm commitment denominated in a foreign currency is hedged with a forward exchange contract, which of the following statements is/are correct?

    I.   Even though the firm commitment is hedged, a net gain or loss can be reported.

    II. As a result of hedging the firm commitment, an otherwise unrecognized asset or liability may have to be recognized.

    A. I only.

    B. II only.

    C. Both I and II.

    D. Neither I nor II.

Hedging Asset/Liability, Available for Sale, and Foreign Operations

AICPA.090121FAR-SIM

412. On December 12, 20X8, Averseco entered into a forward exchange contract to purchase 100,000 units of a foreign currency in 90 days. The contract was designated as and qualified as a fair value hedge of a purchase of inventory made that day and payable in March 20X9. The relevant direct exchange rates between the foreign currency and the dollar are as follows:

	Spot Rate	Forward Rate (for March 12, 20X9)
December 12, 20X8	$0.88	$0.90
December 31, 20X8	0.98	0.93

At December 31, 20X8, what amount of foreign currency transaction net gain or loss should Averseco recognize in income as a result of its foreign currency obligation and related hedge contract? (Ignore premium/discount and present value considerations.)

    A. $-0-

    B. $3,000

    C. $7,000

    D. $10,000

AICPA.090235FAR-SIM

413. Which of the following statements concerning the hedging of an investment in a foreign operation is/are correct?

    I.   The hedged item is the result of translating the foreign operation's financial statements.

    II. Only forward contracts can be used to hedge an investment in a foreign operation.

    A. I only.

    B. II only.

    C. Both I and II.

    D. Neither I nor II.

Speculation and Summary

AICPA.090243FAR-SIM

414. In which of the following hedges using a forward contract will at least a portion of any currency exchange gain or loss on the hedging instrument be reported as a translation adjustment in other comprehensive income?

    A. Forecasted transaction hedge.

    B. Firm commitment hedge.

    C. Investment in available-for-sale securities hedge.

    D. Net investment in foreign operations hedge.

AICPA.090862FAR

415. On December 1 of the current year, Bann Co. entered into an option contract to purchase 2,000 shares of Norta Co. stock for $40 per share (the same as the current market price) by the end of the next two months. The time value of the option contract is $600. At the end of December, Norta's stock was selling for $43, and the time value of the option was now $400. If Bann does not exercise its option until January of the subsequent year, which of the following changes would reflect the proper accounting treatment for this transaction on Bann's December 31, year-end financial statements?

    A. The option value will be disclosed in footnotes only.

    B. Other comprehensive income will increase by $6,000.

    C. Net income will increase by $5,800.

    D. Current assets will decrease by $200.

Conversion of Foreign Financial Statements

Introduction to Conversion of Foreign Financial Statements

AICPA.090168FAR-SIM

416. Operating transactions denominated in a foreign currency are converted to the functional currency using the:

    A. Historic exchange rate.

    B. Current exchange rate.

    C. Average exchange rate.

    D. Forward exchange rate.

AICPA.090262FAR-SIM

417. Which one of the following best describes the currency in which the final consolidated financial statements are presented?

 A. The local currency.
 B. The reporting currency.
 C. The functional currency.
 D. The temporal currency.

Conversion Using Translation

AICPA.090246FAR-SIM

418. A subsidiary's functional currency is the local currency which has not experienced significant inflation. The appropriate exchange rate for translating the depreciation on plant assets in the income statement of the foreign subsidiary is the:

 A. Exit exchange rate.
 B. Historical exchange rate.
 C. Weighted average exchange rate over the economic life of each plant asset.
 D. Weighted average exchange rate for the current year.

Conversion Using Remeasurement

AICPA.090272FAR-SIM

419. Papco, a U.S. entity, has a subsidiary, Sapco, located in a foreign country. Sapco is essentially a sales unit for Papco. After remeasuring Sapco's financial statements from the foreign currency to Papco's reporting currency, Papco determined that it had a loss on the remeasurement. How should Papco report the loss in its consolidated financial statements?

 A. As an extraordinary loss.
 B. As income from continuing operations.
 C. As an item of other comprehensive income.
 D. As a deferred item until the subsidiary is sold.

AICPA.090308FAR-SIM

420. Papco, a U.S. entity, has a subsidiary, Sapco, located in a foreign country. Sapco is essentially a sales unit for Papco. Sapco prepared the following shortened financial statements in its local currency, the FCU, for the fiscal year ended December 31, 20X8:

Statement of Net Income and Comprehensive Income (20X8)	FCUs (in 000)
Sales	12,000
COGS	(4,000)
Depreciation Expense	(1,000)
Other Expenses	(3,000)
Net Income	4,000
Other Comprehensive Income	0
Comprehensive Income	4,000
Retained Earnings (20X8)	
Beginning Retained Earnings (end 20X7)	6,000
Add: Net Income (20X8)	4,000
Deduct: Dividends (20X8)	(1,000)
Ending Retained Earnings	9,000
Balance Sheet (12/31/20X8)	
Cash and Account Receivable	2,000
Inventory	6,000
Fixed Assets	10,000
Total Assets	18,000
Liabilities	2,000
Common Stock	7,000
Retained Earnings	9,000
Subtotal	18,000
Accumulated Other Comprehensive Income	0
Total Liabilities + Equity	18,000

The following exchange rates were available:

Historic exchange rate when Sanco was established by Panco:	1 FCU = $1.200
Historic exchange rate when Sanco's fixed assets were acquired:	1 FCU = $1.250
Weighted average exchange rate for 20X8:	1 FCU = $1.300
Spot exchange rate at date dividend declared:	1 FCU = $1.290
Spot exchange rate at December 31, 20X8:	1 FCU = $1.310

Which one of the following is the amount (in 000) of Sapco's inventory in U.S. dollars?

 A. $6,000
 B. $7,200
 C. $7,800
 D. $7,860

Remeasurement, Translation, and IFRS

AICPA.082044FAR-III.C.I

421. Gordon Ltd., a 100% owned British subsidiary of a U.S. parent company, reports its financial statement in local currency, the British pound. A local newspaper published the following U.S. exchange rates to the British pound at year end:

Current rate	$1.50
Historical rate (acquisition)	1.70
Average rate	1.55
Inventory (FIFO)	1.60

Which currency rate should Gordon use to convert its income statement to U.S. dollars at year end?

A. $1.50
B. $1.55
C. $1.60
D. $1.70

AICPA.090295FAR-SIM

422. Which one of the following sets shows the correct reporting of an adjustment (gain or loss) that results from translation and one that results from remeasurement of financial statements from a foreign currency to a reporting currency?

	Translation Adjustment	Remeasurement Adjustment
A.	Net Income	Net Income
B.	Net Income	Other comprehensive income
C.	Other comprehensive income	Net Income
D.	Other comprehensive income	Other comprehensive income

Leases

Background, Short-Term Leases, and Operating Leases

aq.brgd.short.term.op.001_0818

423. On 1/31/Y1, Clay Company leased a new machine from Saxe Corp. The following data relate to the lease transaction at its inception:

Lease term	10 years
Annual rental payable at beginning of each lease year	$50,000
Useful life of machine	15 years
Implicit interest rate	10%
Present value of an annuity of 1 in advance for 10 periods at 10%	6.76
Present value of annuity of 1 in arrears for 10 periods at 10%	6.15
Fair value of the machine	$400,000

The lease has no renewal option, and the possession of the machine reverts to Saxe when the lease terminates. At the inception of the lease, Clay should record a lease liability of

A. $400,000.
B. $338,000.
C. $307,500
D. $0

aq.brgd.short.term.op.002_0818

424. Marnie Company enters into a two-year lease. The terms of the lease do not transfer ownership and do not contain a bargain purchase option. The lease is for 60% of the asset's economic life and represents 80% of its fair value. The asset is not a specialized asset and does have alternative uses. How should Marnie classify and record the lease?

A. The lease is classified as an operating lease, and no lease liability is recorded at the inception because it does not meet finance lease criteria.
B. The lease should be classified as a short-term lease because it is for only two years.
C. The lease should be classified as an operating lease, and a lease liability should be recorded at the inception of the lease.
D. The lease should be classified as a finance lease, and a lease liability should be recorded at the inception of the lease.

Finance Lease Basics

aicpa.aq.cap.lease.001_0818

425. Arena Corp. leased equipment from Bolton Corp. and correctly classified the lease as a Finance lease. The present value of the minimum lease payments at lease inception was $1,000,000. The executory costs to be paid by Bolton were $50,000, and the fair value of the equipment at lease inception was $900,000.

What amount should Arena report as the lease liability at the lease's inception?

A. $900,000
B. $950,000
C. $1,000,000
D. $1,050,000

Finance Lease—Lessee

assess.AICPA.061209FAR_0818

426. Koby Co. entered into a finance lease with a vendor for equipment on January 2 for 7 years. The equipment has no guaranteed residual value. The lease required Koby to pay $500,000 annually on January 2, beginning with the current year. The present value of an annuity due for 7 years was 5.35 at the inception of the lease.

What amount should Koby capitalize as leased equipment?

A. $500,000
B. $825,000
C. $2,675,000
D. $3,500,000

assess.AICPA.921157FAR-P1-FA_0818

427. On January 1, 20X4, Harrow Co. as lessee signed a 5-year noncancelable equipment lease with annual payments of $100,000 beginning December 31, 20X4. Harrow treated this transaction as a finance lease. The five lease payments have a present value of $379,000 at January 1, 20X4 based on interest of 10%.

What amount should Harrow report as interest expense for the year ending December 31, 20X4?

A. $37,900
B. $27,900
C. $24,200
D. $0

Sales Type Leases—Lessor

AICPA.901126FAR-TH-FA_0818

428. In a lease that is recorded as a sales-type lease by the lessor, interest revenue

A. Should be recognized in full as revenue at the lease's inception.
B. Should be recognized over the period of the lease using the straight-line method.
C. Should be recognized over the period of the lease using the effective interest method.
D. Does not arise.

Direct Financing Leases—Lessor

aq.lessor.direc.fin.001_0818

429. On January 1, Year 1, Bear Company leased an asset to Cub Company and appropriately accounted for the lease as a direct financing lease. The asset has a fair value of $36,000 and a carrying amount of $30,000. The lease has an implicit rate of 6% and a third-party guaranteed residual value of $5,000. The lease term is three years, and the asset has a five-year useful life. Lease payments of $11,897 are due at the end of the year, and the present value factor of an ordinary annuity at 6% for three years is 2.67301. The present value of a single sum at 6% and three years is .83962. Assume a rate of 15.85% amortizes the net lease receivable to zero over the lease term. What amount should Bear record as the amortization of deferred gross profit associated with the first lease payment made December 31, Year 1?

A. $2,595
B. $2,160
C. $4,755
D. $0; there is no deferred gross profit

aq.lessor.direc.fin.004_0818

430. The interest rate applied to the net lease receivable is

A. The rate that amortizes the gross lease receivable to zero at the end of the lease term.
B. The rate that amortizes the net lease receivable to zero at the end of the lease term.
C. The implicit interest rate.
D. The incremental borrowing rate.

Sale Leasebacks and Disclosures

aq.lease.back.disc.003_0818

431. In a sale-leaseback transaction, the seller-lessee has leased back the asset and has retained physical possession of the property. The gain on the sale should be recognized at the time of the sale-leaseback when the lease is classified as a(n)

	Finance Lease	Operating Lease
A.	Yes	Yes
B.	No	No
C.	No	Yes
D.	Yes	No

aq.lease.back.disc.004_0818

432. The following information pertains to a sale and leaseback of equipment by Mega Co. on December 31, Year 1:

Sales price	$400,000
Carrying amount	$300,000
Monthly lease payment	$3,250
Present value of lease payments	$36,900
Estimated remaining life	25 years
Lease term	1 year
Implicit rate	12%

What amount of gain on the sale should Mega report at December 31, Year 1?

A. $0
B. $36,900
C. $39,000
D. $100,000

Additional Aspects of Capital Leases

aq.add.aspect.lease.001_0818

433. Louie the lessee leased an asset for a three-year lease term. Louie appropriately accounted for the lease as a finance lease and recorded a right-of-use asset for $45,000. The asset has a useful life of four years. How much amortization expense should Louie record each year?

A. $15,000
B. $11,250
C. $0, for a finance lease, the lessor will record amortization expense for the right-of-use asset
D. $0, Louie will record depreciation expense, not amortization expense.

aq.add.aspect.lease.003_0818

434. When accounting for an initial direct cost, the lessee will

A. Calculate the present value of the initial direct cost using the present value factor of a single sum associated with the lease term and include this amount in the lease liability.
B. Include the initial direct cost at its cost in the calculation of the right-of-use asset.
C. Include the initial direct cost at its cost in the calculation of the lease liability.
D. Calculate the present value of the initial direct cost using the present value factor of a single sum associated with the lease term and include this amount in the right-of-use asset.

Not-for-Profit Organizations

Introduction to Types of Not-for-Profit Entities and Standard Setting

aq.intro.nfp.001_2017

435. Which one of the following is a voluntary health and welfare organization?

A. Nursing home
B. Clinic
C. Charity raising money for underprivileged children
D. Hospital

AICPA.083791FAR-SIM

436. The primary standards-setting body for a public museum that receives the majority of its funding from local property taxes is the

A. American Institute of CPAs (AICPA).
B. Financial Accounting Standards Board (FASB).
C. Government Accountability Office (GAO).
D. Governmental Accounting Standards Board (GASB).

Financial Reporting

aicpa.aq.fin.report.006_17

437. Kind Nurses Assoc. is a voluntary health and welfare organization. Nurses are paid to visit homes of elderly people and are reimbursed for mileage and supplies. Which of the following items should Kind record as a support activity expense in its statement of functional expense?

A. Nurses' mileage expense.
B. Payment for nurses' employee benefits.
C. Payment for nurses' supplies.
D. Fundraising costs.

aicpa.aq.fin.report.007_17

438. Which of the following financial statements would provide information about the ongoing revenues and expenses associated with a voluntary health and welfare organization?

A. The statement of activities.
B. The statement of cash flows.
C. The statement of functional expenses.
D. The statement of financial position.

aq.fin.report.001_2017

439. A voluntary health and welfare organization had the following asset inflows:

Cash gifts	$40,000
Membership dues	8,000
Dividend income	5,000
Interest income	3,000
Donated supplies	2,000

How should these items be reported?

	Revenues	Public Support
A.	$16,000	$42,000
B.	$2,000	$56,000
C.	$56,000	$2,000
D.	$10,000	$48,000

Donations, Pledges, Contributions, and Net Assets

aicpa.aq.don.pledg.cont.007_17

440. When should a conditional pledge to a nongovernmental not-for-profit organization be recognized as revenue?

   A. Immediately.
   B. When the cash is received.
   C. When the pledge conditions are met.
   D. At the beginning of the next fiscal period.

AICPA.130701FAR_1017

441. Which of the following types of information would be included in total net assets in the statement of financial position for a nongovernmental not-for-profit organization?

   A. Total current net assets and total other assets
   B. Total current assets and restricted assets
   C. Net assets with a donor restriction, net assets without a donor restriction, and total net assets
   D. Unrestricted net assets, restricted net assets, and total current assets.

aq.don.pledg.cont.004_1017

442. Home Care, Inc. (Home Care), a nongovernmental voluntary health and welfare organization, received two contributions in 20X3. One contribution of $250,000 was restricted for use as general support in 20X4. The other contribution of $200,000 carried no donor restrictions. What amount should Home Care report as contributions with a donor restriction in its 20X3 statement of activities?

   A. $0
   B. $250,000
   C. $450,000
   D. $200,000

Special Issues—Recent Developments

aq.spec.iss.001_1017

443. CIBA, a nonprofit performing arts organization, received a contribution of a term endowment and a regular endowment from two external donors. These endowments should be reported on the statement of activities as:

	Term Endowments	Regular Endowments
A.	Temporarily restricted	Permanently restricted
B.	Net assets with donor restriction	Net assets with donor restriction
C.	Temporarily restricted	Temporarily restricted
D.	Net assets without donor restriction	Net assets with donor restriction

AICPA.130710FAR

444. At which of the following amounts should a nongovernmental not-for-profit organization report investments in debt securities?

   A. Potential proceeds from liquidation sale
   B. Discounted expected future cash flows
   C. Quoted market prices
   D. Historical cost

Special Industries: Healthcare and Colleges

Healthcare Organizations

aq.healthcare.001_2017

445. The Johnson Hospital, a private, not-for-profit hospital, received the following revenues in the current year:

Proceeds from the sales of the hospital's flower shop	$60,000
Dividends and interest revenue not restricted	$20,000
Cash contributions for the renovation of the children's ward in the hospital	$200,000

Which of these amounts should be reported as other revenues and gains (other revenue) on the statement of operations?

A. $280,000
B. $60,000
C. $80,000
D. $260,000

AICPA.060233FAR-AR

446. Terry, an auditor, is performing test work for a not-for-profit hospital. Listed below are components of the Statement of Operations:

Revenue relating to charity care	$100,000
Bad debt expense related to patient accounts receivable	70,000
Net assets released from restrictions and used for operations	50,000
Other revenue	80,000
Net Patient Service Revenue (includes revenue related to charity care)	500,000

What amount would be reported as total revenues, gains, and other support on the Statement of Operations?

A. $460,000
B. $530,000
C. $580,000
D. $630,000

Colleges and Universities

aq.colleges.001_1017

447. A private, not-for-profit university receives $100,000 that, according to the donor, must be spent for computers. On the last day of the year, $67,000 of this amount was properly spent. No time restriction was set for the use of these computers. In addition, students were charged tuition of $300,000 but were also awarded $110,000 in financial aid. For net assets without a donor restriction, what was the total amount of revenue, contributions, and reclassifications?

A. $257,000
B. $290,000
C. $400,000
D. $367,000

AICPA.101163FAR

448. How should state appropriations to a state university choosing to report as engaged only in business-type activities be reported in its Statement of Revenues, Expenses, and Changes in Net Position?

A. Operating Revenues
B. Nonoperating Revenues
C. Capital Contributions
D. Other Financing Sources

State and Local Governments

State and Local Government Concepts

Introduction to Governmental Organizations

AICPA.083758FAR-SIM
449. Which of the following has the highest level of authority for setting GAAP for nongovernmental not-for-profit organizations?

    A. GASB
    B. FASB
    C. FASAB
    D. AICPA

AICPA.083759FAR-SIM
450. Which of the following sources of financial resources is unique to governmental entities?

    A. Proceeds from bonds
    B. Grant proceeds from the federal government
    C. Charges for services
    D. Proceeds from taxation

GASB Concepts Statements

aicpa.aq.gas.concept2.001_17
451. Which of the following should be considered part of one of the three primary user groups of the external financial reports of a state government?

    A. Citizens of a neighboring state.
    B. Advocate groups within the state.
    C. Preparers of state government financial reports.
    D. Internal managers in the executive branch of the state government.

AICPA.110588FAR-SIM
452. The City of Palo Alto's Service Efforts and Accomplishments Report for Fiscal Year 2010 reported that the average response to fire calls within 8 minutes occurred on 90% of the fire calls in 2010. This rate met the benchmark target goal of 90%. According to GASB's conceptual framework, this information is classified as a measure of

    A. Effort.
    B. Output.
    C. Outcome.
    D. Efficiency.

Fund Accounting

AICPA.08.12.12-SIM
453. Which of the following activities would *most likely* be accounted for in a proprietary fund?

    A. Street, curb, and sidewalk maintenance and repairs
    B. Wastewater and sewerage services
    C. Police protection
    D. Tax assessor and collection activities

AICPA.083760FAR-SIM
454. Which of the following funds is not a fiduciary fund type?

    A. Police and fire pension trust fund
    B. Motor pool fund
    C. Historical society private-purpose trust fund
    D. County and city tax collection fund

assess.AICPA.FAR.fund.acct-0038
455. Seaview City received a pass-through grant from the state. The money is to be distributed to families who, as determined by the state, are eligible for summer camp scholarships for their children. Seaview does not have administrative or direct financial involvement in the program. In which fund should Seaview record the grant?

    A. Agency.
    B. General.
    C. Internal service.
    D. Enterprise.

Measurement Focus Basis of Accounting

AICPA.060230FAR-TH-AR
456. Dayne County's general fund had the following disbursements during the year:

Payment of principal on long-term debt	$100,000
Payments to vendors	500,000
Purchase of a computer	300,000

What amount should Dayne County report as expenditures in its governmental funds Statement of Revenues, Expenditures, and Changes in Fund Balances?

A. $300,000
B. $500,000
C. $800,000
D. $900,000

AICPA.130703FAR

457. How should a city's general fund report the acquisition of a new police car in its governmental fund statement of revenues, expenditures and changes in fund balances?

A. Noncurrent asset.
B. Expenditure.
C. Expense.
D. Property, plant and equipment.

aicpa.aq.focus.basis.acct.001_17

458. What basis of accounting should be used when preparing a governmental funds statement of revenues, expenditures, and changes in fund balances?

A. Accrual basis of accounting.
B. Modified accrual basis of accounting.
C. Modified cash basis of accounting.
D. Cash basis of accounting.

aicpa.aq.focus.basis.acct.002_18

459. Which of the following transactions should be reported as a liability in the general fund financial statements?

A. An amount that is due within one year of the balance sheet date
B. An amount to be paid from current financial resources
C. An amount set aside to pay for an unfilled contract
D. Principal on long-term debt due 90 days after the balance sheet date

Budgetary Accounting

aq.budg.acct.0001_0318

460. When the budget for the General Fund is recorded, the required journal entry will include

A. A credit to Appropriations.
B. A credit to Estimated Revenues.
C. A debit to Encumbrances.
D. A credit to Fund Balance

aq.budg.acct.0002_0318

461. If a state law requires that local governments prepare General Fund and special revenue fund budgets on a basis that differs from the basis of accounting required by generally accepted accounting principles (GAAP):

A. The actual amounts in the budgetary comparison schedule should be reported on the GAAP basis.
B. The actual amounts in the budgetary comparison schedule should be reported on the GAAP basis; a separate budget-basis comparison schedule should be prepared for the appropriate state oversight body.
C. The actual amounts in the budgetary comparison schedule should be reported using the government's budgetary basis.
D. Only a separate budget-basis comparison schedule should be prepared for the appropriate state oversight body.

AICPA.120639FAR

462. On January 1, Fonk City approved the following general fund resources for the new fiscal period:

Property taxes	$5,000,000
Licenses and permits	400,000
Intergovernmental revenues	150,000
Transfers in from other funds	350,000

What amount should Fonk record as estimated revenues for the new fiscal year?

A. $5,400,000
B. $5,550,000
C. $5,750,000
D. $5,900,000

Encumbrance Accounting

aq.encumb.acct.0001_0318

463. The Encumbrances control account of a county is decreased when

	Goods are Ordered	Goods are Received
A.	No	Yes
B.	Yes	No
C.	No	No
D.	Yes	Yes

aq.encumb.acct.0002_0318

464. When computers are ordered by the city controller's office, the purchase order should be recorded in the General Fund as a debit to

A. Encumbrances.
B. Expenditures.
C. Appropriations.
D. Equipment.

AICPA.110594FAR

465. Encumbrances would *not* appear in which fund?

   A. Capital Projects.
   B. Special Revenue.
   C. General.
   D. Enterprise.

aicpa.aq.encumb.acct.008_18

466. A government's police department reports appropriations of $10,000, encumbrances of $2,000, and expenditures of $5,000. What is the amount of available appropriations for the police department?

   A. $3,000
   B. $5,000
   C. $7,000
   D. $8,000

Deferred Outflows and Deferred Inflows of Resources

aq.def.outflows.0001_0318

467. Which of the following neither increases nor decreases fund balance of the General Fund during the current period?

   A. Deferred inflows of resources
   B. Expenditures
   C. Other financing uses
   D. Revenues

aq.def.outflows.0002_0318

468. Excel City was awarded a $900,000 federal operating grant for use in Year 20X2. On December 1 of year 20X1, half of the grant money was received by the city. The journal entry to record receipt of the grant funds will include

   A. A credit to Grant Revenues of $450,000.
   B. A credit to Deferred Inflow of Resources—Grant Award in the amount of $900,000.
   C. A credit to Deferred Inflow of Resources—Grant Proceeds in the amount of $450,000.
   D. No entry until the grant resources are expended.

AICPA.140410FAR-SIM

469. In Year 20x1 a local government levied $5,000,000 in special assessments. The assessments are due and payable in five equal installments at the beginning of each of the next five fiscal years, starting in Year 20x2. Assume that all installments are collected four months (120 days) into the year that they are due. At the end of Year 20x2, the Special

Assessment Debt Service Fund would report the $4,000,000 remaining levy as:

   A. Revenues.
   B. Liabilities.
   C. Deferred inflow of resources.
   D. Deferred outflow of resources.

Net Position and Fund Balance

aicpa.aq.net.pos.001_17

470. A government's assets include inventory of $2 million, roads constructed for $25 million with accumulated depreciation of $10 million, and equipment acquired for $5 million with accumulated depreciation of $1 million. Its liabilities include an outstanding balance of $5 million for bonds payable issued to construct the roads and a $1 million short-term loan for inventory purchases. What amount should be reported as the net investment in capital assets in the government-wide statement of net position?

   A. $26 million
   B. $25 million
   C. $14 million
   D. $10 million

AICPA.101140FAR-SIM

471. A Special Revenue Fund may report a positive amount in each of the following fund balance classifications *except:*

   A. Restricted.
   B. Committed.
   C. Assigned.
   D. Unassigned.

AICPA.110591FAR

472. In preparing Chase City's reconciliation of the Statement of Revenues, Expenditures, and Changes in fund balances to the Government-Wide Statement of Activities, which of the following items should be subtracted from the changes in fund balances?

   A. Capital Assets Purchases.
   B. Payment of long-term debt principal.
   C. Internal Service Fund increase in Net Position.
   D. Book value of capital assets sold during the year.

Governmental Funds

aicpa.aq.gov.funds.001_17

473. A city received a $9,000,000 federal grant to finance the construction of a homeless shelter. In which fund should the proceeds be recorded?

    A. Permanent
    B. General
    C. Capital project
    D. Special revenue.

AICPA.090812FAR

474. During the current year, Wythe County levied $2,000,000 in property taxes, 1% of which is expected to be uncollectible. During the year, the county collected $1,800,000 and wrote off $15,000 as uncollectible. What amount should Wythe County report as Property Tax Revenue in its Government-Wide Statement of Activities for the current year?

    A. $1,800,000
    B. $1,980,000
    C. $1,985,000
    D. $2,000,000

AICPA.101172FAR

475. Brandon County's General Fund had the following transactions during the year:

Transfer to a Debt Service Fund	$100,000
Payment to a Pension Trust Fund	500,000
Purchase of equipment	300,000

What amount should Brandon County report for the General Fund as other financing uses in its Governmental Funds Statement of Revenues, Expenditures, and Changes in Fund Balances?

    A. $100,000
    B. $400,000
    C. $800,000
    D. $900,000

Proprietary Funds

AICPA.120646FAR

476. At the beginning of the current year, Paxx County's enterprise fund had a $125,000 balance for accrued compensated absences. At the end of the year, the balance was $150,000. During the year, Paxx paid $400,000 for compensated absences. What amount of compensated absences expense should Paxx County's enterprise fund report for the year?

    A. $375,000
    B. $400,000

C. $425,000
D. $550,000

AICPA.130704FAR

477. Which of the following statements is the most significant characteristic in determining the classification of an enterprise fund?

    A. The predominant customer is the primary government.
    B. The pricing policies of the activity establish fees and charges designed to recover its cost.
    C. The activity is financed by debt that is secured partially by a pledge of the net revenues from fees and charges of the activity.
    D. Laws or regulations require that the activity's costs of providing services including capital costs be recovered with taxes or similar revenues.

AICPA.941121FAR-AR

478. The following transactions were among those reported by Corfe City's Electric Utility Enterprise Fund for 20X5:

Capital contributed by subdividers	$900,000
Cash received from customer households	2,700,000
Proceeds from the sale of revenue bonds	4,500,000

In the Electric Utility Enterprise Fund's Statement of Cash Flows for the year ended December 31, 20X5, what amount should be reported as cash flows from capital and related financing activities?

    A. $4,500,000
    B. $5,400,000
    C. $7,200,000
    D. $8,100,000

Fiduciary Funds

AICPA.083774FAR-SIM

479. In a Tax Agency Fund, revenues must be recognized:

    A. When measurable and available.
    B. On the cash basis.
    C. To extent fund expenditures.
    D. None of the above. Revenues are not reported in Agency Funds.

AICPA.090815FAR

480. Harland County received a $2,000,000 capital grant to be equally distributed among its five municipalities. The grant is to finance the construction of capital assets. Harland had no administrative or direct financial involvement in the construction. In which fund should Harland record the receipt of cash?

    A. Agency Fund.
    B. General Fund.
    C. Special Revenue Fund.
    D. Private-Purpose Trust Fund.

AICPA.120641FAR

481. A government makes a contribution to its pension plan in the amount of $10,000 for year 1. The actuarially-determined annual required contribution for year 1 was $13,500. The pension plan paid benefits of $8,200 and refunded employee contributions of $800 for year 1. What is the pension expenditure for the general fund for year 1?

    A. $8,200
    B. $9,000
    C. $10,000
    D. $13,500

Format and Content of Comprehensive Annual Financial Report (CAFR)

The Comprehensive Annual Financial Report

aicpa.aq.comp.ann.fin.001_17

482. A government-wide statement of net position **must** include which of the following?

    A. Prior-year comparative financial data.
    B. Primary government fiduciary fund data.
    C. A consolidation of all government-wide activities.
    D. A distinction between governmental and business-type activities.

AICPA.110590FAR

483. Jonn City entered into a capital lease for equipment during the year. How should the asset obtained through the lease be reported in Jonn City's government-wide Statement of Net Position?

    A. General Capital Asset.
    B. Other Financing Use.
    C. Expenditure.
    D. Not reported.

Determining the Financial Reporting Entity

aq.det.fin.rep.0001_0318

484. Which of the following factors would **not** indicate that a potential component unit (PCU) imposes a financial burden or provides a financial benefit to a primary government?

    A. The primary government has an ongoing financial interest in a joint venture, which pays its surpluses to the joint venture participants.
    B. The primary government is entitled to the PCU's resources.
    C. The primary government is obligated for the PCU's debt.
    D. The primary government is able to approve and modify the PCU's budget.

aq.det.fin.rep.0002_0318

485. Which of the following is evidence of fiscal independence for the purpose of considering whether one legally separate organization is a component unit of another?

    A. The budget of the potential component unit must be approved by the primary government.
    B. The primary government is legally obligated to finance the deficits of the potential component unit.
    C. The potential component unit sets user fees without authority of the primary government.
    D. The primary government can veto, overrule, or modify decisions made by the potential component unit's governing body.

AICPA.110593FAR

486. If a city government is the primary reporting entity, which of the following is an acceptable method to present component units in its combined financial statements?

    A. Consolidation.
    B. Cost method.
    C. Discrete presentation.
    D. Government-wide presentation.

Major Funds and Fund-Level Reporting

aq.major.funds.0001_0318

487. A major governmental fund is one that has one or more elements (e.g., assets, liabilities, revenues, or expenditures) that is at least

    A. 10% of the corresponding element(s) of total governmental funds and 5% of the corresponding element(s) of total governmental and enterprise funds combined.

B. 10% of the corresponding element(s) of total governmental funds and 5% of the corresponding element(s) of total governmental, enterprise funds, and fiduciary funds combined.

C. 5% of the corresponding element(s) of total governmental funds and 10% of the corresponding element(s) of total governmental and enterprise funds combined.

D. 5% of the corresponding element(s) of total governmental funds and 5% of the corresponding element(s) of total governmental and enterprise funds combined.

aq.major.funds.0002_0318

488. Use the following information to determine whether the Special Revenue and the Debt Service Funds should be reported as major funds based on asset amounts provided.

Special Revenue Fund Assets	$750,000
Debt Service Fund Assets	$300,000
Total Governmental Fund Assets	$8,000,000
Total Governmental Fund and Enterprise Fund Assets	$10,000,000

A. The Special Revenue Fund should be reported as major.

B. The Debt Service Fund should be reported as major.

C. Neither the Development Special Revenue Fund nor the Debt Service Fund should be reported as major.

D. Both the Special Revenue Fund and the Debt Service Fund should be reported as major.

AICPA.021109FAR-AR

489. According to GASB 34, *Basic Financial Statements-and Management's Discussion and Analysis-for State and Local Governments*, certain budgetary schedules require supplementary information.

What is the minimum budgetary information required to be reported in those schedules?

A. A schedule of unfavorable variances at the functional level.

B. A schedule showing the final appropriations budget and actual expenditures on a budgetary basis.

C. A schedule showing the original budget, the final appropriations budget, and actual inflows, outflows, and balances on a budgetary basis.

D. A schedule showing the proposed budget, the approved budget, the final amended budget, actual inflows and outflows on a budgetary basis, and variances between budget and actual.

Deriving Government-Wide Financial Statements from Fund-Level Financial Statements

aq.deriv.gov.recon.001_2017

490. Excel City's store supply internal service fund provides services only to general government departments. During 20X1, the internal service fund reported operating revenue of $50,000 and operating expenses of $35,000. What amount of adjustment is needed to convert the governmental funds Statement of Revenues, Expenditures, and Changes in Fund Balance to governmental activities in Excel City's government-wide Statement of Activities?

A. Increase revenue by $50,000.
B. Increase expenses by $35,000.
C. Decrease revenue by $15,000.
D. Decrease expenses by $15,000.

aq.deriv.gov.recon.003_2017

491. Which of the following items would result in an increase in the reconciliation of governmental funds changes in fund balance to governmental activities changes in net position in the government-wide statement?

A. Depreciation
B. Capital outlay expenditures
C. Bond proceeds
D. Book value of capital assets sold

Typical Items and Specific Types of Transactions and Events

Interfund Transactions, Construction Projects, and Infrastructure

AICPA.090128FAR-SIM

492. A city's General Fund contributes $150,000 to its Debt Service Fund to meet upcoming debt service requirements for a general obligation serial bond. The General Fund should report this as a(n):

A. Expenditure of $150,000.
B. Capital Contribution of $150,000.
C. Operating Transfer of $150,000.
D. Interfund Loan of $150,000.

AICPA.901156FAR-TH-AR

493. On March 2, Year 1, Finch City issued 10-year general obligation bonds at face amount, with interest payable March 1 and September 1. The proceeds were to be used to finance the construction of a civic center over the period April 1, Year 1, to March 31, Year 2. During the fiscal year ended June 30, Year 1, no resources had been provided to the Debt Service Fund for the payment of principal and interest.

    The liability for the general obligation bonds should be recorded in the:

    A. General Fund.
    B. Capital Projects Fund.
    C. Government-wide financial statements.
    D. Debt Service Fund.

Long-Term Liabilities Other Than Bonded Debt

aq.lngtrm.liab.0001_0318

494. Pollution remediation obligations should be recognized if which of the following obligating events has occurred?

    I.   A violation of a pollution prevention permit has occurred.
    II. The government is named or will be named as the responsible or potentially responsible party to a remediation.
    III. The government is compelled to take remediation action due to imminent endangerment to the public health.
    IV. All of the above items are obligating events that would require recognition of a pollution remediation obligation.

    A. Choice I
    B. Choice II
    C. Choice III
    D. Choice IV

aq.lngtrm.liab.0002_0318

495. Which of the following is **not** properly reported in the government activities of the government-wide financial reports?

    A. The long-term portion of claims and judgments
    B. Tax-supported general obligation bonds
    C. Revenue bonds issued by an enterprise fund
    D. Obligations under capital leases used to finance general capital assets

AICPA.101242FAR-SIM

496. Big City recently lost a lawsuit relating to an incident involving one of their police officers. A judgment was rendered against the city, and, immediately prior to the current fiscal year end, the city was ordered to pay a total of $500,000. $100,000 is due immediately and the remaining is to be paid in installments of $100,000 per year for an additional four years. How will the external financial statements of the city be affected in the year the court case was settled?

    A. The General Fund statements should report both expenditures and a claims and judgments liability of $500,000.
    B. The General Long-Term Liabilities accounts should report a $500,000 liability.
    C. The General Fund statements should report expenditures and a current liability of $100,000, and the Custodial Fund should report a liability of $400,000.
    D. The General Fund statements should report expenditures and a current liability of $100,000, and the government-wide statements should report a long-term liability of the present value of the $400,000.

Terminology and Nonexchange Transactions

aq.terminology.0001_0318

497. Sales taxes are an example of which category of nonexchange transactions?

    A. Derived tax revenue
    B. Imposed tax revenue
    C. Government-mandated nonexchange transaction
    D. Voluntary nonexchange transaction

AICPA.101164FAR

498. What is the major difference between an Exchange Transaction and a non-Exchange Transaction for governmental units?

    A. The relationship between the amount of value given and received.
    B. Time requirements and whether the transaction is required by law.
    C. Purpose restrictions placed upon fund balances.
    D. Whether resources acquired can be further exchanged.

Special Items—Recent Developments

AICPA.083782FAR-SIM

499. In January 2010, Red County acquired the right to draw water from a lake on the property of a privately owned ranch in exchange for a cash payment of $20 million. The annual volume of water that can be drawn is unlimited. The county's rights under the contract expire in 10 years (2020); however, the contact provides the opportunity to renew the water rights for an additional 10 years (to 2030) for no additional payment, subject to the mutual agreement of the two parties. The county believes that it will request the renewal. The county expects the other party to agree to the renewal since the ranch is a significant user of the county's water supply and is a major employer of Red County residents. The county operates on a calendar fiscal year. The county should recognize in its 2010 Government-Wide Financial Statements:

A. $20 million expense in its Statement of Activities.
B. $10 million expense in its Statement of Activities.
C. $2 million amortization expense in its Statement of Activities.
D. $1 million amortization expense in its Statement of Activities.

AICPA.083786FAR-SIM

500. Which of the following is not one of the five information classification sections that must be included in the Statistical Section of the CAFR?

A. Operating information.
B. Demographics information.
C. Revenue Capacity information.
D. Fund Balance information.

Answers and Explanations

1. **Answer: D**

   The FASB is currently the rule-making body for GAAP. The Board has codified well over one hundred Statements of Financial Accounting Standards, and Interpretations of those standards. The FASB is a private-sector body, the third such body serving as the entity which creates GAAP for U.S. businesses. The FASB has no authority to enforce GAAP, however.

2. **Answer: A**

   The FASB has no official connection with the U.S. Government although the SEC, an agency of the federal government, can modify or rescind an accounting standard adopted by the FASB.

3. **Answer: B**

   A proposed standard may cause firm earnings to fall, for example when they are adopted. Firms will be concerned that lower earnings may make it more difficult to sell stock or to secure loans. As a result, negative economic consequences become a focal point for arguments against the proposed standard.

4. **Answer: C**

   One of the objectives of the FASB in setting standards is to develop rules that are unbiased. FASB statements generally do not reflect any reporting bias.

   For example, the requirement to expense all research and development costs is uniform across all firms and does not favor one firm over another.

5. **Answer: C**

   At least four of the seven members of the FASB must vote in favor of a proposed Statement of Financial Accounting Standards.

6. **Answer: B**

   The audit of the financial statements by independent third parties provides assurance that the financial statements are fairly presented in all material respects. As part of the audit, the auditor should perform risk assessment procedures to identify and assess the risk of material misstatement due to error or fraud, which includes understanding the corporation's internal control over financial

reporting. The auditors do not prepare the information, nor do they have employment ties with either the reporting firm or the intended audience of the financial statements. However, even the audit of financial statements is not a perfect protection as indicated by the frequency of fraud and audit failure.

7. **Answer: B**

   The Accounting Standards Updates (ASU) are the final version of the new accounting guidance. ASUs are how the Codification is amended.

8. **Answer: A**

   The best way to approach this question is by thinking through the effect on cash basis expenses for the change in the prepaid and accrued expenses. The expenses reported on a cash basis are 35,200. Prepaid expenses increased by 500; which means that more cash was paid than expense incurred. Therefore, the 500 should be deducted from the cash basis expense to derive accrual basis expense. Accrued expenses decreased by 450; which means more cash was paid than expenses incurred. Therefore, the 450 should be deducted from the cash basis expense to derive the accrual basis expense. The correct answer is $35,200 - 500 - 450 = 34,250$.

9. **Answer: C**

   The approach on this question is to first calculate the cash-based operating expenses. Cash-based operating expenses are $150,000. The next step is to adjust the cash-based expense for the prepaid and accrued expenses. Beginning of the year prepaid expenses were paid in the prior year, but the expense was incurred (or consumed) in the current year, and end of the year prepaid expenses were paid this year but will be consumed next year. Therefore, you add the beginning of the year prepaid and subtract the end of the year prepaid expenses from the cash-based number.

   Cash-based expenses will also be adjusted for the accrued expense. Beginnings of the year accrued expenses were not paid last year, but were last year's expense item paid this year. End of the year accrued expenses were not paid this year, but are this year's expense paid next year. Therefore, you subtract beginning of the year accrued and add end of the year accrued expenses to the cash-based number.

Cash-based operating expenses	$150,000
Add the beginning of the year prepaid expenses	10,000
Subtract the end of the year prepaid expenses	(15,000)
Subtract the beginning of the year accrued expenses	(5,000)
Add the end of the year accrued expenses	25,000
Accrual-based operating expenses	$165,000

10. **Answer: B**

An increase in prepaid expenses indicates that more cash was paid than expensed (5,000). An increase in accrued liabilities indicates that more expense was accrued than paid (12,000). The reconciliation of operating expense to cash paid is: 100,000 + 5,000 − 12,000 = 93,000.

11. **Answer: A**

The Accounting Standards Codification is updated through the issuance of Accounting Standards Updates (ASU) by the FASB.

12. **Answer: B**

The Codification includes all authoritative GAAP for nongovernmental entities.

13. **Answer: D**

IFRS are not U.S. GAAP and thus are not included in the Codification.

14. **Answer: B**

Changes and updates to the Codification are accomplished through Accounting Standards Updates (ASUs).

15. **Answer: D**

The primary objective of financial reporting is to provide decision-useful information to the financial statement user.

16. **Answer: A**

Relevance and faithful representation are the two primary qualitative characteristics of financial information.

17. **Answer: D**

The question is asking which of the following terms captures predictive value. Predictive value along with confirmatory value is a component of relevance.

18. **Answer: C**

The monetary unit assumption provides the basis for using the home-country currency as the reporting basis in the financial statements and also tends to imply that the unit of currency is stable (little or no inflation or deflation).

19. **Answer: A**

LCM departs from historical cost because it provides an ending valuation below cost when market value is below cost. The inventory is actually written down to a value below what was originally paid. This is one of the few such departures.

20. **Answer: A**

Fair value is a market-based measurement, not an entity-specific measurement. A market-based measurement is the price the entity would receive to sell an asset or pay to transfer a liability and takes into consideration risk and restrictions.

21. **Answer: C**

Establishing new measurement requirements for financial instruments, or for any other asset or liability, is not one of the purposes of the fair value framework. Measurement requirements or elections are determined by other pronouncements; the "Fair Value Measurement" pronouncement establishes standards to be followed in determining (measuring) fair value when it is used.

22. **Answer: A**

If Able Co. intends to elect to implement the fair value option for its investment in Baker's debt, it must make its election on the date it first recognizes the investment, which is January 15, 2008.

23. **Answer: A**

If an asset was acquired from the acquiring firm's majority shareholder, an auditor likely would be especially concerned as to whether or not the price paid to acquire the asset was fair value of the asset because an entity and its majority shareholder are related parties. Related party transactions may not be at arm's length and, therefore, may require special attention of an auditor and special disclosures related thereto.

24. **Answer: B**

The income approach to fair value measurement of an asset measures fair value by converting future amounts to a single present amount. Discounting future cash flows would be an income approach to determining fair value.

25. **Answer: C**

Level three inputs are unobservable.

26. **Answer: B**

An entity's assumptions may be used as inputs in determining fair value. Those assumptions would be level 3, unobservable inputs, but would be used when adequate observable inputs were not available to make fair value determinations.

27. **Answer: D**

Neither Statement I nor Statement II is correct. Quoted market prices should not be adjusted for a "blockage factor" when a firm holds a sizable portion of the asset being valued (Statement I). A "blockage factor" occurs when an entity holds a sizable portion of an asset (or liability) relative to the trading volume of the asset or liability in the market. Using a "blockage factor" would adjust the market value for the impact of such a large block of securities being sold, but is not permitted in determining fair value. Additionally, quoted market prices in markets that are not active because there are few relevant transactions can be used in determining fair value (Statement II). Such prices would be considered level 2 factors, observable inputs but not in active markets.

28. **Answer: C**

This response is a false statement—internally generated cash flow projections are not an observable input.

29. **Answer: D**

Both Statements I and II are correct. The intended purposes of financial statement disclosures required of a firm that elects to

use fair value measurement are to facilitate comparisons both across firms and for differently measured financial assets and liabilities of a single firm.

30. **Answer: C**

Disclosure requirements when fair value measurement is used are differentiated between items measured at fair value on a recurring basis and items measured at fair value on a nonrecurring basis. Items measured at fair value on a recurring basis are adjusted to (measured at) fair value period after period; an example would be investments held-for-trading. Items measured at fair value on a non-recurring basis are adjusted to (measured at) fair value only when certain conditions are met; an example would be the impairment of an asset.

31. **Answer: C**

Combined disclosures about fair value measurements required by all pronouncements are not required, but are encouraged.

32. **Answer: B**

SEC is the abbreviation for the Securities and Exchange Commission, and as such, is not included in the definition of IFRS, International Financial Reporting Standards. IAS 8, para. 5

33. **Answer: B**

The **IASB Framework for the Preparation and Presentation of Financial Statements** has converged with the FASB's SFAC 8. The concept of faithful representation, includes completeness, neutrality, and free from error.

34. **Answer: B**

This answer is correct because the IASB Framework has five elements: asset, liability, equity, income, and expense. The definition given is that of income. Note that income includes both revenues and gains.

35. **Answer: A**

According to the IASB's Framework, recognition is "the process of incorporating in the Balance Sheet or Income Statement an item that meets the definition of an element and satisfies the criteria for recognition." The element must be both probable that any future economic benefit will flow to or from the entity and have a cost or value that can be measured with reliability. IASB Framework, para. 82-83.

36. **Answer: C**

    Relevance and faithful representation are the two fundamental qualitative characteristics of financial information (IASB Framework 5-18).

37. **Answer: A**

    Recognition is the process of incorporating an item in the financial statements when it meets the definition of the element and satisfies the criteria for recognition. That criteria states that there is the probability of future economic benefit associated with the item that will flow to or from the entity and that the item has a cost or value that can be measured with reliability. IASB Framework, para. 82-83.

38. **Answer: C**

    Both statements are correct. IFRS for SMEs is based on accrual basis accounting (Statement I) and, generally, IFRS for SMEs may be used as an alternative to using OCBOA (Statement II).

39. **Answer: C**

    Under IFRS for SMEs, the FIFO and weighted average cost assumptions of cost flow may be used for inventory valuation purposes, but the LIFO cost flow assumption may not be used.

40. **Answer: C**

    Under IFRS for SMEs, goodwill is assumed to have a limited life and is amortized over that life, or a period not to exceed 10 years if the life cannot be reasonably estimated. Under U.S. GAAP, goodwill is assumed to have an unlimited life and is not amortized.

41. **Answer: D**

    Under IFRS, the classified Statement of Financial Position has just two classifications: Current and Non-current. Both assets and liabilities are divided into these two classifications, with Non-current being the default category.

42. **Answer: D**

    All of the items listed would appear on the Income Statement when using IFRS.

43. **Answer: D**

    Reporting accounts receivable at net realizable value is a departure from the principle of historical cost. Accounts receivable is usually aged by some method and reported at net realizable value.

44. **Answer: A**

    Current assets are calculated as follows:

Cash	185,000
Accounts receivable, net	725,000
Reclassification of o/s receivable	(200,000)
Total current assets	710,000

45. **Answer: A**

    Accumulated depreciation is a contra account. The asset account Equipment is reported on the Balance Sheet as the net of accumulated depreciation. As such, the accumulated depreciation account has a credit balance, reducing the Equipment account from its historical cost balance to its carrying or book value.

46. **Answer: B**

    In a multi-step Income Statement, gross profit (margin), operating profit (margin), and pretax income from continuing operations are determined. The focus is on the determination of operating profit rather than simply income from continuing operations. Gross profit (margin) is shown as a separate item.

47. **Answer: A**

    If the accountant forgets to record salary expense in the Statement of Income, then net income is too high. Salary expense would be a decrease from revenues, resulting in lower net income.

48. **Answer: C**

    All items are included in net income except the prior year adjustment to amortization expense and the unrealized gain on the AFS securities. The pre-tax income is $1,878,000 and after 30% taxes the net income is $1,314,600.

49. **Answer: C**

    By definition, comprehensive income includes all changes in enterprise equity during a period except those changes resulting from transaction between the enterprise and its owners (e.g., investments by owners, dividends to owners, etc.). Therefore, comprehensive income includes net income plus/minus changes in equity that do not enter into the determination of net income (called items of "other comprehensive income"). Currently, there are four possible items of other comprehensive income:

1. Minimum additional pension liability adjustment
2. Unrealized gains and losses on debt investments classified as available-for-sa
3. Gains and losses resulting from translating financial statements expressed in a foreign currency (foreign currency translation) and losses/gains on related hedges
4. Gains and losses on the effective portion of cash flow hedges

For Rock Co. comprehensive income would be computed as:

Net income (includes the gain on sale)	$400,000
Items of other comprehensive income:	
Foreign currency translation gain	100,000
Unrealized gain on available-for-sale debt security	20,000
Comprehensive income	$520,000

50. Answer: C

Comprehensive income (CI) is the sum of net income (NI) and other comprehensive income (OCI). In this case, NI = $110,000 ($800,000 sales − $600,000 CGS − $90,000 expenses). The unrealized holding gain is an item of OCI. There are four types of OCI items in all. This firm has only one of them. Thus, CI = $110,000 NI + $30,000 OCI = $140,000.

51. Answer: B

The components of comprehensive income are: Net Income, Unrealized gain/loss on AFS debt securities, foreign currency translation adjustment, unrecognized gain/loss on pension benefits, and deferred gain/loss on certain hedging transactions. Therefore, the Comprehensive income of Palmyra Co is $11,000 − 3,000 + 2,000 = $10,000.

52. Answer: D

The Statement of Changes in Equity reconciles all of the beginning and ending balances in the equity accounts. The statement shows the opening balance then details all changes in the accounts, ending with the closing balance.

53. Answer: D

If the par value of the stock is $2, and the increase in the common stock account is $2,000, then $2,000/$2 = 1,000 shares issued. The average issue price is the sum of the par value ($2) and the additional paid-in capital ($10,000/1,000 shares, or $10), which totals $12.

54. Answer: C

All changes in items affecting equity on the Balance Sheet are reported in the Statement of Owner's Equity. Both treasury stock and retained earnings are equity items.

55. Answer: C

This statement generally requires a significant amount of analysis to uncover the cash flows reported within. The adjusted trial balance presents ending account balances. The Statement of Cash Flows reports changes in cash by category. Cash flows are changes in cash and are categorized by type and reported in three categories: operating, investing, and financing.

56. Answer: C

The cash balance at the end of the year equals the cash balance at the beginning of the year, $27,000, plus the net sum of the three categories of cash flows: $351,000 operating − $420,000 investing + $250,000 financing. The ending balance is $208,000.

The $40,000 proceeds from land sale are included in the net cash outflow from investing activities.

57. Answer: A

Operating activities come from adjustments to reconcile net income to net cash flows and through analyzing the change in current asset and liability accounts. Net income − increase in inventory − decrease in accounts payable $70.000 − $40 000 − $30 000 = $0

58. Answer: C

Financing cash flows are those between the firm and the parties providing it with debt and equity financing. Financing cash flows are the major sources of nonoperating cash inflows and repayments of those amounts to the providers. For example, borrowings and proceeds from stock issuance, retirements of debt, treasury stock purchases, and dividends paid are all financing cash flows. Interest paid, however, is an operating cash flow.

59. Answer: B

Dividends paid to shareholders are a financing activity. The payment of interest on bonds is an operating activity, and payments to acquire shares of Marks Co. stock are investing activities.

60. Answer: C

Cash flows from financing activities are those associated with how the company is financed, such as with borrowing or equity. Therefore, the proceeds from the sale of the building would not be included in financing activities. The proceeds from the issuance of common stock (250), convertible bonds (100), and borrowing on the line of credit (200) are all cash inflows from financing activities. The payment of dividends (300) is a cash outflow from financing activities. $250 + 100 + 200 - 300 = 250$.

61. Answer: C

The disclosure requires cash paid in interest during the period. The best way to answer this type of question is with a T-account:

Interest Payable

	15,000 Beginning balance (given)
Interest paid (solve for) 30,000	20,000 Interest expense (given)
	5,000 Ending balance (given)

62. Answer: D

When bond discount is amortized, a portion of the discount is recognized as expense. The result is that interest expense exceeds the amount of cash paid with each interest payment. The discount is gradually amortized over the bond term as additional interest expense because the firm received less than the amount due at maturity. The operating activity section of the indirect method begins with net income and ends with net cash flow from operations. Income is reduced by the interest expense that exceeds the cash interest paid by the amount of discount amortization. Therefore, the discount amortization is added back, yielding a reduction in net cash flow from operations equal to the amount of cash interest paid.

63. Answer: A

The accounts receivable increase represents sales included in net income but not yet collected and is subtracted because income was increased by an amount exceeding cash collections. The accounts payable increase represents purchases of inventory included in cost of goods sold not yet paid for. This amount is added because income was reduced by an amount exceeding cash payments.

64. Answer: A

The summary of significant accounting policies footnote presents information that helps assist users in understanding the recognition, measurement, and disclosure decisions made by the firm.

GAAP allows many choices. In the long-term construction contracts area, GAAP allows both the completed contract and percentage of completion methods. The result of applying each method significantly affects both the Income Statement and Balance Sheet.

A user is much better equipped to evaluate the firm's financial performance and position with the knowledge of the revenue recognition method used by the firm.

65. Answer: D

The summary of significant accounting policies footnote describes the important accounting choices made by the firm for financial reporting purposes. Such policies affect recognition, measurement, and disclosure.

For example, in some areas of revenue recognition, GAAP allows a choice from among several methods of recognition and measurement. This footnote discloses the choices made by the firm to help users understand the reported amounts of revenue and affected accounts in the Income Statement and Balance Sheet.

Different methods produce different reported amounts.

66. Answer: A

This disclosure will give the financial statement reader information about concentration of credit risk related to the receivables that are all in the same industry.

67. Answer: B

This is not one of the four sources noted in the applicable standard. It is specifically noted as a source not included in the accounting standard.

68. Answer: C

This is an internal policy matter and is not listed as a specific attribute for disclosure in the standard.

69. Answer: C

Disclosures are required when the event is reasonably possible. The event is not required to be probable.

70. **Answer: B**

The breach of contract occurred before the 20x8 balance sheet date. This is a recognized subsequent event. The $0.2 million adjustment is simply part of the entire amount that is known before issuance of the 20x8 statements. Note that if the settlement occurred after the issuance or availability of the 20x8 statements, only the $2 million loss is recognized in the 20x8 statements; the remaining $0.2 million is recognized in 20x9.

71. **Answer: C**

This is a subsequent event that did not exist at the balance sheet date but occurred before the financial statements were issued. The company is required to make a footnote disclosure describing the nature of the event and an estimate of the financial effect, or a statement that an estimate cannot be made. Recognition is inappropriate because the condition existed after the balance sheet date.

72. **Answer: A**

The estimated disposal gain is $240 [($250 − $10) proceeds] − $200 book value, or $40. Estimated disposal gains are not recognized, only estimated losses. Next year, the actual disposal gain will be recognized. Nonfinancial assets are not written up in value.

73. **Answer: A**

The after tax net loss on the disposal of the division is the net asset value, ($2,700,000 of assets − $1,700,000 of liabilities) $1,000,000, less the selling price of $800,000. The result is a net loss of $200,000 before tax. After 30% taxes, the net loss is $140,000.

74. **Answer: B**

AR turnover is the ratio of sales to average AR or $1,400,000/[($120,000 + $100,000)/2] = $1,400,000/$110,000 = 12.73. Thus AR "turns over" 12.73 times per year. In days, AR turns over every 28.7 days = 365/12.73. If the year is divided into 12.73 parts, each part is 28.7 days long.

75. **Answer: A**

The quick ratio is the quotient of very liquid current assets to total current liabilities. Inventories and prepaids are not included in the numerator because they are not considered sufficiently liquid. As such, it is a more stringent test of liquidity than the current ratio. In this case, the

quick ratio consists of: cash + net AR + marketable securities divided by current liabilities: ($60,000 + $180,000 − $8,000 + $90,000)/$400,000) = .805. The closest answer is 0.81 to 1.

76. **Answer: A**

Inventory turnover is the ratio of cost of goods (CGS) sold to average inventory. First, calculate CGS = beginning inventory $100,000 + purchases $700,000 − ending inventory $300,000 = $500,000. Then, average inventory = (beginning inventory + ending inventory)/2 = ($100,000 + $300,000)/2 = $200,000. Turnover = $500,000/$200,000 = 2.5.

77. **Answer: B**

From the given information, (asset turnover) = 2 = sales/(average total assets). (AR turnover) = 10 = sales/(average AR). Therefore, (average total assets) are 5 times (average AR). (average total assets) = 5(average AR) = 5($200,000) = $1,000,000.

78. **Answer: B**

First, we must compute the amount of debt. Since Assets = Liabilities + Stockholders' Equity, we have 760,000 = ? + (150,000 + 215,000). Thus, debt = $395,000. Debt to Equity is 395,000/(150,000 + 215,000) = 1.08

79. **Answer: B**

Rate of return on assets is the ratio of net income for a period to average total assets for the same period.

$150,000/[($2,000,000 + $3,000,000)/2] = 6%.

80. **Answer: C**

Consolidation occurs for all entities under common control. Control is defined as more than 50% direct (or indirect) ownership of another entity.

81. **Answer: C**

Both book values and fair values of a subsidiary's assets and liabilities will need to be determined at the date of acquisition in order to prepare consolidated financial statements after a business combination.

82. **Answer: A**

Transactions between affiliated entities, called intercompany transactions, can originate with either the parent company or a subsidiary company.

83. **Answer: C**

    The difference between (fair) market value and book value of inventories would be recognized by adjusting inventories to fair value on the consolidated balance sheet.

84. **Answer: C**

    Whether the parent carries its investment in the subsidiary using the cost method or the equity method would be of concerning in preparing consolidated financial statements at the end of the operating period following a business combination but would not be of concern in preparing financial statements immediately following the combination. When consolidated financial statements are prepared immediately following a combination, there has been no period over which the parent has "carried" the investment on its books. Therefore, the method it WILL (going forward) use is not of concern immediately after the combination.

85. **Answer: C**

    If the parent uses the equity method to carry on its books the investment in a subsidiary, the carrying value of the investment will change as the equity of the subsidiary changes. However, if the parent uses the cost method, the carrying value on its books normally will not change.

86. **Answer: A**

    Although the cost of the investment was equal to book values, the cost of the investment was greater than the fair values, because the carrying amount of Scarp's building was more than its fair value. For consolidated statement purposes, the building would be written down to its lower fair value, and the excess of cost over fair values would be assigned to recognize goodwill. Since for consolidated purposes the building has a lower fair value than its carrying value, the depreciation expense taken on the carrying value would be greater than the depreciation expense for consolidated purposes. Thus, depreciation expense would be decreased in the consolidating process, and goodwill would be recognized.

87. **Answer: C**

    Under the cost method of carrying an investment in a subsidiary, the parent does recognize its share of the subsidiary's dividends declared and, ultimately, the cash received in payment of the dividend. The dividend income (CR.) so recognized by the parent would be

eliminated in the consolidating process against the retained earnings decrease (DR.) recognized by the subsidiary.

88. **Answer: A**

    The purpose of the reciprocity is to bring the investment account (on the worksheet) in balance with the subsidiary's retained earnings **as of the beginning of the period being consolidated**. Therefore, only the undistributed income of the subsidiary since the business combination up to the beginning of the period being consolidated (January 1, 2009) will be the reciprocity entry at the end of 2009. The undistributed income from October 1 to December 31, 2008 (the beginning of 2009) is net income (+$3,000) less dividends declared and paid (−$1,000), or $2,000.

89. **Answer: C**

    The NCI ownership after the issuance of shares is 36% (9,000 / 25,000) multiplied by the total equity of Sage of $700,000 (500,000 + 200,000) or $252,000 ($700,000 × .36).

90. **Answer: A**

    The change in Parent's equity ownership would reduce the investment in Subsidiary by $4,500.

Investment balance before sale of securities ($150,000 × 90%)	$135,000
Investment balance after sale of securities (($150,000 + 24,000) × 75%)	130,500
Decrease in investment in Subsidiary	$4,500

91. **Answer: A**

    When a parent uses the equity method to account for its investment in a subsidiary, the parent will recognize on its books during the year its share of the subsidiary's income (or loss) and its share of dividends declared by the subsidiary. Therefore, in the consolidating process, those entries (and any other equity-based entries made by the parent) must be reversed so that the elements that make up those entries (revenues, expenses, etc.) can be individually recognized on the consolidating worksheet and the consolidated financial statements.

92. **Answer: D**

    Noncontrolling interest at the date of the business combination should be the noncontrolling interest proportionate share of total fair value at that date, including goodwill. The total fair value of Shaw (including goodwill) at the date Ritt acquired 80% of Shaw's common stock would be $1,218,750 ($975,000/.80). The noncontrolling interest would be .20 × $1,218,750 = $243,750, the correct answer. The investment eliminating entry made immediately following the business combination would be:

DR: (Various) Identifiable Net Assets	$1,100,000	
Goodwill	118,750	
CR: Investment in Shaw		$975,000
Noncontrolling Interest (in Shaw)		243,750

93. Answer: B

The transaction between Parco and Subco should be eliminated, because they are affiliated entities, but the transaction between Subco and Noco should not be eliminated, because Noco is not affiliated with Subco (or Parco).

94. Answer: A

All intercompany transactions (i.e., transactions between affiliated firms) must be eliminated in the consolidating process, including not only transactions between a parent and its subsidiaries, but also transactions between affiliated subsidiaries. The consolidated financial statements must reflect accounts and amounts as though intercompany transactions never occurred.

95. Answer: B

If an intercompany inventory transaction is not eliminated in the consolidating process, consolidated financial statements would show an overstatement of sales. Sales would be overstated by the amount of the intercompany sales reported by the selling affiliate. All intercompany sales and related purchases must be eliminated, even if they do not result in a profit or loss.

96. Answer: C

Even though the intercompany inventory sale from Strawco to Pine was at no profit or loss (at Strawco's cost to manufacture), the intercompany sale and purchase, nevertheless, must be eliminated. Otherwise, consolidated sales and purchases (cost of goods sold) will be overstated. Therefore, the elimination related to the intercompany inventory transaction will be for $12,000, the cost of the sale from Strawco to Pine.

97. Answer: A

The total amount of cost of goods sold (COGS) should equal the cost to parties outside of the consolidated entity. Tulip reported $600,000 and Daisy reported $400,000 of COGS, a total of $1,000,000. However, $100,000 of Daisy's COGS is the amount paid to Tulip and should be eliminated from the consolidated financial statements. Therefore, $900,000 should be reported on the consolidated statement of income.

98. Answer: B

There are two ways to approach this solution. First, take the difference in carrying values 72,000-48,000 = 24,000. The 24,000 is the incremental amount Cinn carries the equipment over the carrying amount of Zest. The 24,000/3 = 8,000 OR, compute the depreciation for each company: Cinn is 72,000/3 = 24,000 Zest is 80,000/5 = 16,000 Since Cinn is 100% owned by Zest, the equipment cannot be depreciated by a greater amount through an intracompany sale. The difference is 24,000 – 16,000 = 8,000.

99. Answer: B

An intercompany sale of a fixed asset at a profit will result in the buying affiliate overstating depreciation expense by the amount of depreciation taken on the intercompany profit, and an intercompany sale at a loss will result in an understatement of depreciation expense taken by the buying affiliate. When an intercompany sale of a fixed asset results in a loss, the carrying value of the asset will be understated by the amount of the loss. As a result, depreciation expense taken by the buying affiliate will be understated by the amount of depreciation that would have been taken on the intercompany loss.

100. Answer: D

The liability and investment related to intercompany bonds are eliminated only on the consolidating worksheet. They are not written off the books of either the issuing or the investing affiliate. From the perspective of the separate companies, the liability and investment related to the bonds continue to exist, but for consolidated purposes, they have been constructively retired.

101. **Answer: D**

The premium or discount on a bond investment is the difference between the par value of the bonds and the price paid for the bonds in the market. If the price paid is more than par value, there is a premium on the bond investment. If the price paid is less than par value, there is a discount on the bond investment. In this case, the price paid for the investment ($200,000) is less than the par value of the bonds ($250,000) by $50,000. Therefore, there is a $50,000 discount on Pico's investment.

102. **Answer: C**

Statement I and Statement III are correct; Statement II is not correct. Under IFRS, the guidelines for determining whether or not to consolidate an entity are more principles-based than are U.S. GAAP (Statement I). Under IFRS, the basic guideline is that an entity must be consolidated when another entity has the ability to govern the financial and operating policies of the entity to obtain benefits from it. U.S. GAAP has a specific two-tiered assessment process that must be followed to determine whether or not an entity should be consolidated. Under both U.S. GAAP and IFRS, there are circumstances under which a majority-owned subsidiary does not have to be consolidated (Statement III). U.S. GAAP does not require consolidation of a majority-owned subsidiary when the investor cannot exercise control of the subsidiary. IFRS does not require consolidation of a majority-owned subsidiary under certain conditions when the parent will be consolidated with a higher-level parent.

103. **Answer: A**

Goodwill can only be recognized if it is acquired by purchase.

104. **Answer: C**

This answer is correct because it is not one of the three conditions required to exclude a subsidiary from consolidation. The three required conditions are: (1) it is wholly or partially owned and its other owners do not object to nonconsolidation; (2) it does not have any debt or equity instruments publicly traded; and (3) its parent prepares consolidated financial statements that comply with IFRS.

105. **Answer: B**

The correct answer is Astro's equity of $200,000 plus Bio's equity of $60,000, less Astro's investment in Bio of $8,000, or $200,000 + $60,000 − $8,000 = $252,000. Astro's investment in Bio must be eliminated to prevent double counting of the $8,000 – once as an investment on Astro's books and again as net assets (to which the investment has a claim) on Bio's books.

106. **Answer: A**

The amount that should be included in sales is the amount of sales with unrelated parties. In this case, that is the $250,000 sales by Branch to unaffiliated entities.

107. **Answer: D**

Only an acquisition form of business combination will require the preparation of consolidated financial statements. In the merger and consolidation forms of business combination, only one firm will remain after the combination. Therefore, there will not be two (or more) sets of financial statements to consolidate.

108. **Answer: C**

When a subsidiary is in bankruptcy, it is under the control of the bankruptcy court and, therefore, not under the control of the parent. When a parent cannot exercise financial and/or operating control of a subsidiary, the subsidiary would not be consolidated, but would be reported as an unconsolidated subsidiary by the parent.

109. **Answer: D**

The consolidated statements would include not only Parco, but also all three of its subsidiaries, for a total of four.

110. **Answer: A**

The Division of Corporate Finance oversees the compliance with the securities acts and examines all filings made by publicly held companies.

111. **Answer: B**

The main pronouncements published by the SEC are the Financial Reporting Releases (FRR) and the Staff Accounting Bulletins (SAB).

112. **Answer: B**

Form 10-K is the annual report filed with the SEC.

113. Answer: A

A nonaccelerated filer is defined by the SEC as an entity with less than $75 million in public market value.

114. Answer: A

Form 10-Q is the form for quarterly filing by a public entity with securities listed in the United States.

115. Answer: A

The market share of the company's product is not a required disclosure. The company may chose to voluntarily present this information, but it is not a required disclosure.

116. Answer: D

Regulation S-X governs the form and content of financial statements and financial statement disclosures for publicly traded entities.

117. Answer: B

One year of preferred stock dividends is subtracted from income in the numerator of EPS because the stock is cumulative. The amount of dividends declared does not affect the calculation. The bonds are not relevant because basic EPS does not assume conversion of the bonds. The calculation is: Basic EPS = [$200,000 − (8,000 × $20 × .10)]/25,000 = ($200,000 − $16,000)/25,000 = $7.36.

118. Answer: A

Earnings per share is: (net income − preferred dividends)/common shares outstanding. Preferred stock dividends are $100 × 10% × 20,000 shares = $200,000. Earnings per share is (2,000,000-200,000)/200,000=$9 per share.

119. Answer: C

In general, the dividends subtracted in computing basic EPS are (1) the annual dividend commitment on cumulative preferred whether or not declared or paid, and (2) declared dividends on noncumulative preferred whether paid or not. The firm has negative income. This answer means that the dividends reduce the numerator further – beyond the loss. The final numerator amount is less than (more negative than) the loss. Also, arrear dividends are never included in EPS because they were subtracted in computing EPS in a previous year.

120. Answer: B

More than one approach is available to compute WA (each yields the same answer) but perhaps the easiest is to weight each item separately going forward to the end of the year. This approach yields 139,008 = [100,000(12/12) + 30,000(9/12) + 36,000(7/12)] (1.05) − 35,000(4/12). The beginning shares are outstanding the entire year (12/12). The next two items are weighted for the fraction of the year they are outstanding. Stock dividends and splits are retroactively applied to all items before their issuance – hence the multiplication by 1.05. The treasury shares are removed from the average for 4/12 of the year – these shares already reflect the stock dividend.

121. Answer: B

The weighted average shares outstanding are calculated as follows:

$$(\{[400,000+(200,000\times 9/12)]\times 3\} - 300,000\times 3/12) = 1,575,000$$

$(1,574,999 \quad rounded)$.

122. Answer: C

The stock dividend is considered to be outstanding since the beginning of the year. The weighted average is therefore: 100,000+24,000+ (5,000X6/12) = 126,500.

123. Answer: C

Firms may use the proceeds from the exercise of stock options for any purpose. However, to promote uniformity in reporting, and to reduce the dilution from exercise, the assumption is that the proceeds are used to purchase the firm's stock on the market. This reduces the net number of new shares outstanding from assumed exercise.

124. Answer: A

Earnings per share is calculated by dividing earnings (profit) available to common stockholders by weighted average number of shares of common stock outstanding. If the denominator is decreased by purchasing treasury stock, then the EPS result is increased.

125. Answer: D

Potential investors and current investors are interested in the future earnings potential of the entity. Thus, they are interested in the earnings per share on continuing income, which would be the $10.50 per share. The EPS attributed to discontinued operations cannot be used in predicting future earnings, as they are one-time events.

126. **Answer: C**

Earnings per share (EPS) is calculated on net income available to the common stockholders, $130,000 − $20,000, or $110,000, divided by weighted average shares of common stock outstanding, 50,000. The EPS = $110,000 / 50,000 = $2.20

127. **Answer: B**

The entity must disclose the amount of revenues received from a single customer that total 10% or more of total revenues.

128. **Answer: B**

FAS No. 131 requires that a public business enterprise report financial and descriptive information about its reportable operating segments.

129. **Answer: B**

The worker's compensation claim should be reported in the period incurred, the third quarter. This is a transaction that occurred in the third quarter and does not impact other quarters.

130. **Answer: C**

Interim income tax expense equals the difference between (1) the total income tax through the end of the interim period at the estimated annual tax rate, and (2) the income tax expense recognized in previous interim periods of the same year. For the second quarter, income tax expense therefore is computed as ($10,000 + $20,000)(.25) − $1,500 = $6,000.

131. **Answer: C**

The fundamental principle underlying interim reporting is that interim reports should be considered an integral part of the annual reporting period. This has important implications for interim reporting. There are exceptions to this principle, however.

132. **Answer: C**

Pure accrual basis accounting is not an other comprehensive basis of accounting. The concept of "other comprehensive basis" means a comprehensive basis of accounting other than pure (or full) accrual accounting.

133. **Answer: C**

When the cash basis or the modified cash basis of accounting is used, the title Income Statement, which is appropriate when the accrual basis of accounting is used, should be replaced by the title Statement of Cash Receipts and Cash Disbursements. This helps distinguish that the statement is not based on full accrual accounting consistent with U.S. GAAP.

134. **Answer: A**

Both nontaxable income items (e.g., life insurance proceeds from the death of an officer) and nondeductible expenses (e.g., premium cost of life insurance on an officer) would be recognized in financial statements prepared using an income tax basis of accounting.

135. **Answer: D**

To qualify for simplified hedge accounting, one of the criteria is that both the swap and the hedged borrowing are linked to the same index.

136. **Answer: B**

The PCC allows private companies to amortize goodwill over a period to not exceed 10 years.

137. **Answer: D**

The cash balance is $20,200: the sum of the checking account balance and the petty cash. Because it has a maturity of less than three months, the only cash equivalent is the $7,000 of commercial paper. The final sum of these two accounts is $27,200.

138. **Answer: C**

The first three items in the list are included in cash and cash equivalents. If no restrictions apply, cash in checking accounts ($350,000) is always included in cash. Per ASC Topic 305, cash equivalents are short-term, highly liquid investments that are readily convertible into cash and have maturities of three months or less from the date of purchase by the entity. Common examples are Treasury bills, commercial paper, and money market funds. In this case, the cash equivalents are the money market account ($250,000) and the Treasury bill ($800,000). Therefore, total cash and cash equivalents is $1,400,000 ($350,000

+ $250,000 + $800,000). The maturity of the Treasury bond was at least 12 months (3/1/X4 to 2/28/X5) from the date of purchase; therefore, it should not be reported in cash and cash equivalents. The reason for the three-month rule is to minimize price fluctuations due to interest rate changes. A security with a fluctuating price is not "equivalent" to cash. One year is too long a time to expect interest rates to remain stable.

139. **Answer: B**

The correct cash balance is the balance per the checkbook ($12,000) plus the $1,800 check written to the vendor, for a total of $13,800.

This check reduced the balance in the checkbook but was not mailed. Thus, the amount remains in Grey's cash balance at the end of the year. The bank statement balance is not the correct balance because information about transactions affecting cash near the end of the month, recorded by Grey, did not reach the bank by the cutoff date.

140. **Answer: D**

The reconciliation should be as follows:

Book balance	$32,300
Less bank fees	(15)
Less NSF check	(120)
Plus deposit transposition error (285 – 258)	27
Corrected book balance	$32,192

141. **Answer: A**

Only amounts adjusting the balance per books require an adjusting entry because only those amounts explain why the firm's recorded cash balance is not the same as the true cash balance. Common adjustments of this type include bank service charges, notes collected, and interest. The firm cannot alter the bank balance.

142. **Answer: C**

The reconciling items that need to be adjusted to the bank balance are: checks outstanding (−1,500) and deposit in transit (+350). The net cash after the reconciliation is: Bank balance $54,200 − 1,500 + 350 = $53,050. The bank service charge and insufficient funds are already

reflected in the bank balance. The error is on Hilltop's books, not on the bank statement, and therefore it does not need to be included in the reconciliation.

143. **Answer: C**

$5,000(1 − .30)(1 − .20)(.98) + $200 = $2,944.

The chain trade discounts are applied to each successive net amount as shown in the calculation, and the cash discount of 2% is then applied to the final invoice amount.

The cash discount applies because the payment was made within 15 days of purchase. The goods were shipped FOB shipping point. Therefore, title transferred to Burr at the shipping point, meaning Burr bears the shipping charges. Because Pitt prepaid them as an accommodation, Burr must reimburse Pitt for the $200, the last term in the calculation leading to $2,944.

144. **Answer: C**

This answer is correct. The first step is to determine sales for year 1. The cost of goods sold in year 1 is $280,000 ($350,000 purchases less $70,000 ending inventory). Note that beginning inventory is zero because the company began operations in year 1. Since all merchandise was marked to sell at 40% above cost, year 1 credit sales are $392,000 ($280,000 cost of goods sold × 140%). The second step is to determine the ending balance in accounts receivable.

145. **Answer: E**

This answer is correct. The solutions approach is to determine the journal entries necessary to (1) reestablish and (2) collect the account receivable. The entry to reestablish the account would be

Accounts receivable	xx	
Allowance for doubtful accounts		xx

The entry to record collection would be

Cash	xx	
Accounts receivable		xx

The net effect is an increase in a current asset account, cash, and an increase in a contra asset account, allowance for doubtful accounts.

146. **Answer: D**

Under the allowance method for uncollectible accounts there is no impact on the balance sheet or net income when the receivable is written off. The estimated uncollectible is recognized at the time of the sale; therefore, when the account is written, off the allowance and the accounts receivable are both reduced resulting in no effect on the income statement or balance sheet.

147. **Answer: A**

The data on write-offs and recoveries is not relevant. The aging method computes a required ending allowance balance based on the aging schedule. That required ending balance is the sum of the products of the receivables in each age category and the uncollectible percentage: $120,000(.01) + $90,000(.02) + $100,000(.06) = $9,000.

The write-offs and recoveries do affect the preadjustment allowance balance and therefore the amount of uncollectible accounts expense to recognize. In this case, the preadjustment balance is $19,000 ($22,000 − $7,000 + $4,000), which means no uncollectible accounts expense would be recognized in 2004 because the preadjustment balance is more than sufficient (exceeds the $9,000 required balance).

148. **Answer: D**

The amount of the adjustment to get the $50,000 debit balance to a $90,000 (3% × $3,000,000) credit balance is $140,000.

149. **Answer: B**

This question requires a determination of the pre-adjustment balance in the allowance account, and the ending balance. The difference between these two amounts is the increase in the account needed, which is also the amount recognized as bad debt expense. The aging method first determines the required ending balance in the allowance account, and then places the amount needed to increase the account to this required balance into the allowance account.

The pre-adjustment allowance balance = Beginning balance − Write-offs + Recoveries = $30,000 − $18,000 + $2,000 = $14,000

The ending allowance balance = $350,000 ending gross AR − $325,000 ending net value of AR = $25,000

Therefore, bad debt expense is the amount needed to bring the allowance balance up to

the ending balance of $25,000. The increase needed is $11,000 ($25,000 − $14,000).

150. **Answer: B**

The note from Alpha Co. is a short-term asset. It is reported at the face value of $10,000. The note from Omega is discounted as a single sum for two time periods at 8% to be reported at $10,000 × .857 = $8,570.

151. **Answer: B**

Total interest revenue is the amount received over the term of the note less the present value of the note: 5($5,009) − $19,485 = $5,560.

Leaf paid $19,485 for the note, and will receive 5($5,009) over the note term. The difference is interest revenue.

152. **Answer: C**

The note receivable should be reported at the present value of the nine remaining payments. The first payment was made at the date of the sale. The remaining nine payments comprise an ordinary annuity as of December 31, 2005 because the next payment is due one year from that date.

Therefore, the present value and reported note value on that date is 6.25($10,000) = $62,500.

153. **Answer: C**

Total interest over the life of the note equals the total amount paid by Ace over the life of the note less the proceeds to Ace. The proceeds equal the present value of the payments at the 9% yield rate. The annual payment is found using the 8% rate because that rate is contractually set and determines the annual payment.

The annual payment P is found as: $20,000 = P(3.992). P = $5,010

Total interest revenue = total payments by Ace − proceeds to Ace = 5($5,010) − $5,010(3.89) = $5,560.

154. **Answer: C**

Maturity value of the note: $500,000(1.08)	$540,000
Less discount to the bank: $540,000(.10)(6/12)	(27,000)
Equals proceeds to Roth	$513,000

The bank charges its discount on the maturity amount, for the period it holds the note. In effect, it is charging interest on interest yet to accrue (for the last six months). This procedure is followed because the maturity value is the amount at risk.

155. **Answer: C**

In a pledge arrangement, the title remains with the originator, in this case with Milton Co.

156. **Answer: A**

The net cash received when the receivables were factored was $80,000 × .85 (100% − 10% − 5%) = $68,000.

157. **Answer: D**

The firm is contingent for the maturity amount, which for a noninterest-bearing note is the face value. If the maker of the note fails to pay the bank or financial institution with whom Davis discounted the note, Davis would be called on to pay the entire maturity amount.

158. **Answer: A**

A loan impairment is recorded by reducing the net book value of the receivable to the present value of probable future cash inflows, discounted at the original rate in the receivable. The original rate is used because the loan continues to exist. The loss to the firm is measured at the rate existing when the original loan was created. The difference between the book value and present value, at the date of recognizing the impairment, is recorded as an expense or loss. There is no reason to report overstated assets.

159. **Answer: A**

The interest method recognizes interest revenue each year until the note is collected because the note was written down to present value when the impairment was recorded. The estimated future cash flows to be received include interest, which is recognized over the remaining term of the note. The cost recovery method recognizes interest revenue only after cash equal to the new carrying value is collected. During Year 3, total collections surpassed the $25,000 new carrying value. $3,000 of interest revenue is recognized under this method in Year 3 ($28,000 − $25,000).

160. **Answer: D**

A CGU is the smallest group of assets that can be identified that generates cash flows

independently of the cash flows from other assets.

161. **Answer: A**

Since there is no beginning or ending inventory, the cost of goods sold equals the cost of materials used ($50,000), the direct labor costs ($75,000), and the ($30,000) or $155,000. The other costs, advertising, staff salaries, and bad debt expense, are not part of cost of goods sold.

162. **Answer: D**

The term f.o.b. destination means that title transfers to the buyer when it arrives at the destination. A liability is recorded when the title transfers.

163. **Answer: D**

The correct ending inventory balance is $1,710,000 ($1,500,000 + $90,000 + $120,000).

The $90,000 of merchandise is included because it was shipped before year-end and the title was transferred to Herc at the shipping point (before year-end). The $120,000 also is included because the goods have not been shipped. The FOB designation is irrelevant because the goods have not yet reached a common carrier.

164. **Answer: C**

Beginning inventory	$90,000
Plus purchases	124,000
Less write-off	(34,000)
Less ending inventory	(30,000)
Equals cost of goods sold	$150,000

The write-off cannot be counted in cost of goods sold because it is a decrease in inventory not associated with sales.

165. **Answer: B**

Cost of goods sold is determined (in a periodic inventory system) as:

Beginning Inventory + Net Purchases = Goods Available for Sale − Ending Inventory = Cost of Goods Sold

Net Purchases includes any purchase discounts (or allowances) and other cost of getting the goods in place and condition for resale, including freight-in. Freight-out (to customers)

is a selling cost. Therefore, Azur Co.'s cost of goods sold would be:

Beginning Inventory $30,840

+ Net Purchases $107,940

= Goods Available for Sale $138,780

− Ending inventory 20,560

= Cost of Goods Sold $118,220

Note net purchase is computed as

+ Purchases $102,800

− Net Purchases 107,940

= Goods Available for Sale $138,780

− Purchases Discounts (10,280)

+ Freight-in 15,420

166. **Answer: B**

The perpetual method recognizes each purchase and sale at the time it occurs. The total value of cost of sales using perpetual LIFO is (($6 \times \$55) + (2 \times \$50) + (7 \times \$60)) = \$850$, as shown in the table below.

			Trees remaining	Cost of trees sold
Begin Inv		10 @ $50	10 @ $50	
March 4	purchased	6 @ 55	10 @ $50 6 @ 55	
March 12	sold	8 @ 100	8 @ 50	6 @ $55 = $330 2 @ $50 = 100
March 20	purchased	9 @ 60	8 @ 50 9 @ 60	
March 27	sold	7 @ 105	8 @ 50 2 @ 60	7 @ $60 = 420
March 30	purchased	4 @ 65	8 @ 50 2 @ 60 4 @ 65	
				Total cost = $850

167. **Answer: A**

Under a perpetual inventory system, the cost of goods sold (COGS) is determined at the time of each sale. In a perpetual FIFO inventory system, the cost of each sale (COGS) would be based on the cost of the earliest acquired goods on hand at the time of the sales. The cost of the most recently acquired goods would remain in ending inventory. In a perpetual LIFO inventory system, the cost of each sale (COGS) would be based on the cost of goods acquired just prior to the sale. The cost of the earlier acquired goods would remain in inventory.

Under a periodic inventory system, the costs of goods sold (COGS) and ending inventory are determined only at the end of the period. In a periodic FIFO inventory system, the cost of sales for the period (COGS) would be based on the cost of the earliest acquired goods available during the period. The cost of the most recently acquired goods would remain in ending inventory. In a periodic LIFO inventory system, the cost of sales for the period (COGS) would be based on the last goods acquired during the period. The cost of the earliest acquired goods would remain in ending inventory. The above descriptions can be summarized as follows for determination of COGS:

Inventory System/ Method	Cost of goods sold determined using FIFO	Cost of goods sold determined using LIFO
Perpetual	Earliest goods acquired	Latest goods acquired prior to each sale
Periodic	Earliest goods acquired	Latest goods acquired during the period

Since cost of goods sold for the period would be the same under both perpetual FIFO and periodic FIFO, ending inventory would be the same under both perpetual FIFO and periodic FIFO. Cost of goods sold (and ending inventory) would not be the same under perpetual LIFO as under periodic LIFO because the perpetual system recognizes cost of goods sold based on the cost of goods acquired just prior to each sale, whereas the periodic system recognizes cost of goods sold based on cost of goods acquired prior to the end of each period.

168. **Answer: B**

A periodic system does not record the cost of each item as it is sold; nor does it maintain a continuously current record of the inventory balance. Rather, cost of goods sold is the amount derived from the equation: Beginning inventory + Purchases = Ending inventory + Cost of goods sold. A count of ending inventory establishes the inventory remaining at the end of the period, but there is no recording of cost of goods sold during the period. Cost of goods sold is the amount that completes the equation. Thus, cost of goods sold is really the cost of inventory no longer with the firm at year-end – an amount that includes shrinkage. Inventory shrinkage refers to breakage, waste, and theft. Shrinkage cannot be identified directly with a periodic inventory system.

169. **Answer: A**

FIFO assumes the sale of the earliest goods first. With rising prices, the earliest goods reflect the lowest prices. Therefore, cost of goods sold under FIFO is the lowest of the cost flow assumptions. With the lowest cost of goods sold, gross margin and income are the highest among the available cost flow assumptions (LIFO and average being the others).

170. **Answer: A**

FIFO produces the same results for periodic and perpetual systems. FIFO always assumes the sale of the earliest goods acquired. Therefore, unlike LIFO periodic, goods can never be assumed sold before they are acquired. Cost of goods sold and ending inventory are the same under FIFO for both a periodic and a perpetual system.

171. **Answer: C**

Ending inventory would decrease because under LIFO, the latest items purchased (and therefore the most costly) are considered sold, leaving the earliest items purchased (and therefore the least costly) in inventory. This is opposite to the effect under FIFO.

The same is true for net income because now, under LIFO, cost of goods sold is increased relative to FIFO because the cost of the latest and most costly items are considered sold first.

172. **Answer: C**

The question provides the ending inventory for 2007 at current cost by layer. The sum of the current cost column ($200,000) is the current cost of the entire inventory at the end of 2007. The sum of the base-year cost for the three years is $150,000. Hence, under this assumption, the ratio of current cost for the total inventory at the end of 2007 to the base-year cost is 1.33 ($200,000/$150,000). This index is then multiplied by the 2007 layer in base-year dollars to derive the increment to DV LIFO ending inventory.

173. **Answer: B**

Beginning inventory of $50,000 is at base-year dollars and the current year increase of $30,000 is also at base-year dollars. The current year layer must be converted to current year costs ($30,000 × 1.10) = $33,000. Ending dollar value LIFO is the beginning dollar value LIFO (in this case it was adopted in January so the beginning inventory must be $50,000) plus the current year layer of $33,000 or $83,000. Note that the sentence "The designated market value of Stitch's inventory exceeded its cost at year end" is a distracter. It is simply stating that there is not an issue with the lower of cost or market since cost is lower.

174. **Answer: D**

This response is correct for both answers. The gross profit method can be used to estimate interim inventory, and the gross profit method is a periodic inventory system.

175. **Answer: A**

The gross margin method of estimating inventory is used to solve this problem. The cost of inventory lost cannot be identified by count but it can be estimated.

First, an estimate of cost of goods sold is subtracted from the cost of goods available on the date of the flood yielding the total amount of inventory that would have been present on May 1.

Second, the amount of inventory not lost is subtracted from the May 1 estimated total inventory. The result is an estimate of the amount lost.

With gross profit being 40% of sales, cost of goods sold must be 60% of sales, on average. Therefore, the estimate of cost of goods sold is $150,000 (.60 × $250,000). Beginning inventory ($35,000) + Purchases ($200,000) = Goods available = $235,000. Subtracting $150,000 of cost of goods sold yields $85,000 of inventory on May 1 ($235,000 – $150,000).

With $30,000 of inventory still accounted for, the amount of lost inventory at cost is $55,000 ($85,000 – $30,000).

176. **Answer: C**

When items are purchased as a group, the total cost of the group is allocated to the individual items based on fair value. Replacement cost is the appropriate value to use in this case.

The total replacement cost of the items is $1,100 ($400 + $700). Therefore, Item A is allocated 4/11 of the purchase cost, or $364 = ($400/$1,100)$1,000.

177. **Answer: D**

Although the result is approximate, by excluding net markdowns from the denominator of the cost-to-retail ratio, the ratio is a smaller amount, resulting in a lower ending inventory valuation.

178. **Answer: A**

The retail method measures beginning inventory and net purchases at both cost and retail. It then applies the average relationship between cost and retail (based on beginning inventory and purchases) to ending inventory at retail to determine ending inventory at cost. Purchase returns reduce net purchases at both cost and retail because returns represent amounts included in gross purchases that are not available for sale.

179. **Answer: C**

This is a two-step process. First, DV LIFO is applied to retail dollars to determine the layer added in current-year retail dollars. Then, the FIFO cost-to-retail ratio (C/R) is applied to convert that layer to cost. Finally, this layer is added to beginning inventory at cost to yield ending inventory at cost. The calculation is:

EI retail, current index = $2,000 + $40,000-$28,000 = $14,000

EI retail, base = $14,000/1.6 = $8,750

Increase in EI retail, base = $8,750-$1,600 = $7,150

Increase in EI retail, current = $7,150(1.6) = $11,440

C/R (use FIFO, not LCM) = $12,000/$40,000 = .30

Increase in EI, cost = .30($11,440) = $3,432

EI, cost = $800 + $3,432= $4,232

180. **Answer: A**

The DV LIFO retail process applies the DV LIFO method to retail dollars, and then deflates the retail layer added, now reflecting current prices, to cost, using the cost-to-retail ratio. The calculations are:

Ending inventory, retail, at base = $450(1.00/1.15) = $391

Increase in retail, current = $111(1.15/1.00) = $128

Increase in cost = $128(.42) = $54

Ending inventory at cost = ($80 + $30) + $54 = $164

181. **Answer: B**

The easiest way to answer a question like this is to make up simple numbers. The following simple numbers were made up to fit the abstract information in the question. Lower of cost or market states you record the inventory at the lower of original cost or market value (replacement cost) within the range of a ceiling and a floor. The numbers below show that replacement cost is lower than original cost and within the floor and ceiling. Replacement cost is the correct answer.

Original cost	$10
Net realizable value	9
Replacement cost	8
NRV less normal PM	7

182. **Answer: C**

Inventory must be carried at lower of cost (such as LIFO or market. Market is replacement cost subject to a ceiling and floor. The ceiling for replacement cost is net realizable value (selling price less cost to complete) and the floor is net realizable value less normal profit margin. Use simple numbers to help solve this abstract question. In this question original cost (assume = 100) is greater than market ((replacement cost) assume = 80). Market (80) is greater than net realizable value (assume = 70). Market is subject to a ceiling of net realizable value (70). In this case the inventory would be valued at net realizable value.

183. **Answer: D**

Use the equation BI + PUR = EI + CGS. When EI is understated, CGS must be overstated to maintain the equation. Net income, therefore, is understated (20x5). Then next year, BI is also understated because BI for 20x6 is EI for 20x5. Using the equation, if BI is understated, CGS is also understated to maintain the equation.

184. **Answer: D**

Counterbalancing simply means that the effect of the inventory error in the second year is opposite that of the first year. Discovery in year two provides an opportunity for the firm to correct year two beginning retained earnings, which is overstated by the error in year one. The overstatement of inventory in year one caused cost of goods sold to be understated and income overstated in year one. The prior period adjustment, dated as of the beginning of year two, is a debit to retained earnings for the after-tax effect of the income overstatement in year one. Inventory is credited for the amount of the overstatement. This allows year two to begin with corrected balances.

185. **Answer: C**

Both qualities are required for a loss to be recognized. The firm must honor a contract in a later period by paying more than current cost and, thus, is in a loss position at the end of the current year.

186. **Answer: C**

Under IFRS, the inventory would be carried at the lower of cost or NRV. The NRV at the end of Year 2 is $75.

187. **Answer: A**

Under IFRS, inventory is carried at the lower of cost or net realizable value. Recovery of previous write-downs is allowed. Therefore, in year 2, the company can recover the previous write-down of $20 ($100 – 80) but cannot write the inventory above the original cost. The entry to record the recovery is a debit to inventory and credit to expense or cost of goods sold for $20.

188. **Answer: C**

IFRS reports inventory at lower of cost or net realizable value. Net realizable value is the selling price less the cost to complete or dispose of the inventory. The net realizable value is the selling price of $1,000 less the cost to complete of $100, or $900. Net realizable value is less than the cost ($910) so the inventory is reported at $900.

189. **Answer: D**

Depreciation expense should begin on the date that the asset is placed into service and therefore, contributing to the generation of revenues. The depreciation expense should begin on February 1, Year 2.

190. **Answer: B**

A useful life of at least three years is NOT a requirement for classification of a plant asset. The plant asset must have a useful life extending more than one year beyond the Balance Sheet date.

191. **Answer: D**

Only assets used in current operations are included in the category of property, plant and equipment (PPE) on the balance sheet. Assets that are held for sale are reclassified from PPE to 'assets held for sale' and are no longer depreciated. This question is an example of a question framed in the null form. That is, the question wants you to find the exception. This response states the asset will be valued at historical cost—that is false. An asset held for sale is reported at net realizable value.

192. **Answer: C**

The costs capitalized to the land are all costs to get the land ready for use (development). Those costs are: the cost of the land, the real estate taxes in arrears, and the attorney fee for the title search.

193. **Answer: C**

The gain or loss on the sale of an asset is part of continuing operations as it is expected that a company will sell existing assets from time to time as the assets are replaced.

194. **Answer: D**

This response includes all the costs to get the equipment ready for use. The rearrangement costs and the wall removal costs were needed to put the equipment into use. The rearrangement costs made the production more efficient.

195. **Answer: C**

The amounts necessary to get the land ready for its intended purpose attach themselves as a part of the total cost of the land. This would be the: $2,500+625+135,000+16,000=$154,125

196. **Answer: C**

The sum of the four listed costs is $120,000, which exceeds fair value of $105,000. Therefore, the asset is capitalized at $105,000, the lesser of the two amounts. Subtracting the $10,000 residual value yields $95,000 depreciable cost-the total depreciation over the life of the asset.

197. Answer: A

The firm has committed to a fixed price but must recognize the loss in the period the decline in price occurred, much like under lower-of-cost-or-market. Inventory is not reduced because the firm has not purchased the inventory under contract. There is no asset to reduce, but the decrease in net assets is accomplished by recording the liability for the portion of the purchase price that has no value.

198. Answer: B

The average accumulated expenditures for purposes of capitalizing interest during construction of the warehouse includes the land cost, but the interest is capitalized to the warehouse only. The land is not under construction.

199. Answer: C

Neither debt issuances were identified as the construction loan. Therefore, the interest rate must be determined based on the weighted average of the interest on all of the debt outstanding during the year. The calculation is as follows:

	$6,000,000 × .08 =	$480,000
	$8,000,000 × .09 =	$720,000
Totals	$14,000,000	$1,200,000
	$1,200,000 / $14,000,000 =	8.57%

200. Answer: A

Interest is capitalized on the project's average expenditures times the interest during that period. Key here is to use the 5% annual interest over the three months (April, May, and June).

Average expenditures:	$\frac{500,000 + 800,000 + 1,500,000}{3}=$	933,333
Interest rate for 3-month period:	.05 × 3/12	× .0125
Capitalized interest:		11,666

201. Answer: B

Post-acquisition expenditures, which increase the useful life (assuming normal maintenance) or the utility (usefulness or productivity) of the asset, are capitalized. Such expenditures provide value for more than one year. The original useful life of an asset assumes regular maintenance. Therefore, regular maintenance does not increase the intended useful life of the asset.

202. Answer: C

When the cost and accumulated depreciation of a component or portion of a larger asset is identifiable, and that component or portion is replaced, the replacement is treated as two separate transactions: (1) disposal of the old component (for zero proceeds in this case, due to the fire damage) and (2) purchase of the new component.

Thus, a loss equal to the book value of the old component is recognized for (1) and the amount paid to purchase the new component is capitalized as a separate purchase for (2).

203. Answer: B

The gain or loss on the disposal of an asset is the difference between the net book value (NBV) and the selling price. The annual depreciation of the machine is $9,000 ($90,000/10 years). The asset was held for 9.5 years, so accumulated depreciation is $85,500. NBV is $4,500 ($90,000 less accumulated depreciation of $85,500). The sale is a gain of $500 because the selling price is greater than the NBV ($5,000 − $4,500).

204. Answer: A

This is a change in estimate and is handled currently and prospectively by allocating the remaining book value at the beginning of year 6 over the revised estimate of remaining years at that point. Through the beginning of year 6, the asset has been used five years. Therefore, seven years remain in the original book value. The book value at the beginning of year 6 is 7/12 × $48,000 or $28,000. The remaining useful life of seven years is extended to 10. Therefore, depreciation expense for year 6 is $28,000 × 1/10 or $2,800.

205. Answer: C

Net equipment at end of 20X4: $344,000 − $128,000 =	$216,000
Equipment purchase	50,000
Book value of equipment sold	(9,000)
Depreciation in 20X5	?
Equals net equipment at end of 20X5: $379,000-$153,000 = $226,000	

Solving for depreciation yields $31,000 depreciation for 20X5.

206. **Answer: D**

Salvage value is the portion of the asset's cost not subject to depreciation. Total depreciation, under any method, is limited to depreciable cost (cost less salvage value). The declining balance methods do not subtract salvage when computing depreciation. Care must be taken to avoid depreciating an asset beyond salvage value.

207. **Answer: C**

The carrying amount (book value) of a depreciable asset is its original cost less accumulated depreciation. Under sum-of-the- years' digits method of calculating depreciation expense (and, therefore, accumulated depreciation), the net depreciable cost (original cost less estimated salvage value) is multiplied by a factor consisting of:

Numerator = the number of years the current year is from the end of the life of the asset

Denominator = the sum of numbers (digits) for each year in the life of the asset

For Spiro, the net depreciable cost is $20,000-$2,000 = $18,000. Since the equipment has an estimated useful life of four years, the sum of the digits for each year would be $1 + 2 + 3 + 4 = 10$, the denominator for calculating each year's depreciation. Depreciation for the four years would be:

Year	Depreciable cost		Factor		Annual depreciation	Accumulated depreciation	Carrying value				
20X3	$18,000	×	4/10	=	$7,200	$7,200	$20,000	−	7,200	=	$12,800
20X4	18,000	×	3/10	=	5,400	12,600	20,000	−	12,600	=	7,400
20X5	18,000	×	2/10	=	3,600	16,200	20,000	−	16,200	=	3,800
20X6	18,000	×	1/10	=	1,800	18,000	20,000	−	18,000	=	2,000
Total	18,000	×	10/10	=	18,000	18,000					2,000

Thus, at the end of 20X5 the carrying amount is $3,800, which also can be calculated as salvage value $2,000 + (1/10 \times \$18,000) = \$2,000 + \$1,800 = \$3,800$.

208. **Answer: D**

The successful efforts method capitalizes only the cost of exploration efforts that locate the resource. As such, only those efforts that yield a probable future benefit are capitalized. This is a direct application of the asset definition, which requires that an asset have a probable future benefit.

209. **Answer: A**

The depletion rate = ($40 + $100 + $60)/20 = $10/ton. Depletion = 2,000,000($10/ton) = $20,000,000. Depletion for a period is the cost of the deposit allocated to the inventory removed for the period. In this case, the entire amount is included in cost of goods sold because there is no ending inventory. However, if there had been ore left at the end of the period, the $10/ton rate would have been applied to the units remaining. That would not change the answer to the question, however.

210. **Answer: D**

The depletion rate = [$40 + (.25)($100) + $60]/20 = $6.25/ton. Depletion = 2,000,000($6.25/ton) = $12,500,000. Because all the ore removed was sold, cost of goods sold includes the entire amount of depletion and the extraction costs. Cost of goods sold = $12,500,000 + $10,000,000 = $22,500,000. Note, that extraction costs is included in inventory (and therefore, cost of goods sold), but not in the deposit (and therefore, not in depletion).

211. **Answer: B**

The test for impairment for an asset in use is whether the carrying value (book value) is less than its recoverable cost. An asset's recoverable cost is the sum of its estimated net cash inflows projected for its remaining life.

When book value > recoverable cost, the carrying value is not recoverable. In other words, the asset is booked at more than the sum of its future net cash inflows.

For example, if an asset's carrying value is $100 and its recoverable cost is $80, then its carrying value is not recoverable (only $80 is recoverable). The AMOUNT of the loss recognized is the difference between carrying value and fair value, but that difference is not used for TESTING whether an asset is impaired.

That difference is not the condition leading to the impairment loss.

212. **Answer: A**

Recovery of impairment losses is prohibited under U.S. GAAP.

213. **Answer: A**

The net book value of the asset at the time of impairment was $150,000: $250,000 cost less $100,000 accumulated depreciation (4 years of depreciation at $25,000 a year). After the impairment of $30,000, the net book value is $120,000 ($150,000 − 30,000). The remaining life is 6 years and annual depreciation is $20,000.

214. **Answer: D**

Determination of impairment for an asset held in use is a two-step process. First the carrying value (CV) is compared to the recoverable cost (undiscounted cash flows). Since the CV is more than the recoverable cost, the second step must measure the impairment loss. The impairment loss is measured as the difference between CV and fair value (FV). The CV is $100 million and the FV is $80 million so the impairment loss is $20 million.

215. **Answer: A**

Under IFRS the impairment loss can be recovered if the asset is held for use or disposal.

216. **Answer: C**

The greater of fair value less cost to sell or value in use is the recoverable amount according to IFRS.

217. **Answer: A**

When remeasurement to fair value is used, it must be applied to the entire class or components of PPE.

218. **Answer: D**

Under IFRS an increase in an assets fair value above original cost are recorded in a revaluation surplus account and any decreases in an assets fair value below the original cost are recorded as losses to the income statement. Therefore, the 10,000 decrease in year 1 would have been recorded as a loss to the income statement and the 15,000 increase in year 2 would be recorded as a 10,000 gain to the income statement and 5,000 gain in revaluation surplus (OCI).

219. **Answer: B**

Under component depreciation, the asset is separated into component parts, and each part is depreciated over its useful life. The bus would be separated into three parts and depreciated as follows:

Bus	65,000	÷ 20 years	=	3,250
Engine	25,000	÷ 10 years	=	2,500
Seats	10,000	÷ 8 years	=	1,250
Total	100,000			7,000

220. **Answer: C**

Gains and losses from nonmonetary exchanges that have commercial substance are recognized immediately.

221. **Answer: C**

The gain on an exchange of nonmonetary assets is based on the fair value and book value of the asset exchanged. The land with a fair value of $50,000 is given for machinery. The company is using the land as legal tender. The gain will be the difference between the book value and the fair value of the asset given or $50,000 − $20,000 = $30,000.

222. **Answer: C**

When a transaction lacks commercial substance and cash is paid, the new asset is recorded at the book value of the old asset plus any cash given. Campbell has the same economic position as before the exchange – a different truck used in the same manner and $700 less cash. The new truck is the BV of the old asset ($3,000) plus the cash paid ($700) or $3,700.

223. **Answer: A**

This is an exchange with no commercial substance because the exchange was one truck for another. When cash is given and there is no commercial substance, a gain is not recognized. This transaction is an even exchange in value. Charm gave the old truck with a net book value of $3,000 ($10,000 – 7,000) plus $2,000 in cash, or a total of $5,000. The consideration given of $5,000 equals the fair value of the new truck, $5,000.

224. **Answer: B**

When commercial substance is lacking, gains are recognized in proportion to the amount of cash received.

225. **Answer: D**

The fair value of the advertising services provided can be reliably measured by reference to a nonbarter transaction for similar advertising with a different counterparty (SIC Interpretation 31, para 5).

226. **Answer: B**

The method of payment used to acquire an investment does not help determine the correct accounting treatment of the investment. While the method of payment determines what will be "credited" upon acquisition of the securities, it will not enter into the subsequent accounting treatment of the investment.

227. **Answer: B**

An investor may elect to use fair value to account for or measure some investments that otherwise would be accounted for using the equity method (Statement II). However, an investor is not required to use fair value to account for all equity investments (Statement I).

228. **Answer: B**

The minimum level of voting ownership considered to give an investor significant influence over an investee is 20%. In the absence of other relevant factors, an investor is considered to have significant influence over an investee if it owns 20%–50% of the voting securities of the investee.

229. **Answer: B**

The investment in Swedberg is initially measured and recorded at the price paid for the shares including the brokerage fees. The subsequent measurement of an equity investment is at fair value.

230. **Answer: A**

The entries related to the investment in Pear are as follows:

DR: Investment in Pear	150,340	
CR: Cash		150,340

(to record the purchase of Pear (($25 × 6,000) + $340)

DR: Investment in Pear	11,660	
CR: Unrealized gain		11,660

(to adjust investment to fair value of 162,000 ($27 × 6,000)

(162,000 – 150,340)

DR: Cash	2,400	
CR: Dividend income		2,400

(to record dividend income ($0.40 × 6,000))

DR: Cash	115,775	
CR: Investment in Pear		108,000
CR: Gain on sale		7,775

(to record the sale of 4,000 shares of Pear at $29 per share)

Cash = (($29 × 4,000) – 225 = 115,775)

Investment in Pear = ($27 × 4,000 = 108,000)

Gain = (115,775 – 108,000)

231. **Answer: A**

When there is no influence over the investee and the equity investments carried at fair value, cash dividends are recorded as dividend income.

232. **Answer: C**

The costs associated with determining fair value are not taken into consideration when assessing whether fair value is readily determinable. The costs listed in this response are the typical and reasonable costs that the entity would incur to determine fair value.

233. **Answer: C**

Investments in equity securities are reported at fair value if the control is not significant and there is a readily determinable fair value.

If the control is not significant and there is not a readily determinable fair value, then the entity may elect to use the cost method. In this situation, only the investment in Kemo Inc. qualifies to be reported using the cost method.

234. **Answer: B**

An investment in equity securities of another entity gives the investor an ownership interest and, therefore, the ability to vote in corporate elections. An investment in the debt of another entity does not give the investor an ownership interest or the right to vote in corporate elections. An investment in the debt of another entity establishes a debtor-creditor relationship, not an ownership relationship.

235. **Answer: B**

Because Catco owned only 12% of Dexco's common stock during the period October 1–December 31, 200X, it would not have been able to exercise significant influence over Dexco and would have used the fair value method. Because the purchase of an additional 18% of Dexco's common stock would have given it a total of 30%, in the absence of other factors, it would be presumed to have significant influence over Dexco and, therefore, would have used the equity method during the period January 1–December 31, 200Y.

236. **Answer: C**

The investor must disclose the accounting policy for the investee. It is possible for the investor to use equity method accounting or elect the fair value option to account for the investee. The users of the financial statement need to know the basis for the equity accounting and if the investment included intercompany profits or other items that could impact the carrying value.

237. **Answer: B**

The unrealized loss would be credited to the other comprehensive income account to reclassify the holding loss as a realized loss in the income statement for Year 2. For purposes of illustration, assume the available-for-sale (AFS) securities were originally purchased for $5 and that the loss during Year 1 was $1. The related entries would be:

Purchase:	DR. AFS Securities	$5	
	CR. Cash		$5
Year 1	DR. OCI (holding loss)	$1	
	CR. AFS Securities		$1
Year 2:	DR. Cash	$4	
	CR. AFS Securities		$4
	DR. Loss on AFS Securities	$1	(Income Statement)
	CR. OCI (holding loss)		$1 (B/S, Accumulated OCI)

The last entry (above) reclassifies the holding loss to recognize a realized loss on sale.

238. **Answer: B**

Only realized gains (from sale or reclassification) on available-for-sale securities are recognized in income for the period. The unrealized changes in fair value are recorded in owners' equity.

239. **Answer: A**

When the decline in fair value is considered to be other-than-temporary, the unrealized losses in OCI are reclassified to earnings.

240. **Answer: B**

An available-for-sale security is valued at fair value at the balance sheet date, and any temporary decline in value is recorded in other comprehensive income for the period. However, because the decline was permanent (not temporary in nature), the available-for-sale security should be written down to fair value, and the amount of the write-down should be recorded in the income statement as a loss. Subsequent increases in the fair value of the available-for-sale security would be included in other comprehensive income in the year of the increase.

241. **Answer: D**

Held-to-maturity investments in bonds are reported at amortized cost. The discount or premium at purchase is amortized during the term of the bonds so that the carrying value is equal to face value at maturity. This is the amount to be received at maturity. The purchase price, exclusive of accrued interest, is $215,000 ($220,000 − $5,000). Accrued interest is not included in the investment carrying value. The premium paid on the bonds is $15,000 because the face value of the bonds is $200,000 (200 × $1,000). The term of holding the bonds is from October 1, 2014, to January 1, 2021, a period of six years and three months, or 75 months. The period from purchase to the December 31, 2015, balance sheet is 15 months. Amortization of the premium reduces the investment carrying amount because only face value, which is less than the amount paid for the investment, will be received at maturity. Therefore, the ending 12/31/15 investment carrying value is $212,000 = $215,000 − ($15,000 × 15/75 = $3,000).

242. **Answer: B**

When a bond is purchased at a discount, the price paid is less than face value. Any cash paid to the seller for accrued interest is debited to interest receivable, not to the bond investment. Thus, the carrying value is the portion of the total amount paid attributable to the total bond price, exclusive of accrued interest. The carrying value must be less than the cash paid to the seller, which includes accrued interest.

243. **Answer: C**

An unrealized gain on held-to-maturity securities is disclosed only in the notes to the financial statements. Gains are reflected in the financial statements only when they are realized (i.e., upon sale or for other than temporary declines in value). The year-end financial statements would present the held-to-maturity portfolio at cost. Parenthetical or footnote disclosure would indicate their market value.

244. **Answer: B**

North is the investee because it issued the bonds, but neither South nor East is an investee. Since East owns the bonds on December 31, it is the investor. Since South did not issue the bonds and does not own the bonds on December 31, it is neither an investor nor an investee.

245. **Answer: B**

Because Plack Co. owns only 2% of Ty Corp. stock, it does not have significant influence over Ty and will use fair value to account for its investment. Plank's dividend will be determined by the number of shares of Ty that it owns

multiplied by the amount of dividend per share. The calculation is:

2/14 Purchase	10,000 shares
4/30 Stock dividend	2,000 shares
12/15 Total shares owned	12,000
Dividend rate	$2
Total Dividend income	$24,000

The stock dividend would be recorded by Plack as a memorandum entry to adjust the per-share original cost, so it is based on the total 12,000 shares now owned.

246. **Answer: D**

Stock dividends are not recognized in the accounts at receipt, at fair value or any other value. Rather, they reduce the cost per share under both methods. The original cost is spread over more shares.

The investor's percentage of the firm has not changed as a result of the stock dividend, but the investor has more shares (as do all investors). When the shares received as a dividend are sold, the reduction in cost basis increases the gain or reduces the loss.

247. **Answer: D**

Under any method used to account for an investment in common stock, the investor records a stock dividend received by a memorandum entry to increase the number of shares owned. Since the cost of the investment does not change, the per share cost of the stock decreases.

248. **Answer: A**

If Clarion does not elect the fair value option for valuing its financial assets, the rules of ASC Topic 320 apply. Both the Company X stock investment and the Company Y bond available-for-sale security investment would be reported at fair value. However, only the $21,000 unrealized gain associated with the Company X stock trading security investment would be reported in earnings of the period. The unrealized gain of $5,000 on the Company Y bond available-for-sale security investment would be reported in other comprehensive income (OCI). The Company Z bond held-to-maturity security investment would be reported at amortized cost.

249. Answer: C

ASC Topic 320 requires that held-to-maturity securities be carried at amortized cost and that available-for-sale and trading securities be carried at fair value (FV). Therefore, Ott's investment portfolio is reported at 12/31/Y1 at the following amounts:

Bond		Amount reported
Mann Co.	$10,000	cost
Kemo, Inc.	10,000	FV
Fenn Corp.	9,000	FV
	$29,000	

250. Answer: A

Both transfers from held-to-maturity to held-for-trading classifications and from held-for-trading to held-to-maturity classifications can occur in the accounting for debt investments.

251. Answer: D

Fair value is the valuation basis used when debt investments are transferred between classifications. Conceptually, the existing carrying value is written off and the current fair value is written on in the new classification, with any difference being an unrealized gain or loss.

252. Answer: B

Statement II is correct; Statement I is not correct. The business model test used in evaluating debt instruments for classification purposes is concerned with the investor's intent. Specifically, did the investor make the investment to collect cash flows from interest and return of principal, rather than to make a profit on sale of the investment (Statement II)? While there is a single category for equity investments (at fair value), there are two categories for debt investments (at amortized cost and at fair value) (Statement I).

253. Answer: B

Under IFRS No. 9, investments in debt securities made under an entity's business model plan to make and hold such investments solely to receive cash from interest and principal repayment, and when there is no accounting mismatch, should be reported at amortized cost. Amortized cost is par value ($100,000) plus the unamortized premium ($3,500), or $100,000 + $3,500 = $103,500, the correct answer.

254. Answer: A

Under IFRS, changes in fair value may be reported in profit/loss or in other comprehensive income, depending on whether or not the investment is held for trading purposes or not. If an investment in equity securities is held-for-trading purposes (i.e., to make a profit on price appreciation), changes in fair value will be reported through profit/loss. If an investment in equity securities is not held-for-trading purposes, the investor may elect to report changes in fair value through other comprehensive income.

255. Answer: D

Once a project reaches technological feasibility, then the research and development cost can be capitalized. The costs of registering a patent can be capitalized as an intangible asset because if the entity is registering the patent, most likely the project has reached technological feasibility.

256. Answer: A

Unless there is evidence otherwise, amortization is on a straight-line basis. This intangible has a 10-year life and has a residual value. The annual amortization is 4,000 per year (50,000 − 10,000 = 40,000 / 10 years).

257. Answer: C

Litigation costs can be capitalized only if the defense of the patent was successful.

258. Answer: A

Once the lowest level of identifiable cash flows is identified for a division or unit, the next step would be to test the recoverability of the carrying amount of the division's assets. This is done by comparing the fair value of the unit to the carrying amount to determine if further steps are necessary.

259. Answer: D

For public business entities, goodwill is not amortized; rather, it is tested for impairment at least annually or when factors indicate a potential impairment. There is no requirement as to the timing of the impairment testing other than that the testing be completed at the same time every year.

260. Answer: C

This is a quantitative measure of the implied goodwill. The question asked which of the responses is not a qualitative factor used in the pre-step for goodwill impairment. This response is incorrect also because implied goodwill is determined by comparing the fair value of the reporting unit to the fair value of the identifiable assets – not by using a discount model.

261. Answer: A

The recoverability test is applied to definite-life intangible assets. The patent is the only definite-life intangible asset listed. The first step of the impairment test of a definite-life intangible is to compare the asset's book value (BV) to the recoverable cost. Recoverable cost is the sum of the net cash flows attributable to using the asset and from the ultimate disposal. If the BV is greater than the recoverable costs, then the asset is potentially impaired. The second step is to compare the BV to the fair value (FV). If the BV is greater than the FV, the asset is written down to FV. The impairment loss equals BV – FV.

262. Answer: A

Under IFRS goodwill impairment is measured in a one-step process. The carrying value of the CGU is compared to the recoverable amount. If the CV > recoverable amount the goodwill is impaired. The impairment loss is the recoverable amount – the CV. In this case $32,000 – $45,000 = ($13,000) loss.

263. Answer: C

Redesign of a product prerelease would be considered R&D because it is discovering new technology, process, or function of the product.

264. Answer: C

Equipment that is used in research and development activities and has alternative future uses should be depreciated over its estimated useful life. During the time that the equipment is used for R&D activities the depreciation will be recorded as R&D expense.

265. Answer: B

Research costs are associated with the discovery of new knowledge or the development of new products, services, processes or techniques.

Development costs are the translation of the research into a plan or design. The costs included in R&D are $75,000 + 22,000 and the depreciation associated with the equipment used in R&D ($150,000 / 5 years = $30,000) and the R&D services paid to a third party $23,000 = $150,000. The receipt of payment from a third party is not netted against the R&D costs.

266. Answer: C

Research and development (R&D) costs are expensed until the point the project reaches technological feasibility, at which point the costs can be capitalized. Therefore, all costs prior to July 31 are expensed as R&D. This software coding and testing ($200,000 and $100,000) should be expensed as R&D.

267. Answer: C

Both option I. and III. are the criteria for determining if the cloud computing arrangement contain a software license.

268. Answer: C

The cost of developing software for internal purposes is expensed up to the "application development stage" at which point the effort appears to be leading to a useable application. After that point, costs are capitalized. With a three-year useful life and $10 million capitalized cost, the amortization expense is one-third, or $3.33 million.

The useful life of the product is used rather than the useful life of the equipment because new software can be developed after three years for use on that equipment.

269. Answer: C

The greater of fair value less cost to sell or value in use is the recoverable amount according to IFRS.

270. Answer: B

Under IFRS impairment losses associated with identifiable intangibles are recoverable. Impairment losses associated with goodwill are NOT recoverable.

271. Answer: C

This question has three debt instruments that need to be categorized into current or long-term. The line of credit is due in one year so it is all current. The secured note is due in 5 annual installments so 1/5 is current and 4/5 is long-term. The balloon note is due in 3 years so it is all long term.

Instrument	Current	Long-term
Line of credit	250,000	0
Secured	150,000	600,000
Balloon	0	300,000
Total	400,000	900,000

272. **Answer: B**

This question requires you to think about how liabilities are accrued. If Hemple is holding funds for a mortgage company, it is a liability for Hemple. The liability would be increased when escrow monies are deposited and decreased when there is payment made on behalf of customers. The funds are also earning interest and 10% of that interest is charged as a maintenance fee to the customer. A T-Account will help demonstrate this:

Escrow Liability

Taxes paid from escrow 1,450,000 Maintenance fees	Beginning Balance
	1,200,000 Escrow receipts
	40,000 Interest earned
	210,000 Ending Balance

273. **Answer: A**

Only the bonus is a liability of the firm as of 12/31/Year 1. That amount was earned and granted in Year 1 and thus is recognized in the Year 1 balance sheet because it is not due for payment until Year 2. Dividends are not liabilities until declared. There is no unpaid declared dividend at 12/31/Year 1.

274. **Answer: B**

This question has two costs that occurred during the year. You are asked how much of these costs would be recognized in year 1. The $15,000 of maintenance cost is for a 1 year period beginning March 1. The maintenance cost would be allocated 1/12 evenly over the life of the service period or $1,250 a month × 10 months in year 1 = 12,500. The $5,000 modification to the software has increased its functionality and therefore should be capitalized and amortized over the life of the software $5,000 / 5 years = $1,000/year. The total expense recognized in year 1 would be $12,500 + 1,000 = $13,500.

275. **Answer: B**

Only costs that are attributable to employee service already rendered can be accrued. The firm has received no benefit for services that employees have not yet rendered. The firm owes employees nothing for future services and therefore has no liability for these amounts and no cost or expense should be recognized.

276. **Answer: A**

The wage limit on unemployment tax is $10,000. Thus, the total accrued liability, which is also the unemployment tax amount, is 5($10,000)(.02) = $1,000.

277. **Answer: D**

A loss that is probable to occur but cannot be reasonably estimated is disclosed in the notes to the financial statements.

278. **Answer: B**

The beginning warranty liability in year 1 is $100,000 (1,000 units × $100) less the first year warranty costs of $12,000, equals the first year ending balance $88,000.

279. **Answer: C**

Under U.S. GAAP, impairment testing is a two step process. The first step compares the assets' carry value (CV) to its undiscounted cash flows (UCF). In this problem the CV > UCF; therefore the asset is potentially impaired and we must go to the second step. The second step compares the assets CV to its fair value (FV). In this problem the FV < CV and the asset is written down to its FV. $170 million – $135 million = $35 million impairment loss.

280. **Answer: D**

Contingent gains are not recognized in the accounts. At most, footnote disclosure is considered acceptable reporting. This is the best answer because no amount in the range of possible values is *more likely* than any other. The $100,000 amount was not known when the financial statements were published.

281. **Answer: A**

In the interest of conservatism and disclosure, the guarantee should be disclosed. It is not required to be accrued because the probability is remote that the firm will have to pay the note.

282. Answer: A

A provision is a present obligation. This is one of the ways a liability can be treated as a contingent liability under international standards. If the provision involved a probable outflow, then it would be recognized, but would not be a contingent liability.

283. Answer: A

A probable (> 50%) outflow of benefits is implied, and the amount is estimable. This is a recognized liability for international accounting standards, not a contingent liability.

284. Answer: A

The interest payable is comprised of the following:

$100,000, 12% note	(100,000 × .12 × 3/12)	$3,000
$75,000, 10% note	(75,000 × .10 × 3/12)	1,875
		$4,875

There is no interest accrued on the noninterest bearing note because it is for less than one year.

285. Answer: C

The first payment included interest of $22,500 (.09 × .25 × $1,000,000). Note that interest rates are always expressed for an annual period. Only 25% of year elapsed from Sept. 30 to the end of the year. The rest of the payment ($241,700 = $264,200 − $22,500) is principal. The note payable balance at Dec. 31 therefore is $758,300 ($1,000,000 − $241,700).

Expanded explanation:

1. The note payable has a stated interest rate of 9%,
2. payments are made quarterly,
3. first payment was issued after 3 months on December 30 in the amount of $264,200, and
4. the question is asking for the note payable amount to be recorded on the balance sheet on December 31 of the same year.

The payment made on December 30 is part interest, part principal. The amount to be recorded on the balance sheet on December 31 is principal only.

Interest for quarter 1 = $1,000,000 × 9% × ¼ = $22,500

- Payment of $264,200 = $22,500 interest + x principal
- Solve for principal amount = $241,700

- Remaining note to be shown on balance sheet on December 31 is $1,000,000 − $241,700 principal payment = $758,300

The next payment would be calculated in a similar manner; however, interest would be paid on the remaining principal balance of $758,300.

286. Answer: D

The accrued interest covers the period from the borrowing to 12/31/X5 because no interest has yet been paid. The interest is also compounded (this is a stumbling point easily missed).

The 20X5 ending balance in accrued interest payable therefore includes interest on 20X4's accrued interest:

20X4: $10,000(.12)(10/12)	$1,000
20X5: ($10,000 + $1,000)(.12)(12/12)	1,320
Total accrued interest payable, December 31, 20X5	$2,320

287. Answer: B

When the yield rate (effective interest rate) exceeds the stated or coupon rate, the bond sells at a discount. For example, the only way a 5% bond can yield 6% is to sell below face value. The discount represents interest expense over and above the periodic cash interest paid because the full face value is paid at maturity. The discount is recorded as debit contra account to bonds payable. This extra amount of interest is recognized by amortizing the discount recorded at issuance. The journal entry for periodic interest is: dr. Interest Expense, cr. Discount, cr. Cash. In this way, interest expense exceeds the cash interest paid at each interest payment date.

288. Answer: A

The carrying value of the bonds after the first interest payment is $363,600 which reflects $3,600 of discount amortization. Because discount amortization increases the carrying value of the bond by reducing the discount, the carrying value (and amount received at issuance) must have been $3,600 less or $360,000 ($363,600 − $3,600). As discount is amortized, the carrying value gradually increases to the maturity (face) value over the bond term.

289. Answer: D

Legal and accounting fees	$45,000
Printing of the prospectus	55,000
Underwriting fees	85,000
Total bond issue costs	$185,000

Bond issue costs are those costs incurred to facilitate the issuance of the bonds. All of the above costs contribute to that effort.

290. **Answer: D**

The total amount received, which is called proceeds on the bond issue, is: .99($1,000)(600) + .10(3/12)(600)($1,000) = $609,000.

The first factor is the total bond price, exclusive of accrued interest. The second factor is the accrued interest since 4/1/Y5.

When bonds are issued between interest dates, the cash interest since the most recent past interest payment date must be collected from the bondholders because a full six months' interest is paid on the following interest date.

291. **Answer: A**

This question is a basic discount amortization scenario. The carrying amount of the bond will increase by the amount of the discount amortization each period until the carrying amount is $100,000 at maturity. Adding cells E2+D3 together will add the discount amortized for the period to the carrying amount of the bond, giving the new carrying amount at the end of the period.

292. **Answer: C**

IFRS provides that financial liabilities may be reported at amortized cost or at the fair value through profit or loss (FVTPL). If FVTPL is elected, the resulting gain or loss is recognized in profit or loss for the period.

293. **Answer: C**

The $1,000,000 loan was successfully refinanced on a long-term basis and therefore was moved to the noncurrent liability category. The refinancing took place before the financial statements were issued, thus meeting the requirements for reclassification on a long-term basis. The remaining items are all current: $750,000 accounts payable + $400,000 short term borrowings + $100,000 current portion of mortgage payable = $1,250,000 total current liabilities.

294. **Answer: B**

Only the principal portion of the mortgage note is current. The short-term debt has been refinanced and reclassified as noncurrent. The deferred tax liability relating to depreciation is noncurrent.

295. **Answer: C**

The question asks for the book value amount to be compared to the price paid for the bonds retired when the gain or loss on retirement is computed.

The net book value includes the unamortized bond issue costs. The amount of unamortized issue costs relating to the portion of the bond issue retired increases the loss or decreases the gain. The remaining portion of the bond term for the portion of the bond issue retired is the period for which the bond issue costs were not amortized.

Number of semiannual periods in bond term:	15(2) = 30
Number of semiannual periods remaining at 6/2/year 6 =	10(2) = 20
Remaining unamortized bond issue costs: $6,000(20/30)	= $4,000

Net amount to compare to price paid for bonds, to determine gain or loss on retirement, on one-half the bond issue: (1/2)($500,000 − $4,000) = $248,000. A journal entry recording the retirement of one-half the issue helps show why $248,000 is the correct answer.

Bonds payable	250,000	
Bond issue costs		2,000
Cash .98($250,000)		245,000
Gain		3,000

The gain equals the net value of two accounts removed from the books ($248,000) less the amount paid to retire the bonds.

296. **Answer: A**

Book value of bonds retired $600,000 + $65,000	$665,000
Less total market value of bonds retired 600($1,000)(1.02)	(612,000)
Equals gain on retirement	$53,000

The unamortized premium is a component of the book value at retirement. A premium increases the net book value of the bonds because more was paid in than the face value when the bonds were originally issued.

When a liability is retired for less than its book value, a gain is recorded because the firm reduces its liabilities more than the reduction in its cash or other assets used for retirement.

297. Answer: A

In a troubled debt restructuring involving only a modification of terms, the debtor will recognize a gain only if the total undiscounted future cash payments for principal and interest under the new terms are less than the current amount payable for principal and accrued interest.

When the future payments under the new terms are less than the current obligation, the debtor writes down the carrying amount of the liability by the amount of the difference and thus recognizes a gain.

298. Answer: A

Both sets of standards treat settlements as extinguishments with a gain to the debtor for the difference between debt book value and fair value of consideration paid.

299. Answer: C

This transaction increases current liabilities, thus reducing the current ratio. The current ratio is current assets divided by current liabilities. There is no effect on current assets.

300. Answer: C

It must be at least possible that the liability will be called in order for the classification to be downgraded to current.

301. Answer: B

The value of the stock to be issued is $20,000. At time of issuance, the stock price is $25. Therefore, 800 shares are issued ($20,000/$25). The par value of the stock is $2, requiring a credit of $1,600.

302. Answer: A

Shifter paid $5,000 more for the treasury stock than its fair value: 1,000 shares × ($20 − $15). The $2,000 fee (1,000 × $2) offsets that loss yielding a net loss of $3,000.

303. Answer: A

A 5% stock dividend increases outstanding shares by 5%, and a 2-for-1 split doubles outstanding shares. The number of outstanding shares at year-end therefore is 105,000 = 50,000(1.05)(2). Each subsequent dividend or split compounds the previous change.

304. Answer: C

The number of shares outstanding at the end of year 2 = (100,000 + 15,000 + 2,500)2 = 235,000. The beginning outstanding shares of 100,000 is augmented by the issuance of previously unissued stock, and by the reissuance of treasury stock. Stock splits are applied retroactively to all changes in outstanding shares occurring before the split. The split is a nonsubstantive change in shares. Each share after the split is worth half of one share before the split.

305. Answer: A

Treasury shares are considered issued, but not outstanding. At December 31, 20X5:

Number of shares issued = [100,000 (beginning) + 10,000 (new issuance)]2 = 220,000.

Number of shares outstanding = [95,000 (beginning) + 1,000 TS reissuance + 10,000 (new issuance)]2 = 212,000.

306. Answer: C

The net effect of the transactions is to receive cash of $1,200 and issue stock for that amount at $15/share; $1,200/$15 = 80 shares fully paid. Required net changes in balances are (1) common stock, 80($10) = $800, (2) PIC-CS, 80($15 − $10) = $400, (3) cash $1,200. The share purchase contract receivable account is opened and then closed for the same amount. There is no ending balance in that account.

307. Answer: A

Common stock: 20,000($1) = $20,000. Only par value is credited to common stock.

Preferred stock: 6,000($10) = $60,000. Only par value is credited to preferred stock.

Additional paid-in capital (the amount received on issuance in excess of par): Common: 20,000($30 − $1) = $580,000 Preferred: 6,000($50 − $10) = 240,000 Total $820,000

308. Answer: B

When a firm retires preferred stock, cash is paid to the shareholders reducing total owners' equity. Retained earnings can never be increased when shares are retired, redeemed, or converted into another class of stock.

309. Answer: A

The $2 difference multiplied by 500 shares yields $1,000 paid in capital kept by the firm. The journal entry is:

DR: Preferred stock 500($100)	50,000	
DR: PIC—preferred 500($103 – $100)	1,500	
CR: PIC—retirement of preferred		1,000
CR: Cash 500($101)		50,500

310. Answer: A

Income is not affected by treasury stock transactions. When a firm transacts with its owners acting as owners, it cannot profit or report a negative income. In this case, the $3 difference between the $10 reissue price of the treasury stock and its $7 cost is credited to an owners' equity account as paid-in capital from treasury stock transactions. The firm's net worth has increased as a result of its treasury stock purchase and reissuance, but the "gain" is not recognized as earnings.

311. Answer: D

The shares are considered donated treasury shares. Treasury stock and a gain or revenue account are increased by the market value of the stock received in donation (FAS 116). The increase in the treasury stock account decreases the owners' equity, but the gain or revenue increases the owners' equity by the same amount. Therefore, there is no net effect on the owners' equity.

312. Answer: D

Instead of paying $4.5mn in dividends at declaration, the firm decided to issue notes due in five years, calling for the principal amount ($4.5mn), plus five years of simple interest to be paid. The note does not call for compounding.

Therefore, the amount due at maturity is $4.5mn + (5 years)(.10)($4.5mn) = $6.75.

313. Answer: A

A legal liability comes into existence at declaration. The firm has committed itself to paying resources to shareholders from retained earnings on that date.

314. Answer: C

This is a large stock dividend (> 25%); therefore retained earnings is debited for par value. The amount is the par value of the shares distributed in the dividend, or 1,000(.30)($1) = $300. The credit is to common stock for the shares issued.

315. Answer: C

The annual preferred dividend commitment is $120,000 (20,000 × $100 × .06).

The amount paid in 20X5 ($240,000) covers both 20X5, and 20X4 (dividends in arrears). Wood owns 10% of Arlo's preferred stock and, therefore, received $24,000. This amount is recognized as revenue in 20X5.

Dividends in arrears are not recognized until received. The stock dividend is not treated as revenue, but rather reduces the cost per unit of Wood's investment in Arlo's common stock.

316. Answer: C

Preferred represents one-fifth of total par value outstanding ($10,000/$50,000).

	To Preferred	To Common
Arrearage	.08(2)($10,000) = $1,600	
Current year	.08($10,000) = 800	
Matching		.08($40,000) = $3,200

Dividends remaining = $30,000 – $1,600 – $800 – $3,200 = $24,400, which exceeds .04($50,000), so there is enough for both classes of stock to participate at 4%.

	To Preferred	To Common
Participation	.04($10,000 = 400	
Remaining		$24,400 – $400 = 24,000
Total	$2,800	$27,200

317. **Answer: A**

Preferred represents one-fifth of total par value outstanding ($10,000/$50,000).

	To Preferred	To Common
Arrearage	.08(2)($10,000) = $1,600	
Current year	.08($10,000) = 800	
Matching		.08($40,000) = $3,200

Dividends remaining = $7,100 − $1,600 − $800 − $3,200 = $1,500, which is insufficient to provide 4% participation to both classes of stock [.04($50,000) = $2,000]. The remainder is allocated according to total par value.

	To Preferred	To Common
Participation	1/5($1,500) = 300	
	4/5($1,500)	= 1,200
Total	$2,700	$4,400

318. **Answer: B**

Preferred represents one-fifth of total par value outstanding ($10,000/$50,000).

	To Preferred	To Common
Arrearage	.08(2)($10,000) = $1,600	
Current year	.08($10,000) = 800	
Matching		.08($40,000) = $3,200

Dividends remaining = $30,000 − $1,600 − $800 − $3,200 = $24,400, which is allocated according to total par value.

	To Preferred	To Common
Participation	one-fifth($24,400) = 4,880	
	four-fifths($24,400)	= 19,520
Total	$7,280	$22,720

319. **Answer: A**

The issuance of warrants to shareholders does not require a journal entry, because no resources are expended or received. Therefore, in 20X3, there is no effect on owners' equity.

When the warrants are exercised in 20X4, the shareholders pay $30 per share for the stock purchased under the warrants. This issuance is recorded as a normal issuance at $30, even though that is not the market price at the date of issuance. Additional paid-in capital is increased by $10, the difference between the $30 exercise price and $20 par. Issuing warrants or stock has no effect on earnings. A firm does not profit on transactions with owners.

320. **Answer: C**

Retained earnings at December 31, 20X5 would be the sum of the beginning retained earnings

of $630,000 and the net income. Net income is revenue ($3.6mn) − expense ($2.6mn) or $1mn.

However, this did not include taxes. Taxes on $1mn (at the 30% tax rate) are $300,000. This is exactly the same as the pre-paid taxes, so no additional liability exists. The pre-paid just need to be transferred to an expense category.

This makes income $700,000 and ending retained earnings $1.33mn. No adjustment need be made for the accounts receivable, unless Trey is handling this transaction differently for tax (installment method) than for book purposes, which is contrary to the facts presented in the problem.

321. **Answer: C**

The dividend did not affect total OE, because no resources were expended or received. The payment of $0.10 per right reduces OE by a total of 120,000($0.10) = $12,000, because this amount of cash was paid.

322. **Answer: B**

Book value per share of common stock is common stockholders' equity per share of common stock. The portion of owners' equity allocated to preferred stock for this ratio is measured as the liquidation value per share. Therefore, the book value per share equals the net assets of the corporation per share that would be distributed to common shareholders on liquidation of the company, if the market value equaled book value for all assets and liabilities. The preferred shareholders would be paid the liquidation value per share first.

This firm has 1,000 shares of preferred stock outstanding: $100,000/$100 par; and 30,000 shares of common stock ($300,000/$10 par). It also has total owners' equity of $495,000 ($100,000 + $300,000 + $95,000).

For this firm, book value per share is $13.00 = [$495,000 − 1,000($105)]/30,000. Had there been dividends in arrears, they would also be subtracted from total owners' equity in the numerator. However, the preferred stock is non-cumulative, so there could be no dividends in arrears.

323. **Answer: C**

Reducing the par value to $5 creates $250,000 of additional paid-in capital: ($30 − $5)10,000 shares = $250,000. The common stock account is now $50,000: ($5)10,000.

Additional paid-in capital now stands at $400,000 ($150,000 + $250,000).

After absorbing the deficit in retained earnings, $190,000 remains in additional paid-in capital: ($400,000 − $210,000). Retained earnings are now zero.

324. **Answer: D**

Revenue is generated by the entity engaging in its central operations, which may include the sale of goods or the providing of services. Revenue may result in an enhancement of assets (e.g., receiving cash for goods or services) or the reduction or settlement of a liability.

325. **Answer: D**

A contract to which the revenue standard may be applied does not exist at this time, because of the ability to cancel the contract without

penalty or payment of consideration and because work has not begun on the contract performance obligations. At this point, the entities should disregard revenue guidance to contracts.

326. **Answer: D**

Because Holt has prior experience with similar contracts, Holt should use the expected value method, also referred to as the probability-weighted method, to estimate the variable consideration associated with this contract. Holt determines the transaction price using the following probabilities and amounts:

80% chance of $2,600,000 [$2,500,000 + ($100,000 × 1.0)]	=	$2,080,000
10% chance of $2,550,000 [$2,500,000 + ($100,000 × .50)]	=	255,000
5% chance of $2,525,000 [$2,500,000 + ($100,000 × .25)]	=	126,250
5% chance of $2,500,000 [$2,500,000 + ($100,000 × 0)]	=	125,000
		$2,586,250

The total transaction price, using the probability-weighted method is $2,586,250.

327. **Answer: B**

A company should use the expected value method when there are more than two possible outcomes and the company has experience with contracts with similar characteristics. The company can use its experience to appropriately weight the probability of each outcome to calculate the expected value of the variable consideration.

328. **Answer: D**

Wolf should allocate the total contract price of $850,000 to the equipment and the installation based on the proportion of fair value each component represents. The total fair value of the transaction is $900,000 ($850,000 fair value of the equipment plus $50,000 fair value of the installation). The equipment represents 94.44% ($850,000 / $900,000) of the fair value of the transaction, and the installation represents 5.56% ($50,000 / $900,000) of the fair value of the transaction. To allocate the transaction price to the equipment, multiply the total contract price by the proportion of the fair value the equipment represents ($850,000 × .9444). To allocate the transaction price to the installation, multiply the total contract price by the proportion of the fair value the installation represents ($850,000 × .0556). Wolf should allocate $802,740 to sales revenue from the sale of the equipment and $47,260 to service revenue from the installation.

329. **Answer: D**

The stand-alone prices for the performance obligations are totaled, and each stand-alone price per performance obligation is divided by the total of the stand-alone prices to calculate the proportion of the transaction price that will be assigned to each performance obligation. The total transaction price is multiplied by each proportion, and the resulting amount is allocated to the performance obligation.

330. **Answer: C**

By December 31, 20X3, two out of three years covered by the warranty have passed. The Unearned Warranty Revenue account would have one-third of the original amount left in it because Dot would recognize $12,000 of warranty revenue in each of the previous two years. $36,000 − $24,000 = $12,000 OR $36,000 × 1/3 = $12,000. Therefore, $12,000 in unearned warranty revenue would remain at December 31, 20X3.

331. **Answer: B**

The effect of estimated returns is recognized in the month of sale. Net sales to be reported for the current month equal $200,000 less the returns expected on those sales (5%, or $10,000), or $190,000. The actual returns granted in the current month on previous months' sales were recognized as reductions in net sales in those previous months.

332. **Answer: A**

The finder's fee benefits the entire lease term and therefore is allocated evenly over the 10-year lease term. The finder's fee represents a direct, incremental cost that benefits more than one period.

Net rental income	= Rent revenue	− Expenses associated with the property	
	= 50,000	− ($15,000 / 10 + $12,000 + $9,000)	= $27,500

333. **Answer: C**

For a new separate contract to be formed, the additional products must be distinct and the

consideration for the additional products must reflect appropriate standalone pricing.

334. **Answer: C**

Contrary to US GAAP, international standards require a modified version of completed contract—the cost recovery method, when the percentage of completion method is not allowed.

335. **Answer: D**

The gross profit recognized for the first two years must be computed first. Then, the difference between the $500,000 final total gross profit on the project (= $2.5mn − $2mn), and the gross profit for the first two years, is the amount of gross profit recognized in the last (third) year. The percentage of completion at the end of the first two years is 70% (= $500,000 + $900,000)/$2mn). The gross profit recognized through the end of year two is $350,000 [= .70($2.5mn − $2mn)]. Therefore, gross profit for year three is $150,000 (= $500,000 total gross profit on project − $350,000).

336. **Answer: D**

Service cost is included in compensation expense reported for the employees with whom the pension benefits are associated. Because the service cost component is included in the compensation expense line item, the subtotal for income from operations includes its effect.

337. **Answer: D**

The plan is currently underfunded and remains underfunded after the asset increase. Reported pension liability is the underfunded amount, the difference between PBO and plan assets. This firm's reported pension liability decreased from $800,000 to $300,000 ($800,000 − $500,000) owing to the asset increase.

338. **Answer: D**

Accumulated other comprehensive income (AOCI) is impacted by unexpected gains and losses from plan assets and unamortized portions of prior service costs from pension plan amendments. The net gain of $140,000 that has not previously been recognized in pension expense is reported as part of AOCI as a credit balance. The unamortized portion of prior service cost of $210,000 is reported as part of AOCI as a debit balance. The amount reported in AOCI related to the company's defined benefit pension plan is a net debit balance of $70,000.

339. Answer: B

PSC is recognized immediately in pension expense and DBO.

340. Answer: C

Pension gains and losses are recognized immediately and in full in accumulated other comprehensive income. However, they are not subsequently amortized to earnings.

341. Answer: C

OCI is increased through the increase in pension gains/losses—OCI.

342. Answer: C

The employee's full eligibility date occurs seven years from today. At that time, she is fully eligible for 75% coverage. The last three years of her service do not increase the level of her benefit. There is no additional service cost beyond that date, although interest cost will continue. If she were expected to work 15 years after today, her full eligibility would not occur until 15 years from now, at which time she would be fully eligible for 100% coverage and service cost would continue through that date.

343. Answer: C

The excess of plan assets over the benefit liability (accumulated postemployment benefit liability or APBO) is reported as an asset and is classified as noncurrent. The plan assets and APBO are not reported separately but rather are offset. Given the long-term nature of such plans, the asset is classified as a noncurrent asset.

344. Answer: A

Total share-based compensation expense is measured at the grant date by multiplying the number of options by the fair value of each option. The annual share-based compensation expense is calculated by dividing the total share-based compensation expense by the vesting or service period.

The employees were granted 100,000 options, each of which had a fair value of $15 at the grant date. Total shared-based compensation expense is $1,500,000 (100,000 options multiplied by $15). Total shared-based compensation expense of $1,500,000 divided

by the three-year vesting period results in an annual share-based compensation expense of $500,000. Assuming none of the employees forfeit their options, share-based compensation expense of $500,000 will be recognized at the end of years 1, 2, and 3.

345. Answer: C

Total compensation expense is the product of the fair value of one option at the grant date ($5) and the number of options granted (10,000). The result is $50,000 of total compensation expense. This total is allocated equally to each year in the service period. The service period is the period from grant date to vesting date (first exercisable date), or 4 years. Annual compensation expense is $50,000/4 = $12,500.

346. Answer: D

Total compensation expense at grant date is $60,000 (3,000 × $20). The service period is four years (20x5 – 20x8). Annual expense recognized is $15,000 ($60,000/4).

Through 20x6, a total of $30,000 of compensation expense is recognized. After the forfeit, only 2,900 shares remain to be awarded.

Annual compensation expense for the remaining two years before considering forfeited shares is therefore $14,500 [(2,900 × $20)/4].

The expense for the two years associated with the 100 shares forfeited is $1,000 [(100 × $20)/2].

For 20x7, subtracting the reversal of the $1,000 yields $13,500 as the final amount of expense to be recognized.

Another way to calculate the $14,500 is: ($60,000 original total compensation expense – $30,000 expense for x5 and x6 – $1,000 expense for x7 and x8 on forfeited shares)/2.

347. Answer: A

Total compensation expense is computed as the fair value of the stock awarded, and is allocated evenly over the vesting period. The fair value at award date is the fair value used for this computation. The two awards are treated as separate awards, each with four year amortization periods. The total expense for year 2 is the sum of the compensation expense to be recognized for each plan for year 2 and is computed as 10,000($20)/4 + 20,000($25)/4 = $175,000. Total fair value is not updated after the award date.

348. **Answer: B**

Total compensation expense is the product of the number of shares in the award and the market price of stock at the grant date. This amount is recognized over the service period required for the employee to receive or keep the shares.

349. **Answer: D**

From a financial reporting perspective, a primary objective of accounting for income taxes is to recognize and measure the deferred tax consequences (e.g. deferred tax assets and deferred tax liabilities) of temporary differences between pretax financial income and taxable income.

350. **Answer: B**

The company should report a net noncurrent amount on the balance sheet. Because the deferred tax asset is greater than the deferred tax liability, the two netted together result in an overall net noncurrent deferred tax asset amount.

351. **Answer: D**

The future temporary difference at December 31, 20X4 is $9,500, the amount of insurance expense to be recognized for financial-reporting purposes.

The entire $19,000 deduction was taken for tax purposes in 20X4. Therefore, no further deduction will be taken beyond 20X4. The difference is taxable, because future taxable income exceeds future pre-tax accounting income from transactions through 20X4.

The deferred tax liability uses the future tax rate, because that is the rate at which the deferred taxes will be paid. The ending deferred tax liability for 20X4 = $2,375 = .25($9,500).

352. **Answer: D**

Both listed items are permanent differences. These are differences that never reverse and are not used in the determination of deferred tax accounts. Both income tax expense and income tax liability are affected the same way by these items. A deferred income tax liability is based on future taxable differences at the end of the reporting year. There are no such differences. Therefore, there is no deferred tax liability.

353. **Answer: B**

This answer describes one category of temporary difference. In general, a temporary difference is one for which the item's recognition takes place at a different rate or time for financial reporting and the tax return. However, the total impact of the item is the same over its life, for both systems of reporting.

354. **Answer: A**

The tax liability is the tax rate times taxable income = .30($600,000 − $60,000 − $120,000 − $100,000) = $96,000.

The municipal- bond interest is tax exempt, but included in pre-tax accounting income of $600,000 and therefore is subtracted when computing taxable income.

The excess depreciation is also subtracted, because pre-tax accounting income reflects only depreciation recorded for financial accounting purposes.

The proceeds on life insurance are included in pre-tax accounting income, but are not taxable and are therefore subtracted in computing taxable income.

355. **Answer: B**

The effective tax rate is the ratio of income tax expense to pre-tax accounting income. income tax expense equals income tax liability in this case, because there are no temporary differences. Both the interest revenue and life-insurance premiums are permanent differences. The income tax liability is the product of the income tax rate and taxable income. Taxable income is $190,000 ($200,000 − $20,000 non-taxable interest included in the $200,000 + $10,000 non-deductible insurance premiums subtracted from $200,000). The income tax liability (and income tax expense) equal $57,000 (.30 × $190,000). The effective tax rate is .285 ($57,000/$200,000).

356. **Answer: C**

Income tax expense reflects the tax effects of permanent differences as measured by the tax code.

Because there are no temporary differences, income tax expense equals the income tax liability for the period or: $.30($280,000) = $84,000.

This reflects the tax ultimately payable on 20X5 transactions.

Therefore, income tax expense should also reflect that amount, in the absence of temporary differences.

357. **Answer: A**

A change in method of depreciation is treated as an estimate change. The remaining book value is allocated over the remaining useful life of the asset. Therefore, the total future difference between book and tax depreciation as of the beginning of 20X2 remains unchanged. That difference is $18,000, the difference between book and tax depreciation through the end of 20X1. The pattern of reversal of this difference in the future has changed owing the change in method, but the total difference remains unchanged. Therefore, there is no reduction in the deferred tax asset at the beginning of 20X2.

358. **Answer: A**

Income tax expense for the year is a derived amount and is the net sum of the income tax liability and the changes in the deferred tax accounts for the year. The income tax liability is the product of taxable income and the current-year tax rate, or $120,000(.35) = $42,000. The changes in the deferred tax accounts are the differences between the beginning and ending balances of those accounts. From the data, the deferred tax liability increased $5,000 for the year and the deferred tax asset increased $6,000. With the two liabilities increasing a total of $47,000 and the deferred tax asset increasing $6,000, income tax expense is the difference, or $41,000. The tax accrual journal entry is: dr. Income tax expense 41,000; dr. Deferred tax asset 6,000; cr. Deferred tax liability 5,000; cr. Income tax payable 42,000. The increase in the deferred tax asset represents a future reduction in income tax recognized in income tax expense for the current year. The increase in the deferred tax liability represents a future increase in income tax recognized in income tax expense for the current year.

359. **Answer: C**

income tax expense is the net sum of the income tax liability for the year, the changes in the deferred tax accounts, and the change in the valuation account for deferred tax assets.

Tax liability (current portion of income tax expense):	$13,000
Less increase in deferred tax asset: $20,000 − $15,000	($5,000)
Plus increase in valuation account: .10($20,000)	$2,000
Equals income tax expense	$10,000

The increase in the deferred tax asset causes income tax expense to decrease relative to the tax liability, because, as a result of transactions through the end of the current year, future taxable income will be reduced. This reduction is not realized in the current year as a reduction in the tax liability. Therefore, the anticipated future reduction is treated as an asset at the end of the current period. When realized, the asset is reduced in a future year.

The increase in the valuation allowance, which is contra to the deferred tax asset, reduces the deferred-tax-asset effect, because it is an amount of the deferred tax asset not likely to be realized.

360. **Answer: B**

This is the largest amount, which has at least a 50% probability of occurring. The cumulative probability through this amount is 60%. A liability is recognized for the $15,000 of the total $40,000, which has less than a 50% chance of occurring.

361. **Answer: A**

Income tax expense was reduced two years ago by $20,000, but the final benefit upon resolution is $22,000. The $2,000 increase in benefit is recognized in the year of resolution.

362. **Answer: B**

Deferred income tax accounts are not affected by permanent differences, because their effect on income tax is the same as their effect on income tax liability.

But temporary differences and operating loss and tax-credit carry-forwards produce deferred tax accounts. Temporary differences cause both deferred tax liabilities and assets to be recognized. Operating loss and tax credit carry-forwards generate only deferred tax assets.

To fully understand the nature of deferred tax accounts, the types and amounts of I and III are reported in a detailed footnote. For example, depreciation differences are major causes of deferred tax liabilities.

363. **Answer: B**

The unused net operating loss (NOL) at the beginning of the year is $20,000 (= $6,000/.3). The firm pays no tax for the current year, because $12,000 of the NOL is used to absorb the $12,000 of taxable income. $8,000 of the NOL remains to carry forward to the next year. Also, there is a future temporary difference of $20,000 from the future warranty deduction ($30,000 − $10,000 current-year claims). In total, then, the basis for the ending deferred tax asset is $28,000 (= $8,000 + $20,000). The ending deferred tax asset balance is $8,400 (= $28,000 × .3). The beginning deferred tax asset balance is $6,000. Therefore, the deferred tax asset is increased by $2,400 and income tax benefit of that amount also is recorded (credited) in the tax-accrual entry.

364. **Answer: D**

The accrual basis of accounting is required by GAAP. A change from an inappropriate method to the correct method is treated as an error correction. The procedure requires retrospective application, resulting in an after-tax cumulative adjustment to prior years' earnings (called a Prior period adjustment) to the beginning balance in retained earnings.

365. **Answer: A**

The cash basis of accounting is not acceptable under GAAP. Therefore, the change to the accrual basis is a change from an unacceptable method or basis of accounting to an acceptable method or basis. Such a change is treated as an error correction, which is reported as a Prior period adjustment. This adjustment is to the beginning balance in retained earnings for the current year.

366. **Answer: C**

$6,000 is the cumulative pre-tax income difference between the two methods as of January 1, 2005.

The after-tax difference is .70($6,000) or $4,200. Accounting changes are measured as of the beginning of the year of change. The $6,000 represents the total difference in cost of goods sold between the two methods for the entire life of the firm, because under weighted-average, the firm has $6,000 more in inventory than under FIFO at January 1, 2005. This is the "ending" inventory for that firm, as of that date, for the firm's entire existence.

The $6,000 difference completely explains the pre-tax difference in income under the two methods for years up to January 1, 2005; the $4,200 is the after-tax difference.

Cumulative effects are reported net of tax as an adjustment to the beginning balance of retained earnings in the year of the change.

367. **Answer: C**

When it is impossible to determine whether the change is an estimate or a change in accounting principle, the change should be considered a change in **estimate** and accounted for prospectively.

368. **Answer: B**

All publicly traded companies are required to report EPS information. However, only the current year is affected. Restatement of prior-year statements is not required.

369. **Answer: D**

When there is an error in prior period financial statements and those statements are presented with the current year, the error should be corrected in years 1 and 2 so they are comparative to year 3. The effect of the error should be reflected in the year 3 beginning balances of the appropriate assets and liabilities.

370. **Answer: A**

In order for Topco to gain control of Botco, it must own, either directly or indirectly, more than 50% of Botco's voting stock. Since it directly owns 40% of Botco's voting stock, it must acquire control over 10+% more. Also, since Topco owns 60% of Midco, it controls Midco. Therefore, if Midco acquires 11% of Botco, Topco will be able to exercise 51% of Botco's voting stock — 40% directly and 11% indirectly through its control of Midco.

371. **Answer: C**

The requirements of ASC 805 do not apply to combinations between not-for-profit organizations (or to the formation of a joint venture, an acquisition of assets that do not constitute a business, a combination of entities under common control, or the acquisition of a for-profit entity by a not-for-profit organization).

372. **Answer: D**

Only the acquisition method is acceptable in accounting for a business combination. The purchase method and the pooling of interests method of accounting for a business combination are not acceptable methods. The pooling of interests method was eliminated in 2001 and the purchase method was changed to the acquisition method in 2008. Although the acquisition method is a variation of the purchase method, it has sufficiently different requirements that it is not identified as the "purchase method," but rather as the "acquisition method."

373. **Answer: B**

All consideration, including contingent consideration, must be measured at acquisition date fair value. The total consideration transferred is:

Cash	$3,000,000
Stock	10,000,000
Contingent consideration	2,100,000
Total	$15,100,000

374. **Answer: D**

This question implies that the acquisition is a business combination. The costs associated with a business combination are expensed as incurred.

375. **Answer: B**

A noncontractual liability that is more likely than not (greater than 50%) to meet the definition of a liability, should be recorded at acquisition date fair value. This lawsuit is probable to occur and should be recorded as part of the business combination at $5 million.

376. **Answer: D**

Neither Statement I nor Statement II is correct. The value assigned to a noncontrolling interest in an acquiree would not be based simply on the proportional share of that interest in the net assets of the acquiree (Statement I), but rather on the separately determined fair value of the noncontrolling interest. The fair value per share of the noncontrolling interest in an acquiree does not have to be the same as the fair value per share of the controlling interest (Statement II), because there is likely to be a premium in value associated with having control of an entity that the noncontrolling interest would not enjoy.

377. **Answer: B**

The correct calculation would be the fair value of Trace's assets $240,000 – the fair value of the liabilities, $60,000 = $180,000.

378. **Answer: B**

Damon should report a $70,000 gain, calculated as:

Fair value of net assets acquired:	
Assets ($350,000) – Liabilities ($70,000)	= $280,000
Cost of Investment:	
Stock (20,000 shares × $10/share)	= $200,000
Contingent consideration @ fair value	= 10,000
Total cost of investment	= 210,000
FV of net assets > Cost of investment = Gain	= $70,000

379. **Answer: B**

A reacquired right is a right granted by an acquirer to the acquiree prior to a business combination that is reacquired when the acquirer gains control of the acquiree or the asset in a business combination. For example, the acquiree may have acquired the right to use the acquirer's trade name as part of a franchise agreement. A reacquired right is an intangible asset that is amortized by the acquirer over the remaining contractual period of the contract that grants the right.

380. **Answer: C**

A bargain purchase means that the acquirer paid less than the fair market value of the identifiable net assets. The seller must have been under some sort of duress (perhaps eminent bankruptcy) and was willing to accept a price less than the value of the net assets. In this case the acquirer recognizes that gain on the date of the acquisition.

381. **Answer: A**

Financial statement disclosures that enable users to evaluate the nature and financial effects of a business combination must be made both when the combination occurs during the reporting period and when the combination occurs after the reporting period but before the financial statements are released.

382. **Answer: D**

All three statements identify required disclosures. When a bargain purchase occurs in a business combination, the amount of the gain (Statement I), the income statement line item that includes the gain (Statement II), and a description of the basis for the bargain purchase amount (Statement III) must be disclosed.

383. **Answer: B**

Pine will not recognize on its books an investment in Straw. Because the business combination is a legal merger, Pine recognizes on its books almost all of Straw's assets and liabilities, not an investment in Straw. There can be no investment in Straw, because Straw will cease to exist.

384. **Answer: C**

The calculation is:

Fair value (200,000 sh. × $12/sh.)	$2,400,000
Par value (200,000 sh. × $5/sh)	(1,000,000)
Gross additional paid-in capital	$1,400,000
Less: Registration and issuance costs	35,000
Net additional paid-in capital	$1,365,000

The legal and consulting fees ($110,000) were paid in cash and would be expensed in the period incurred. The registration and issuance costs of the common stock are properly deducted from the additional paid-in capital derived from the issuance of the stock.

Acquisition-related costs (expect as noted below) should be expensed in the period in which the costs were incurred and the services are received. These costs, in this case the $110,000 legal and consulting fees incurred in relation to the acquisition, are not included as part of the cost of an aquired business.

The cost of issuing debt and equity securities for the purposes of a business combination are not treated as cost of the acquired business, but should be accounted for generally as follows:

- Debt issuance costs may be either recognized as a deferred asset and

amortized over the life of the debt, or expensed when incurred. In this case, equity was issued in the acquisition, not debt.
- Equity issuance costs reduce the proceeds from the securities issued and, in effect, reduce Additional Paid-in Capital. In this case, the information states $35,000 is incurred for registration and issuance costs for the stock issued.

385. **Answer: A**

The requirement is to identify the statement that correctly describes how goodwill may be recognized under IFRS. Goodwill can be recognized only if it is acquired in a business combination.

386. **Answer: A**

Under IFRS, contingent assets are not recognized. Under U.S. GAAP, contingent assets are recognized if the item meets the criteria of the definition of an asset.

387. **Answer: D**

All financial instruments do not have the same accounting requirements. Because financial instruments cover a variety of assets and liabilities, and are used for different purposes, there are different accounting requirements for different financial instruments, including derivatives.

388. **Answer: A**

Financial assets classified as "Loans and Receivables" are measured at amortized cost, with interest and amortization related to the instrument recognized in current income. This treatment is the same as the treatment under U.S. GAAP for investments held to maturity.

389. **Answer: C**

When it is not practicable for an entity to estimate the fair value of a financial instrument, both information pertinent to estimating the fair value of the instrument and the reasons it is not practicable to estimate fair value must be provided.

390. **Answer: A**

All entities must disclose all significant concentrations of credit risk arising from all financial instruments, whether from a single entity or a group of parties that engage in similar activities and that have similar economic characteristics.

391. **Answer: B**

A contract that has its settlement value tied to an underlying notional amount best describes a derivative financial instrument. The value or settlement amount of a derivative is the amount determined by the multiplication (or other arithmetical calculation) of a notional amount and an underlying. Simply put, a derivative instrument is a special class of financial instrument which derives its value from the value of some other financial instrument or variable.

392. **Answer: B**

The intrinsic value of a call option is the difference between the exercise (strike) price and the market price. This call option has an exercise price of $9 / share and the market price is $10 / share. Therefore, there is a $1 / share intrinsic value (I can buy the stock at a price less than the market). The option is to purchase 100 shares so the total intrinsic value is $100.

393. **Answer: D**

Neither Statement I nor Statement II is correct. Derivative instruments can be used not only for hedging purposes (Statement I), but also for speculative purposes. In addition, derivative instruments can be used not only to hedge fair value (Statement II), but also to hedge cash flows.

394. **Answer: D**

Because Buyco entered into the forward contract (hedging instrument) to hedge the risk of change in the fair value of the raw materials (hedged item), the change in fair value of the forward contract offsets the change in the fair value of the raw materials. Since during 2008 the change in the value of the raw materials decreased more than the value of the forward contract increased, the difference is the amount by which the derivative is ineffective as a fair value hedge. Specifically, the decrease in the value of the raw materials, $500, was offset by the increase in the value of the forward contract of $480, so the hedge was ineffective by $500 − $480 = $20, which is the correct answer.

395. **Answer: C**

A firm commitment has not been recorded (yet) as an asset or liability. A firm commitment occurs when an entity has a contractual obligation or contractual right, but no transaction has been recorded (and no asset or liability recognized) because GAAP requirements for recognition have not yet been met. Nevertheless, the subject matter of the firm commitment is at risk of change in fair value and can be hedged.

396. **Answer: D**

All differences between the change in value of the hedged item and the change in value of the hedging instrument is not recognized in current income. To the extent the change in the fair value of the hedging instrument offsets the change in the fair value of the hedged item, the hedge is effective, and that amount is recognized in other comprehensive income, not current income. To the extent the change in the fair value of the hedging instrument is different than the change in the fair value of the hedged item, the hedge is ineffective, and that amount is recognized in current income.

397. **Answer: D**

Prior service costs that have not been recognized in net periodic pension costs are included in accumulated other comprehensive income.

398. **Answer: C**

All foreign currency hedges are not treated as fair value hedges. While foreign currency hedges of unrecognized firm commitments, investments in available-for-sale securities, and net investments in foreign operations are treated as fair value hedges, foreign currency hedges of forecasted transactions are treated as cash flow hedges, and foreign currency hedges of recognized assets or liabilities may be treated either as fair value hedges or cash flow hedges, depending on management's designation.

399. **Answer: D**

Foreign currency hedges can be used to hedge the risk of exchange rate changes on planned (forecasted) transactions, available-for-sale investments, and accounts receivable/accounts payable (and unrecognized firm commitments and net investments in foreign operations).

400. **Answer: A**

Entities that either issue or hold derivatives (or other contracts used for hedging) must disclose a considerable amount of information concerning their reasons for using derivatives and the outcomes (e.g., gains/losses) of their accounting for the derivatives. Generally, these disclosures must distinguish between instruments used for different purposes (e.g., fair value hedges, cash flow hedges, etc.).

401. **Answer: D**

The definition of a derivative under IFRS does not include the concept of notional amount.

402. **Answer: C**

Foreign currency exchange gains (or losses) on accounts receivable are reported in current income as an item of income from continuing operations.

403. **Answer: A**

A gain or loss on a foreign currency import transaction can be recognized if the transaction is initiated in one fiscal period and settled in either the same fiscal period or a later fiscal period. The effect of exchange rate changes on accounts denominated in a foreign currency should be recognized in the period(s) in which the exchange rate changes. Therefore, if such an account (e.g., account payable) exists in more than one period, the effects of exchange rate changes in either or both periods would result in the recognition of a gain or loss in either or both periods.

404. **Answer: A**

The foreign currency exchange gain that occurred as a result of the exchange rate change should be recognized as a component of income from continuing operations in the income statement. Gains and losses resulting from changes in exchange rates are recognized in current earnings in the period in which the exchange rate changes.

405. **Answer: D**

The event described is a foreign currency (FC) transaction, not FC translation, and the gain (or loss) would be reported as a component of income from continuing operations for the current period.

406. **Answer: A**

At the date Don Co. entered into the transaction, June 19, and agreed to accept euros in satisfaction of its account receivable, it should record the transaction (sale and account receivable) at the (then existing or current) spot exchange rate of .988. Thus, the dollar amount of the account receivable (and sale) would be computed as 200,000 E × .988 = $197,600,

which also is the dollar value that would be received if the transaction were settled at that date.

407. **Answer: B**

While a foreign currency forward exchange contract entered into for speculative purposes is likely to result in a foreign currency loss (or gain) for the contract holder, a foreign currency option contract entered into for speculative purposes is not likely to result in a foreign currency loss for the contract holder.. Since the contract holder has the option of whether or not to exercise the contract option to exchange currencies, it is not likely that the option would be exercised if it would result in a loss.

408. **Answer: B**

While the intent of hedging is to mitigate the risk of loss (or gain) attributable to the item being hedged, hedging does not assure that no gain or loss will be incurred on the hedged item. Only in a perfect hedge does no gain or loss occur. In order to be a perfect hedge, the hedging instrument would need to have a 100% inverse correlation to the hedged item. Such an outcome is rare.

409. **Answer: D**

The net effect of a change in value of a hedged item and its related hedging instrument may be a gain, a loss, or neither a gain nor a loss (a perfect hedge).

410. **Answer: C**

A hedge to offset the risk of exchange rate changes on converting the financial statements of a foreign subsidiary to the domestic (functional) currency would be the hedge of a net investment in a foreign operation. Changes in exchange rates will result in changes in the amount of domestic (functional) currency that will result from converting (translating) financial statements from a foreign currency. Hedges of net investments in a foreign operation are intended to offset that risk.

411. **Answer: C**

Both Statement I and Statement II are correct. Even though a firm commitment is hedged, a net gain or loss can be reported (Statement I) if the changes in value of the firm commitment (hedged item) and the forward contract (hedging instrument) are not identical. Additionally, as a result of hedging a firm commitment, an otherwise unrecognized asset or liability may have to be recognized (Statement II) to offset any gain or loss recognized on the forward contract.

412. **Answer: C**

The net loss will be $7,000. The gain or loss on the payable will be measured as the number of foreign currency units multiplied by the change in the spot rate between the date the liability arose, December 12, and the end of the year, December 31. Thus, the loss on the payable will be 100,000 foreign currency units × ($0.98 − $0.88 = $0.10) = $10,000. The gain or loss on the forward contract (disregarding any premium/discount at initiation of the contract and without using a present value factor) will be measured as the number of foreign currency units multiplied by the change in the forward rate between the date the contract was executed, December 12, and the end of the year, December 31. Thus, the gain on the forward contract will be 100,000 foreign currency units × ($0.93 − $0.90 = .03) = $3,000. The net will be $10,000 − $3,000 = $7,000, the correct answer.

413. **Answer: A**

Statement I is correct; Statement II is not. In the hedging of an investment in a foreign operation, the hedged item is the result of translating the foreign operation's financial statements from a foreign currency to the functional currency (Statement I). The intent of the hedge is to offset changes in the translated results that are caused by changes in exchange rates. Statement II is not correct; either derivatives (e.g., forward contracts) or non-derivatives can be used to hedge an investment in a foreign operation. For example, borrowing in the same foreign currency would hedge the investment, but the borrowing is not necessarily a derivative (e.g., forward contract).

414. **Answer: D**

The hedge of a net investment in foreign operations is a fair value hedge, *but changes in the fair value of the forward contract (hedging instrument) that are equal to or less than the change in the translated value of the financial statements of the foreign operation are reported as a translation adjustment in other comprehensive income.* The change in the forward contract reported as a translation adjustment offsets the change in the value of the translated financial statements of the foreign operation, which also are reported as a translation adjustment.

415. **Answer: C**

An option is a financial derivative and must be reported as either an asset or liability at fair value, with any change in fair value recognized in income of the period that the fair value changes (unless the option is used as a hedge). At the date the option contract was initiated, it had no intrinsic value (the strike price was the same as the current price), but had a time value of $600 (given). At December 31, the time value had decreased to $400, a decline of $200, but the intrinsic value had increased by $6,000, computed as the change in the market price from $40 per share to $43 per share, an increase of $3 × 2,000 shares (the option quantity) = $6,000. Thus, the net change in fair value, and the amount of gain that would be recognized in December 31 financial statements, is + $6,000 − $200 = $5,800, the correct answer.

416. **Answer: B**

Operating transactions denominated in a foreign currency are converted to the functional currency using the current (or spot) exchange rate. The current (or spot) exchange rate is the exchange rate in effect at the current time (or as close thereto as possible); that is, at the time of the transaction or revaluation.

417. **Answer: B**

The reporting currency is the currency in which the final consolidated financial statements are presented (reported).

418. **Answer: D**

The weighted average exchange rate for the current year is the correct rate to use to convert depreciation expense. Since the functional currency is the local currency, the income statement of the subsidiary would be converted using translation, which requires the use of the exchange rate when a revenue/gain was earned or expense/loss was incurred, or the weighted average exchange rate for the year. Since depreciation expense is incurred throughout the year, the weighted average exchange rate normally is the appropriate basis for conversion.

419. **Answer: B**

Under the remeasurement method of converting from a foreign currency to a reporting currency, any resulting loss (or gain) is reported as an item of income from continuing operations in current income.

420. **Answer: C**

Since remeasurement should be used to convert Sapco's financial statements expressed in FCUs to U.S. dollars, inventory should be converted using the historic exchange rate in effect when the inventory was acquired. In this case, the inventory was acquired evenly during 20X8 and the weighted average exchange rate for the year was $1.300. Therefore, the correct dollar amount of Sapco's inventory would be 6,000 FCUs × $1.300 = $7,800.

421. **Answer: B**

Since Gordon prepares its financial statements in its local currency, the British pound, and since the British economy has not been in hyperinflation, Gordon's functional currency would be the British pound, and its financial statements would be converted to U.S. dollars using translation, not remeasurement. Under the translation method of converting, income statement items are converted using the average exchange rate for the period.

422. **Answer: C**

An adjustment resulting from translation of financial statements would be reported in other comprehensive income, and an adjustment resulting from remeasurement would be reported in net income.

423. **Answer: B**

At the inception of a lease, the lessee records a lease liability. To be considered a finance lease, a lease must satisfy any one of the five criteria specified in ASC Topic 842. This lease does not satisfy any of the five criteria. The lease has no bargain purchase option and does not transfer title. The lease term is not 75% or more of the useful life (10 years out of 15 years is 67%), and the PV of the lease payments is not 90% or more of the FV of the asset [(6.76 × $50,000) / $400,000 = 84.5%]. Therefore, this is an operating lease, not a finance lease. The lessee will record a lease liability of $338,000 ($50,000 annual payment multiplied by the present values of an annuity due factor of 6.76).

424. **Answer: C**

The lease exceeds 12 months but does not meet any of the classification criteria for a finance lease. Marnie should classify this lease as an operating lease and record a lease liability at the inception of the lease.

425. **Answer: A**

The lessee capitalizes the lease at the lesser of the present value of the minimum lease payments or the fair value of the leased asset at the inception of the lease. Because the fair value of the equipment is less than the present value of the minimum lease payments, Arena Corp. will report a lease liability of $900,000.

426. **Answer: C**

The amount to be capitalized is the present value of the lease payments. This amount is $2,675,000 ($500,000 × 5.35) and should be equal to the market value of the equipment if the useful life is also 7 years.

Although $3,500,000 (7 × $500,000) will be paid by Koby over the lease term, the difference between that amount and $2,675,000 represents interest to be recognized over the term. The $2,675,000 amount is the current sacrifice required to obtain the use of the equipment and should be close to the purchase price if the equipment is available by purchase.

If Koby invested that amount at the interest rate implied in the lease, the investment would be sufficient to cover all seven payments.

427. **Answer: A**

The beginning lease liability balance at 1/1/X4 is $379,000. That balance is unchanged the entire year because the first lease payment is made 1 year later. Therefore, the interest expense for the first year is $37,900 (.10 × $379,000).

428. **Answer: C**

For all sales-type leases, the lessor uses the effective interest method to compute interest over the period of the lease. The interest revenue recognized each period equals the interest rate implicit in the lease multiplied by the beginning net lease receivable.

429. **Answer: A**

Bear records a net lease receivable of $30,000 and uses an effective interest rate of 15.85%. Bear calculates interest associated with the net receivable of $4,755. Bear also calculates interest based on the gross lease receivable ($36,000) and the implicit interest rate of 6%. Interest associated with the gross lease receivable is $2,160. The amortization of the deferred gross profit is $2,595 ($4,755 – $2,160).

430. Answer: B

The lessor must determine the rate that will amortize the net lease receivable to zero by the end of the lease term.

431. Answer: C

If the leaseback is classified as an operating lease by the seller-lessee, then control of the asset has likely passed to the buyer-lessor and the revenue recognition criteria are met. The seller-lessee may recognize the gain at the time of the sale.

432. Answer: D

The transaction appears to meet the sale criteria for a sale-leaseback. Assuming the buyer-lessor paid cash for the asset and pretending the asset had a cost of $500,000 and accumulated depreciation of $200,000 (made-up numbers to illustrate the journal entry), Mega would record a $100,000 gain and the following journal entry at the time of the sale transaction:

Cash	$400,000
Accumulated depreciation	$200,000
Equipment	$500,000
Gain on sale	$100,000

433. Answer: A

Louie will amortize the asset over the shorter of the lease term or useful life. In this question, the lease term is shorter at three years. The right-of-use asset divided by the three-year lease term results in $15,000 amortization expense each year ($45,000 / 3-year lease term).

434. Answer: B

A cost that qualifies as an initial direct cost will be included in the lessee's calculation of the right-of-use asset at its costs because these costs occur around the time of execution of the lease. Because the costs are included in the right-of-use asset amount, they are effectively amortized over the lease term as the right-of-use asset is amortized.

435. Answer: C

Charity raising money for underprivileged children is correct. The other answer choices are all health care organizations.

436. Answer: D

A museum that receives the majority of its funding from property taxes is most likely a part of a city government and will be subject to accounting and reporting standards established by the Governmental Accounting Standards Board (GASB).

437. Answer: D

Support activities include general administration and fundraising expenses. The nurses' mileage cost, employee benefits, and supplies are expenses necessary to visit the elderly that further the mission of the organization and are classified as a part of "program services" in the statement of functional expenses.

438. Answer: A

The statement of activities is the operating statement for all not-for-profit organizations, which includes voluntary health and welfare organizations.

439. Answer: A

Revenues are membership dues, dividend income, and interest income for a total of $16,000. Public support consists of cash gifts and donated supplies for a total of $42,000.

440. Answer: C

Contribution revenue is recognized when the following characteristics occur: a "condition" does not exist or has been met, it is not part of an exchange transaction, it is made voluntarily, and it does not involve an ownership interest. This answer is correct because the pledge condition (perhaps a condition to "match" the pledge) has been met.

441. Answer: C

ASC 958-201-45-1 requires three categories of net assets: (1) net assets with donor restrictions, (2) net assets without donor restrictions, and (3) total net assets (i.e., 1 plus 2). This is a major change found in ASU 2016-14, which replaced the three categories of net assets previously used (permanently, temporarily, and unrestricted net assets). which is the answer given here.

442. Answer: B

Because the $250,000 cannot be spent until 20X4, a time restriction applies, and the contribution would be classified as net assets with a donor restriction in the 20X3 financial statements. The $200,000 contribution is not restricted and would be reported as contributions without a donor restriction.

443. **Answer: B**

Both endowments are part of net assets with donor restriction. The term endowment allows a portion of the principal to be spend each period. The regular endowment does not allow any of the principal to be spent. Following ASU 2016-14, both endowments are donor-restricted net assets when the contributions were made.

444. **Answer: C**

Unlike for-profit entities, not-for-profit entities do not break debt securities into trading, available-for-sale, and held-to-maturity categories. Following ASC 958-320-35-1, not-for-profits value debt securities at fair value (quoted market price).

445. **Answer: A**

All three items are peripheral in nature and should be included in nonoperating revenues and gains.

446. **Answer: A**

Total revenues, gains, and other support on the Statement of Operations includes net patient revenue, premium revenues (e.g., HMO capitation fees), other revenue, and net assets released from restrictions for operating purposes. Net patient revenues are fees for patient services less contractual adjustments and charity care. Both governmental and not-for-profit hospitals record estimates for uncollectible patient accounts as contra-revenue accounts. The correct answer is $460,000: $500,000 (net patient revenues including charity care) less $100,000 (charity care), less $70,000 uncollectible patient accounts, plus $50,000 (net assets released for operating activities) plus $80,000 (other revenue). Take note that uncollectible accounts other than patient accounts are recorded as bad debt expense by not-for-profit hospitals (ASC 954-605-56-6) and that governmental hospitals will not report bad debt expense since they use a net revenue approach. Moreover, had the net assets released from restrictions not been for operating purposes; such as to acquire fixed assets, the reclassification of net assets released would not be included in total

revenues, gains, and other support section. Rather, the amount would appear after the excess (deficiency) of revenues, gains, and other support over expenses and losses (e.g., the performance indicator) near the bottom of the unrestricted net asset section of the Statement of Operations.

447. **Answer: A**

Tuition revenue is always reported net of scholarships and financial aid. Thus, the net tuition revenue is shown as $190,000. Because the gift is designated by the donor, the $100,000 is initially reported as an increase in net assets with a donor restriction. When $67,000 is properly spent, that amount is reclassified from net assets with a donor restriction to net assets without a donor restriction. Thus, the total increase is $190,000 plus $67,000, or $257,000.

448. **Answer: B**

A state university is an example of a special-purpose government. Since it is engaged only in business-type activities, it should report the financial statements required for Enterprise Funds. In that case, state appropriations to the university are Nonoperating Revenues.

449. **Answer: B**

The Financial Accounting Standards Board (FASB) is the highest level of GAAP for all nongovernmental entities, which includes nongovernmental not-for-profit organizations.

450. **Answer: D**

One of the unique characteristics of government is its power to force involuntary financial resource contributions through taxation. No other form of organization has this power.

451. **Answer: B**

Advocate groups are part of one of three categories of primary users of government financial reports as identified by GASB Concept Statement No. 1: the citizenry (to which the government is accountable to), legislative and oversight bodies (who represent the citizenry), and investors and creditors (those who lend or participate in the lending process). The citizenry group includes citizens, the media, advocate groups, and public finance researchers.

452. Answer: C

The example in the question is an outcome measure. Outcome measures indicate the accomplishments or results that occur because of the services provided.

453. Answer: B

Wastewater and sewerage services are usually provided on a service-fee basis; therefore, they are accounted for in an enterprise fund – one of the two types of proprietary funds. Enterprise funds are also referred to as "business type" funds and use full accrual accounting.

454. Answer: B

A motor pool fund is a type of internal service fund that charges other parts of the government for services provided on a cost-reimbursement basis. An internal service fund is one of the two types of proprietary service funds. Recall the mnemonic "PIPPA" for fiduciary funds – pension trust funds, investment trust funds, private-purpose trust funds, and agency funds.

455. Answer: A

Seaview City is merely acting as an agent for the state and should use an agency fund to receive and then distribute the funds as directed by the state.

456. Answer: D

On the Statement of Revenues, Expenditures, and Changes in Fund Balances, which reports transactions using the modified accrual basis of accounting, repayment of principal on long-term debt, payments to vendors, and purchases of fixed assets are all reported as expenditures.

457. Answer: B

Governmental fund types use the modified accrual basis of accounting which focuses on the "flow of financial resources." Consequently, the use of financial resources is an expenditure rather than an expense without regard to the character of the expenditure (e.g., operating expense or capital expense). Therefore, as this answer states, the new police car (a long-term asset) is recorded as an expenditure in the period of acquisition because it represents an outflow of financial resources. Since it is an immediate expenditure, the General Fund does not list the car as a noncurrent asset. However, in the government-wide Statement of Net Position (not part of this question) the car

would be included in the noncurrent assets and depreciated overtime.

458. Answer: B

Because the measurement focus basis for governmental funds is the flow of current financial resources, the modified accrual basis of accounting is used to prepare governmental fund financial statements.

459. Answer: B

The general fund uses the modified accrual basis of accounting, and liabilities are recognized for those amounts that are to be paid from current financial resources, essentially, related to goods and services of the current year. Recall that according to the 60-day rule, "current financial resources" includes the amount the government receives in the first 60 days of the next fiscal year.

460. Answer: A

Appropriations are credited so that a schedule to compare Appropriations (credits) to Expenditures (debits) results in reporting whether appropriations are under or over spent.

461. Answer: C

Budgets are legally binding on government administrators and lead to the formal recording of the budget, on the basis in which the budget is based, into the ledgers of the General Fund, special revenue funds, and any other funds that are required by law to record a budget. Reporting is on the budget basis. When the budget basis is different from GAAP, a separate schedule is required to reconcile the actual amounts in the budget to the GAAP amounts shown in the statement of revenues, expenditures, and changes in fund balances.

462. Answer: B

Transfers in from other funds are classified as "Other Financing Sources" and are not revenues. The other three amounts are classified as revenues and, for budget purposes, should be included in determining "estimated revenues." The total is $5,550,000.

463. Answer: A

Encumbrances are increased (debited) when goods are ordered and decreased (credited) when goods are received.

464. **Answer: A**

Encumbrances are used to maintain a record of purchase orders issued such as the order by the controller's office for computers.

465. **Answer: D**

Encumbrance accounting is used for budgetary control and, therefore, is commonly used in Governmental Fund types, including the General, Special Revenue, and Capital Projects Funds. It is usually not used by Debt Service Funds since the terms of the debt control spending. It is rarely used by Proprietary Funds so the Enterprise Fund (answer D) is the best choice for this question.

466. **Answer: A**

The amount of available appropriations is calculated as follows: Authorized appropriation amount from the budget less outstanding encumbrances and less expenditures. In this example, $10,000 – $2,000 – $5,000 = $3,000.

467. **Answer: A**

A deferred inflow of resources is the acquisition of net assets by the government that applies to a future reporting period, such as grant monies that are restricted to future periods. Consequently, the grant proceeds are recorded as an asset and a like amount is recorded as a deferred inflow of resources.

468. **Answer: C**

The $450,000 received in 20X1 has a time restriction and is a deferred inflow of resources in 20X1.

469. **Answer: C**

The remaining levy is measureable and available in Year 20x3 through Year 20x6 and is a deferred inflow of resources in Year 20x2.

470. **Answer: C**

Net investment in capital assets is the amount of long-term capital assets, net of accumulated depreciation, less the outstanding balance of capital-related debt. The gross value of the roads and equipment is $30 million. Accumulated depreciation on the roads and equipment totals $11 million and there is $5 million bonds payable outstanding related to the roads. The net investment in capital assets, therefore, is $14 million [$30 – $11 – $5 = $14].

Note that amounts related to inventory are distractors since inventory is not capital asset related.

471. **Answer: D**

Only the General Fund can report a positive amount in Unassigned Fund Balance. In all other Governmental Fund types (including a Special Revenue Fund), if expenditures exceed amounts restricted, committed, or assigned, it may be necessary to report a negative Unassigned Fund Balance. Should that occur, the Assigned Fund Balance is reduced to eliminate the deficit. If a deficit remains after eliminating Assigned Fund Balance, the negative residual should be classified Unassigned Fund Balance.

472. **Answer: D**

At the Governmental-Fund level, the entire proceeds from the sale of capital assets is a financial resource of the fund – it is spendable. Only the gain or loss on the sale of capital assets is reported in the Government-Wide Financial Statements. Therefore, the book value of capital assets should be *subtracted*.

473. **Answer: C**

The primary purpose of a capital project fund is to account for resources dedicated to the acquisition and/or construction of long-term assets, such as this homeless shelter.

474. **Answer: B**

Property taxes are an Imposed Nonexchange Revenue source for which the government receives value without directly giving something in equal value in exchange. In the Government-Wide Financial Statements, a Receivable is recorded when there is an enforceable claim – the property tax levy in this case – and Revenue should be recorded at the amount of Net Estimated Refunds and Estimated Uncollectible Amounts, *in the period for which the taxes are levied* [GASB Codification Section N50.115]. Given the facts in this question, revenue of $1,980,000 should be recognized ($2,000,000 gross levy less 1%, $20,000, estimated uncollectible amount). Had the question asked about revenue recognition in the General Fund, which uses the modified accrual basis of accounting, the answer would be different. In modified accrual accounting the concept of *availability* is an aspect of revenue recognition (GASB Codification Section

P70.104]. Typically, that means that amounts collected during the year and up to 60 days into the next year are recognized in the current year as revenue. While the facts are incomplete in this question regarding the next year, the implication is that $1,800,000 would be recognized as revenues in the current year and $180,000 as deferred inflow of resources in the current year.

475. **Answer: A**

Transfers between funds are classified as Other Financing Sources and Uses. The payment to the Pension Trust Fund pertains to employee and employer contributions to the pension plan and is part expenditure (employer share) and liability reduction (employee share that was due to the Pension Trust Fund). Under the modified accrual basis of accounting used by the General Fund, the purchase of the equipment is an expenditure.

476. **Answer: C**

Enterprise funds use accrual accounting. The amount of compensated absences expense for the current year can be computed as: ending accrued compensated absences ($150,000) plus compensated absences paid ($400,000) less beginning compensated absences ($125,000), which amounts to $425,000.

477. **Answer: B**

There are two types of proprietary funds: (1) Internal Service Funds and (2) Enterprise Funds. Both use accrual accounting. They differ in terms of the primary user of their services and the pricing policy to set fees. Other governmental agencies/departments are the primary user of services provided by an internal service fund and the pricing policy is some portion of routine operating costs (e.g., from 50% to 100%). Motor pools, data processing, and self insurance are some examples of Internal Service Funds. External users are the primary users of services provided by an enterprise fund and the pricing policy is to recover operating costs, depreciation, and to provide for capital maintenance.

478. **Answer: B**

The statement of cash flows for an Enterprise Fund has four sections: (1) cash flows from operating activities, (2) cash flows from noncapital financing activities, (3) cash flows from capital and related financing activities, and (4) cash flows from investing activities. Both capital contributed by subdividers, $900,000, and proceeds from the sale of revenue bonds, $4,500,000, are considered cash flows from capital and related financing activities, therefore $5,400,000 is the correct answer.

The cash received from customer households, $2,700,000, is classified as cash flows from operating activities.

479. **Answer: D**

Agency Funds act as intermediaries in the process of disbursing monies from one governmental entity to another. The government has no claim on the resources in the Agency Fund and does not recognize revenues when it receives the monies or recognize expenses when the monies are disbursed.

480. **Answer: A**

Agency Funds are used to account for assets received on behalf of and paid to other funds, individuals, or organizations. The capital grant described in this question is an example of a pure pass-through grant in which Harland County acts as a conduit to distribute the funds to the five subrecipient municipalities. Hartland County will not record any revenues or expenditures related to the grant and will record a receivable and payable in the Agency Fund that acts as a clearinghouse for the funds.

481. **Answer: C**

Because the question is about the General Fund, which uses the modified accrual basis of accounting, only the $10,000 contribution to the pension plan, which is a use of financial resources in year 1, is recognized as pension expenditure. The Pension Trust Fund would report the $10,000 received from the General Fund as an "Addition" and not as revenue.

482. **Answer: D**

The primary focus of the government-wide financial statements is to report two activities: governmental and business-type. The governmental activities are largely funded by nonexchange transaction revenues, such as property taxes, and business-type activities that rely mainly on user fees.

483. **Answer: A**

The Government-Wide Financial Statements will present both the asset and the liability associated with a capital lease asset.

484. **Answer: A**

A joint venture is a legal entity or other organization that results from a contractual arrangement and that is owned, operated, or governed by two or more participants as a separate and specific activity subject to joint control. "Joint control" means that no single participant has the ability to unilaterally control the financial or operating policies of the joint venture. The joint venture is not included as a component unit. The primary government reports its equity interest in government-wide financial statements and in the affected fund-level statements.

485. **Answer: C**

The ability to raise its fee structure without primary government approval is an example of fiscal independence.

486. **Answer: C**

Two approaches are used for component units: (1) discrete presentation in a separate column of the Government-Wide Financial Statements and (2) blended with the primary government.

487. **Answer: A**

Note also the fiduciary funds and internal service funds are never major funds.

488. **Answer: C**

The General Fund is always a major fund. Other governmental funds are major funds if the element (assets in this question) exceed 10% of total governmental fund assets ($800,000) and 5% of total governmental fund and enterprise fund assets combined ($900,000).

489. **Answer: C**

The Budgetary Comparison Schedule must report the original budget, the amended/final budget, and actual revenues and expenditures. The revenues and expenditures must be reported using the same basis used to prepare the budget: governmental budgets are frequently prepared on a cash or near-cash basis.

490. **Answer: D**

The general government departments have recorded a total of $50,000 in expenditures related to billings from the internal service fund. The conversion to government-wide financial statements requires the elimination of the $15,000 "profit" by decreasing the $50,000 expenditure to $35,000 and reclassifying it as "expense."

491. **Answer: B**

Capital outlay expenditures in the governmental fund-level financial statements are eliminated in converting to governmental-wide financial statements. The adjustment is an increase in reconciling changes in fund balance, at the governmental fund level, to changes in net position at the government-wide level.

492. **Answer: C**

General Fund transfers to the Debt Service Fund to provide for the servicing of debt is an example of a regular, routine, reoccurring transfer of resources between funds to subsidize current activities that are classified as Operating Transfers.

493. **Answer: C**

The government-wide financial statements are used to account for all unmatured long-term indebtedness of the government, except for that debt belonging to Proprietary and similar Trust Funds. The liability for the general obligation bonds should be recorded in this account group.

494. **Answer: D**

All three events are obligating events that require recognition of a pollution remediation obligation.

495. **Answer: C**

Revenue bonds issued by an enterprise fund are reported within business-type activities in government-wide financial statements.

496. **Answer: D**

The $100,000 portion of the judgment due in the current year is reported in the General Fund and will appear as expenditures in the fund-level statements. The unmatured $400,000 portion is reported in the Government-Wide Statements as a liability at present value. The long-term portion of the liability is RECORDED in the Schedule of General Long-term Debt.

497. **Answer: A**

Sales taxes are "derived" from underlying taxable exchange transactions of individuals and businesses.

498. **Answer: A**

Exchange Transactions involve a direct relationship between the charge and the service. Nonexchange Transactions, which are frequent in governments, do not have this relationship (e.g., taxes and fines).

499. **Answer: D**

The county would recognize in its Government-Wide Statement of Net Position a capital asset of $20 million for the acquisition of the water rights in 2010. A capital outlay expenditure of $20 million would be recorded in the county's

Capital Projects Fund Statement of Revenues, Expenditures, and Changes in Net Position. Since there is evidence that the county will seek and be able to acquire renewal of the water rights without incurring additional outlays, the useful life of the water rights is 20 years-the original 10 year term plus the 10 year renewal term. Using straight-line amortization, annual amortization expense of $1 million ($20 million over 20 years) would be recorded in the county's Government-Wide Statement of Activities, starting in 2010.

500. **Answer: D**

GASB Statement No. 44 requires that statistical information be presented in five categories – Financial Trends Information, Revenue Capacity Information, Debt Capacity Information, Demographic and Economic Information, and Operating Information. Fund balance information is not one of the five categories, but for Governmental Funds, Fund Balance Information is required as part of the financial trends information category.

Task-Based Simulations

Conceptual Framework and Financial Reporting

General-Purpose Financial Statements: Statement of Cash Flows

Sources and Uses of Cash

Task-Based Simulation 1

TBSFCO0159

Research		
	Authoritative Literature	
		Help

The Statement of Cash Flows has three primary areas of focus:

- Operating Activities
- Investing Activities
- Financing Activities

You are asked to provide a citation from the codification that provides guidance for the classification of cash inflows associated with investing activities. Where in the codification is specific guidance provided for this area?

Type the topic here.

Correctly formatted FASB ASC topics are 3 digits.

FASB ASC		-		-		-	

❶ Some examples of correctly formatted FASB ASC responses are 205-10-05-1, 323-740-S25-1, 260-10-60-1A, 260-10-55-99, and 115-60-35-128A.

Answer

Research		
	Authoritative Literature	
		Help

section	subsection	paragraph

	FASB ASC	230	-	10	-	45	-	12

230-10-45-12

Financial Accounting Standards Board (FASB): Fair Value Framework

Disclosure Requirements

Task-Based Simulation 2

tbs.gen.is.disc.req.001_17

Account Classifications

Authoritative Literature

Help

You are a senior accountant at Gala Inc. and have been asked to review the table, listed below, that was prepared by a staff accountant. The information will be used to prepare the necessary fair value measurements and related disclosures reported on the financial statements for the fiscal year ended December 31, 20X2.

For each item, refer to the supporting documents in the following Exhibits and in the four questions that follow the Exhibits, click in the associated cell and select from the list to determine the reported value and level in fair value hierarchy.

Email regarding Antal Corp Stock

From: marymethesenior@gala.com
To: timcomptoncontroller@gala.com
Sent: January 4, 20X3 1:54 PM

Tim,

Per your request, I have attached the stock quote for Antal Inc., which trades under the ticker symbol ANTL on the North American stock exchange. We purchased 1,500 shares on March 22, 20X1 for $32.50 per share, plus transaction costs of $78.00. To date, no shares have been sold. We are looking to sell the stock once it trades $38.50.

Please let me know if you need anything else.

Thank you,

Mary Methe
Senior Accountant, Gala Inc.
(245) 567-3456
marymethesenior@gala.com

http://freedomfinance.com/quote/NAEx/ANTL?p=ANTL

FREEDOM FINANCE   **ANTL**   Search

ANTL Corporation (ANTL) *Traded publicly on North American Stock Exchange*	
Close	$35.65
Previous Close	$ 35.5
1 Year Target	39
Today's High /Low	$ 35.75 / $ 35.25
Share Volume	275,057
50 Day Avg. Daily Volume	289,756
52 Week High/Low	$ 38.20 / $ 29.50
Date	December 31, 20X2

Corporate Bond Investment Memo

To: Files of Brother Bear Inc. Corporate Bonds

From: Larry Boyd, Finance Manager

Date: January 8, 20X3

RE: Feb 1, 20X1 purchase of Brother Bear Corporate Bonds

On 1 February 20X1, Gala Corp. purchased 100, $1,000 Brother Bear Inc. Corporate Bonds, carrying semi-annual coupons at the rate of 8% and a maturity of December 31, 20X8, for $89,162. The bonds had an effective interest rate of 10%. At the issuance date, Gala Inc. elected the fair value option.

Because Brother Bear Inc. Corporate Bonds are not traded publicly, management believes that the bonds of Sister Bear Inc. are very similar in nature, credit rating, and business models. Furthermore, management feels that a discount or any other adjustment to the price of Sister Bear Inc. Corporate Bonds is not needed and that the exchange traded price can be used as substitute for pricing of the Brother Bear Inc. Corporate Bonds. See *Exhibit B* for the year end pricing of Sister Bear Inc. Corporate Bonds.

Because the bonds of Brother Bear were purchased at a discount we have included Exhibit A, which shows the amortization of the bond discount using the effective interest method.

Exhibit A: Brother Bear Inc.

Bond Investment – Brother Bear Inc. Effective Interest Method – semi-annual interest receipts 8% Bonds issued at 10%					
Interest Periods	**Interest to be received**	**Interest revenue to be recorded**	**Discount Amortization**	**Unamortized Discount**	**Bond Carrying Value**
Issue Date				$10,838	$89,162
June 30, 20X1	$4,000	$4,458	$458	$10,380	$89,620
December 31, 20X1	$4,000	$4,481	$481	$9,899	$90,101
June 30, 20X2	$4,000	$4,505	$505	$9,394	$90,606
December 31, 20X2	$4,000	$4,530	$530	$8,864	$91,136
June 30, 20X3	$4,000	$4,557	$557	$8,307	$91,693
December 31, 20X3	$4,000	$4,585	$585	$7,722	$92,278
June 30, 20X4	$4,000	$4,614	$614	$7,108	$92,892
December 31, 20X4	$4,000	$4,645	$645	$6,464	$93,536
June 30, 20X5	$4,000	$4,677	$677	$5,787	$94,213
December 31, 20X5	$4,000	$4,711	$711	$5,076	$94,924
June 30, 20X6	$4,000	$4,746	$746	$4,330	$95,670
December 31, 20X6	$4,000	$4,783	$783	$3,547	$96,453
June 30, 20X7	$4,000	$4,823	$823	$2,724	$97,276
December 31, 20X7	$4,000	$4,864	$864	$1,860	$98,140
June 30, 20X8	$4,000	$4,907	$907	$953	$99,047
December 31, 20X8	$4,000	$4,952	$952	$-	$100,000

Exhibit B: **Sister Bear Inc. Corporate Bond Current Market Value; quote obtained from the North American Exchange**

http://americaninvestor.com/quote/NAEx/sisterbearbr?p=STRB

American investor

TICKER: STRB

Dec 31, 20 X2	Coupon	Maturity Date	Close	Yld%	Yr. High	Yr. Low
Sister Bear Inc.	8.0	Dec 31/ X8	83.24	12.0	91.50	83.00

Mutual Fund Brokerage Statement and Stock quote (TLF)

Spirit Trading

INVESTMENT REPORT
January 1, 20X2-December 31, 20X2

Gala Inc. Account # 245-3456GI

Holdings	Quantity Dec. 31, 20x2	NAV per unit Dec.31, 20X2	Value (NAV) Dec. 31, 20X2	Cost	Fees	Total Cost and Fees
Triple Line Enhanced Opportunistic Fund (TLF)	1,000	$25.61	$25,610	$23.58	$250	$23,830
Total	1,000	$25.61	$25,610	$23.58	$250	$23,830

Mutual Funds: 100% of Holdings

Quote obtained from North American Exchange:

http:// Spirittrading.com/quote/NAex/TLF?p=TLF

Mutual Fund Name: Triple Line Enhanced Opportunistic Fund (TLF)

Best Bid/ Offer	25.25/ 25.75
Total Assets	875,000,000
Total Liabilities	234,786,000
Shares outstanding	25,000,000
NAV	25.61
Date	December 31, 20X2

Balance Sheet Walker Holdings LP

STRICTLY PRIVATE & CONFIDENTIAL

Walker Holdings LP

Northridge, TX 345675-2343

Attention: Andy Leiter, Chief Executive Officer, Gala Inc.

Dear Sir,

Per your request, we have provided the balance sheet for the year ended December 31, 20X2 for Walker Holdings, LP in order for your company to properly record value of your investment at Net Asset Value. The quotes and appraisals at fair value were obtained from outside sources. This information is provided for investor use only and should not be shared with anyone outside of the corporation.

Sincerely,

Matt Jacobs GP

Matt JacobS

Walker Holdings LP

Walker Holdings LP
BALANCE SHEET
December 31, 20X2

	Book Value	Fair Value
Cash	$2,500,987	$2,500,987
A/R (net)	1,056,897	1,056,897
Inventory	1,057,000	1,057,000
PP& E (net)	3,543,789	5,500,000
Total Assets	**8,158,673**	**10,114,884**
A/P	545,786	545,786
Mortgages Payable	2,500,870	2,600,870
Loans Payable	500,098	500,098
Total Liabilities:	**3,546,754**	**3,646,754**
Partners' Capital Accounts:		
Gala Inc.	461,192	646,813
Crowder Co.	691,788	970,220
Janel LP	922,384	1,293,626
Cromer Inc.	1,152,980	1,617,033
Walker Inc.	1,383,575	1,940,438
Total Partners' Capital Account	**4,611,919**	**6,468,130**
Total Liabilities and Partners' Capital Account	**8,158,673**	**10,114,884**

For each item, click in the associated cell and select from the list to determine the reported value and level in fair value hierarchy.

Financial Statement Item	Reported Value	Level in the Fair Value Hierarchy
1. 1,500 shares of Antal Corp. (ANTL)	A. $48,828 B. $48,750 C. $53,475 D. $53,553 E. $57,750 F. $57,828	A. Level 3 B. Level 1 C. Level 2 D. Level 4 E. Not included in the fair value hierarchy; disclosure required F. Not included in the fair value hierarchy; NO disclosure required
2. 100 Brother Bear Inc. Corporate Bonds	A. $91,136 B. $91,500 C. $89,162 D. $83,240 E. $83,000 F. $100,000	A. Level 1 B. Level 2 C. Level 3 D. Level 4 E. Not included in the fair value hierarchy; disclosure required F. Not included in the fair value hierarchy; NO disclosure required
3. 1,000 shares of Triple Line Enhanced Opportunistic Fund	A. $25,610 B. $23,580 C. $23,830 D. $25,250 E. $25,750 F. $25,860	A. Not included in the fair value hierarchy; disclosure required B. Level 1 C. Level 2 D. Level 3 E. Level 4 F. Not included in the fair value hierarchy; NO disclosure required
4. Investment in Walker Holdings LP (10%) (Fair Value elected)	A. $461,192 B. $815,867 C. $1,104,489 D. $646,813	A. Level 3 B. Level 1 C. Level 2 D. Level 4 E. Not included in the fair value hierarchy; disclosure required F. Not included in the fair value hierarchy; NO disclosure required

Financial Statement Item	Reported Value						Level in the Fair Value Hierarchy					
	(A)	(B)	(C)	(D)	(E)	(F)	(A)	(B)	(C)	(D)	(E)	(F)
1. 1,500 shares of Antal Corp. (ANTL)	○	○	○	○	○	○	○	○	○	○	○	○
2. 100 Brother Bear Inc. Corporate Bonds	○	○	○	○	○	○	○	○	○	○	○	○
3. 1,000 shares of Triple Line Enhanced Opportunistic Fund	○	○	○	○	○	○	○	○	○	○	○	○
4. Investment in Walker Holdings LP (10%) (Fair Value elected)	○	○	○	○	○	○	○	○	○	○	○	○

Answers and Explanations

Task-Based Simulation 2 Solution

Account Classifications

Authoritative Literature

Help

	Reported Value						Level in the Fair Value Hierarchy					
Financial Statement Item	(A)	(B)	(C)	(D)	(E)	(F)	(A)	(B)	(C)	(D)	(E)	(F)
1. 1,500 shares of Antal Corp. (ANTL)	○	○	●	○	○	○	○	●	○	○	○	○
2. 100 Brother Bear Inc. Corporate Bonds	○	○	○	●	○	○	○	●	○	○	○	○
3. 1,000 shares of Triple Line Enhanced Opportunistic Fund	●	○	○	○	○	○	○	●	○	○	○	○
4. Investment in Walker Holdings LP (10%) (Fair Value elected)	○	○	○	●	○	○	○	○	○	○	●	○

1. **(C)** 1,500 shares of Antal Corp. (ANTL) Reported Value: Fair value measurement is required for Gala Inc.'s investment in Antal Corp. Antal Corp trades on a publicly traded exchange; therefore, a market approach is appropriate and adequate to determine the fair value. Under a market approach fair value is determined by using prices generated by real market transactions for identical or similar items. The fair value of the stock should be determined at the measurement date (December 31, 20X2.) using the exit price on the most advantageous market. In determining the most advantageous market, transaction costs are considered, but not included in the reported value. Therefore, the amount to report on the measurement date would be $53,475 ($35.65 × 1,500.)

    (B) 1,500 shares of Antal Corp. (ANTL) Level in the Fair Value Hierarchy: The Fair Value Hierarchy contains only three levels: Level 1, Level 2, and Level 3. Level 1 amounts include observable quoted prices at the measurement date in active markets for identical items. Level 1 is considered the highest level with the most desirable inputs. Because Antal Corp. trades on an active publicly traded exchange we should classify this investment as Level 1.

2. **(D)** 100 Brother Bear Inc. Corporate Bonds Reported Value: Investments in Bonds are valued using amortized cost. However, the FASB allows companies to make an election to value bonds at fair value. Gala Inc. has elected to value the bonds of Brother Bear at fair value. Management is using the value of the observable (similar) bonds Sister Bear, without any adjustments, to obtain the reported fair value of Brother Bear bonds. The closing price of Sister Bear bonds is 83.24. The reported price should be $83,240 (1,000 × .8324 × 100.)

    (B) 100 Brother Bear Inc. Corporate Bonds Level in the Fair Value Hierarchy: The Fair Value Hierarchy contains only three levels: Level 1, Level 2, and Level 3. Level 2 amounts include observable quoted prices at the measurement date for similar assets or liabilities in active markets. Management should classify this as a level 2 investment in the fair value hierarchy because the bonds of Brother Bear are similar to the bonds of Sister Bear, Sister Bear bonds trade in an active market where prices are observable, and the fair value of Sister Bear can be used to value Brother Bear.

3. **(A)** 1,000 shares of Triple Line Enhanced Opportunistic Fund Reported Value: The fair value of an investment in a mutual fund where the mutual fund's NAV per share is determined and published and the basis for current transactions is fair value. The NAV quote for the mutual fund is $25.61. The reported value should be $25,610 (25.61 × 1,000 shares.)

(B) 1,000 shares of Triple Line Enhanced Opportunistic Fund Level in the Fair Value Hierarchy: The fair value of an investment in a mutual fund where the mutual fund's NAV per share is determined and published and the basis for current transactions is fair value. Because the mutual fund trades on an active publicly traded exchange, management is not using NAV as a practical expedient, rather an observable quoted price at the measurement date in active markets for identical items. Therefore, management should classify this investment as Level 1.

4. **(D)** Investment in Walker Holdings LP (10%) Reported Value: If NAV is communicated to the investor, but is not publicly available, NAV is being used as a practical expedient for fair value. In this situation, management is using the NAV obtained from the balance sheet related to its 10% investment. NAV is determined by looking at the investor's capital account at fair value. For Gala Inc. NAV of its investment is $646,813 ((Assets minus liabilities) × 10 %.)

   (E) Investment in Walker Holdings LP (10%) Level in the Fair Value Hierarchy: If NAV is communicated to the investor, but is not publicly available, NAV is being used as a practical expedient for fair value and is excluded from the fair value hierarchy. In this situation, management is using the NAV obtained from the balance sheet, which is not publicly available. Therefore, management is using NAV as a practical expedient and the investment will not be classified into the fair value hierarchy; however, disclosures about the use of NAV are required.

Consolidated Financial Statements: Intercompany (I/C) Transactions and Balances

Intercompany (I/C) Inventory Transactions

Task-Based Simulation 3

tbs.drs.ic.invntry.001_17

Account Classifications		
	Authoritative Literature	
		Help

Pele Incorporated (Pele) is a client of Callahan and Lowe LP (C&L). During the year, Pele purchased Soccer Strategies Specialists, Inc., (SSS). Since this is the first time that Pele has completed a consolidation worksheet, Pele's controller has asked C&L to review the consolidation prepared for the year ended December 31, 20X7. An associate at C&L has performed an initial review of the consolidation worksheet and has drafted an email to the controller of Pele with comments and required changes. Your manager has asked you to review the email that follows the exhibits and to make any revisions necessary to correct any errors.

Consolidation Worksheet

Consolidation Worksheet – Pele Inc. & Subsidiaries				
Item	**Pele Inc.**	**SSS Inc.**	**Eliminations**	**Consolidation Totals**
Cash	1,024,516	164,274		1,188,790
A/R	237,000	36,364	a. (27,000)	246,364
Inventory	15,030	11,300		26,330
Other Current assets	200,000	2,875		202,875
PP&E, net	2,250,345	800,000		3,050,345
Investment in SSS Inc.	892,513		b. (892,513)	-
Goodwill			b. 331,000	331,000
Accounts Payable	(75,000)	(20,000)	a. 27,000	(68,000)
Accrued Liabilities	(62,000)	(32,000)		(94,000)
Other Current Liabilities	(10,000)	(69,700)	d. 31,454	(48,246)
Non-Current Liabilities	(836,701)	(331,600)		(1,168,301)
Common stock	(600,000)	(25,000)	b. 25,000	(600,000)
APIC	(2,200,000)	(175,000)	b. 175,000	(2,200,000)
Ret. Earnings	(650,000)	(269,000)	b. 269,000	(650,000)
Service revenue	(475,556)	(297,500)		(773,056)
Sales revenue	(13,300)	(2,500)	c. 13,300	(2,500)
Income from SSS Inc.	(92,513)		b. 92,513	-
Cost of revenues	200,000	120,000	c. (13,300)	306,700
Other Expenses	100,000	39,828		139,828
Income Tax Expense	95,666	47,659	d. (31,454)	111,871
Total	$ -	$ -		$ -

Soccer Strategies Specialists Inc. Financial information

Soccer Strategies Specialists Inc. Stock Investment Memo

To: Files of Soccer Strategies Specialists Inc. Stock Acquisition

From: Controller

Date: January 8, 20X8

RE: Soccer Strategies Specialists Inc. financial statements

On June 30, 20X7 Pele Corp. purchased 100 percent of the shares of Soccer Strategies Specialists Inc. for $800,000. As a result, Pele will need to present consolidated financial statements with Soccer Strategies Specialists Inc.

Soccer Strategies Specialists Inc. has provided the following financial statements as of June 30 and December 31, 20X7. See Exhibits A, B, and C.

Exhibit A – Income Statement

	Soccer Strategies Specialists Inc. STATEMENT OF OPERATIONS	
	Six Months Ended June 30, 20X7	Six Months Ended Dec 31, 20X7
Revenues:		
Service revenue	$ 250,000	$ 297,500
Sales revenue	-	2,500
Total Revenues	**250,000**	**300,000**
Cost and revenue:		-
Cost of revenues	100,000	120,000
Other expenses		39,828
	34,925	
Total costs and expenses	**134,925**	**159,828**
Income before income taxes	**115,075**	**140,172**
Provision for income taxes	39,126	47,659
Net income	**$ 75,949**	**$ 92,513**

Exhibit B – Statement of Retained Earnings

Soccer Strategies Specialists Inc.
STATEMENT OF RETAINED EARNINGS

	Six months ended June 30, 20X7	Six months ended Dec 31, 20X7
Retained earnings at beginning of period	$ 193,051	$ 269,000
Net income	75,949	92,513
Cash dividends	-	-
Retained earnings at end of period	**$ 269,000**	**$ 361,513**

Exhibit C – Balance Sheet

Soccer Strategies Specialists Inc
BALANCE SHEETS

	June 30, 20X7	Dec 31, 20X7
ASSETS		
Current assets:		
Cash	$ 154,000	$ 164,274
Accounts Receivable, net	24,000	36,364
Inventory	-	11,300
Prepaid expenses and other current assets	2,500	2,875
Total current assets	**180,500**	**214,813**
Land	800,000	800,000
Total assets	**$ 980,500**	**$ 1,014,813**
LIABILITIES AND SHAREHOLDERS' EQUITY		
Current liabilities:		
Accounts payable	$ 15,000	$ 20,000
Accrued liabilities	28,000	32,000
Other current liabilities	77,200	69,700
Total current liabilities	**120,200**	**121,700**
Non-current liabilities	391,300	331,600
Total liabilities	**511,500**	**453,300**
Shareholders' equity:		
Common shares - $1.00 par value, 25,000 shares authorized, issued, and outstanding	25,000	25,000
Capital in excess of par value	175,000	175,000
Retained earnings	269,000	361,513
Total shareholders' equity	**469,000**	**561,513**
Total liabilities and shareholders' equity	**$ 980,500**	**$ 1,014,813**

Inventory intercompany transaction detail

INVOICE

From: ⚽

Pele Incorporated

856 Rollins Drive
Rockland, NV, 24565-8809

To:

Soccer Strategies Specialists Inc
4863 Indian Ln.
Eastmont, NV 35890

Invoice #6578
Invoice Date: December 20, 20X7
Due Date: February 5, 20X8

Item Description	Quantity	Unit Price	Amount
Soccer Post	133	$100	$13,300
		Subtotal	$13,300
	State sales Tax @4.6%		exempt
		Total	$13,300
		Amount paid:	($1,300)
		Balance Due:	$12,000

Signed: Tom Trainer

Tom Trainer
Manager - Pele Incorporated

CUSTOMER PICKUP

INVOICE

From:

Soccer Strategies Specialists Inc.
4863 Indian Ln.
Eastmont, NV 35890

To:
Corner Kick Suppliers
1328 Eastman Road
Adler Rock, NV, 35978

Invoice #5736
Invoice Date: December 28, 20X7

Item Description	Quantity	Unit Price	Amount
Soccer Post	20	$125	$2,500
		Subtotal	$2,500
		State sales Tax @4.6%	exempt
		Total	$2,500
		Amount paid:	($2,500)
		Balance Due:	-

CUSTOMER PICKUP

Excerpt from Master Inventory Record Files

Pele Incorporated Inventory Record: Soccer Posts

	No. of Units	Unit Cost	Total Cost
Beginning Inventory - 7/1/20X1	200	$90	$18,000
Purchases – 9/7/2015	100	$90	$9,000
Units Available for sale (7/1-12/31)	300		$27,000
Ending Inventory - Soccer Posts	167	$90	$15,030

Soccer Strategies Specialists Inc. Inventory Record: Soccer Posts

	No. of Units	Unit Cost	Total Cost
Beginning Inventory - 7/1/20X1	-	-	-
Purchases - 12/20/20X7	133	$100	$13,330
Units Available for sale (7/1-12/31)	133		$13,330
Ending Inventory - Soccer Posts	113	$100	$11,300

Appraisal Report

From: financemanager@ Pele.com
To: controller@Pele.com
Sent: June 28, 20X7 4:50 PM

Controller,

I have attached the requested report from JB Appraisers to assist your team in pricing the planned purchase of 25,000 shares of Soccer Strategies Specialists Inc. on June 30, 20X7.

In addition, we heard back from other valuation companies and their assessment is that the carrying value of all other assets and liabilities of Soccer Strategies Specialists Inc, not listed in the appraiser's report are already equal to fair value.

We do not expect any material changes to fair value of any assets or liabilities of Soccer Strategies Specialists Inc between the date of this letter and June 30, 20X7.

Please let me know if you need anything else.

Thank you,

Finance Manager
Pele Incorporated
(245) 567-3456

financemanager@Pele.com

ATTACHMENT TO EMAIL

JB Appraisers

June 26, 20X7

1358 Rollins Way
Rockland, NV 24134
Phone: 398-221-1911

Michael Arts, Vice President
Pele Incorporated
856 Rollins Drive
Rockland, NV, 24565-8809
RE: FAIR VALUE APPRAISAL OF LAND AT 365 BUDLER ROAD
Dear Michael,
At your request, JB Appraisers has prepared the attached valuation analysis to assist you with the fair value (FV) of the land located at 365 Budler Road. Our records indicate that Soccer Strategies Specialists Inc. is the current holder of the deed.
The standard of value to be applied in our valuation analysis is fair value: the price that would be paid to sell an asset or paid to transfer a liability in an orderly transaction between market participants at the measurement date as defined in Accounting Standards Codification Topic 820, *Fair Value Measurements*.
The conclusion of our report is:

TOTAL ESTIMATED FAIR VALUE OF LAND: $1,000,000

We feel this information has been completed to the best of our ability. The content of this report will remain confidential. We have retained a copy for our records.
Please contact us with any question regarding this report.
Sincerely,

Pamela Grant

Pamela, Grant –
Senior Appraiser - JB Appraisers
(387)123-5634
pmgrant@jb.com

Accounts Receivable Subledger

Accounts Receivable Subledger - Pele Incorporated December 31, 20X7	
Soccer Strategies Specialists Inc.	$12,000
Low Far Post Sporting Goods Corp.	15,000
Goal time Inc.	79,500
2002 Elite team player training fee	25,000
2001 Elite team player training fee	32,000
2000 Elite team player training fee	36,000
1999 Elite team player training fee	37,500
Total	$237,000

To revise the email, select the needed correction, if any from the list provided. If removal of the entire section of text is the best revision to the email select [Delete] from the list.

From: Manager@C&L.com

To: Controller@Pele.com

Sent: January 23, 20X8 10:54 AM

RE: Consolidation Worksheet

Dear Controller,

We have reviewed the consolidation worksheet prepared for the year ended December 31, 20X7 and have the following comments and requested changes:

	(A)	(B)	(C)	(D)	(E)	(F)	(G)	(H)

While the consolidated worksheet has correctly included the balances of both the parent, Pele Incorporated (Pele) and its wholly-owned subsidiary, Soccer Strategies Specialists Inc., (SSS), some of the consolidated balances require adjustment.

1. The consolidated balance for accounts receivable and accounts payable should be adjusted to a debit balance of
   A. $258,364 and a credit balance of $80,000, respectively.
   B. [Delete Text]
   C. $258,364 and a debit balance of $80,000, respectively.
   D. $12,000 and a debit balance of $12,000, respectively.
   E. $261,364 and a credit balance of $83,000, respectively.
   F. $15,000 and a debit balance of $15,000, respectively.
   G. $237,000 and a credit balance of $75,000, respectively.

   ○ ○ ○ ○ ○ ○ ○ ○

2. The purchase of the 25,000 stock of SSS on June 30, 20X7 had the potential to create goodwill.
   A. The goodwill elimination entry is correct.
   B. [Delete Text]
   C. However, the company purchased the stock of SSS for fair value, therefore no goodwill should be recorded.
   D. The goodwill elimination entry is not correct; the consolidated balance for goodwill should be $223,513.
   E. The goodwill elimination entry is not correct; the consolidated balance for goodwill should be $131,000.
   F. The goodwill elimination entry is not correct; the consolidated balance for goodwill should be $39,891.
   G. The goodwill elimination entry is not correct; the consolidated balance for goodwill should be $239,861.

   ○ ○ ○ ○ ○ ○ ○ ○

3. The balance for PP&E is incorrect.
   A. The correct balance should be $2,850,000.
   B. [Delete Text]
   C. The correct balance should be $4,050,000
   D. The correct balance should be $2,250,000
   E. The correct balance should be $3,381,345
   F. The correct balance should be $3,250,345

   ○ ○ ○ ○ ○ ○ ○ ○

	(A)	(B)	(C)	(D)	(E)	(F)	(G)	(H)

4. Pele and SSS had an intercompany inventory transaction. Because of this transaction, several accounts require review to determine if the proper consolidated balances are presented correctly.

- A. The consolidated ending balance for sales revenue is correct.
  B. [Delete Text]
  C. The consolidated ending balance for sales revenue is not correct. The correct balance should be $10,800 cr.
  D. The consolidated ending balance for sales revenue is not correct. The correct balance should be $2,000 dr.
  E. The consolidated ending balance for sales revenue is not correct. The correct balance should be $2,000 cr.
  F. The consolidated ending balance for sales revenue is not correct. The correct balance should be $2,500 dr.
  G. The consolidated ending balance for sales revenue is not correct. The correct balance should be $10,800 dr.
  H. The consolidated ending balance for sales revenue is not correct. The correct balance should be $15,800 cr.

- A. The eliminating entry for cost of revenues is correct, however no there is no elimination of the profit in ending inventory. The eliminating entry should include a debit to inventory for $13,300.
  B. [Delete Text]
  C. The eliminating entry for cost of revenues and inventory is incorrect. The correct entry should credit cost of revenues for $12,170 and credit inventory for $1,130.
  D. The eliminating entry for cost of revenues and inventory is incorrect. The correct entry should debit cost of revenues for $12,170 and credit inventory for $12,170.
  E. The eliminating entry for cost of revenues and inventory is incorrect. The correct entry should debit cost of revenues for $11,970 and credit inventory for $1,800.
  F. The eliminating entry for cost of revenues and inventory is incorrect. The correct entry should credit cost of revenues for $2,000 and credit inventory for $1,330.
  G. The eliminating entry for cost of revenues is incorrect; the correct entry should be a credit of $11,970.

Once all the changes are made, adjustments to the eliminating entries to account for income taxes at the consolidated level are also required.

We did not find any other issues with the consolidation worksheet. However, please feel free to contact me if there are specific questions.

Regards,

Audit Manager

C&H LP.

(132) 598-4524

manager@C&H.com

Answers and Explanations

Task-Based Simulation 3 Solution

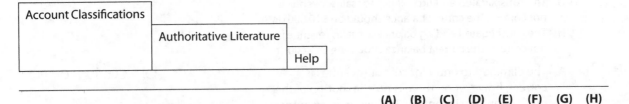

	(A)	(B)	(C)	(D)	(E)	(F)	(G)	(H)

While the consolidated worksheet has correctly included the balances of both the parent, Pele Incorporated (Pele) and its wholly-owned subsidiary, Soccer Strategies Specialists Inc., (SSS), some of the consolidated balances require adjustment.

1. The consolidated balance for accounts receivable and accounts payable should be adjusted to a debit balance of
    A. $258,364 and a credit balance of $80,000, respectively.
    B. [Delete Text]
    C. $258,364 and a debit balance of $80,000, respectively.
    D. $12,000 and a debit balance of $12,000, respectively.
    E. $261,364 and a credit balance of $83,000, respectively.
    F. $15,000 and a debit balance of $15,000, respectively.
    G. $237,000 and a credit balance of $75,000, respectively.

    (A) ○ (B) ○ (C) ○ (D) ○ (E) ● (F) ○ (G) ○ (H) ○

2. The purchase of the 25,000 stock of SSS on June 30, 20X7 had the potential to create goodwill.
    A. The goodwill elimination entry is correct.
    B. [Delete Text]
    C. However, the company purchased the stock of SSS for fair value, therefore no goodwill should be recorded.
    D. The goodwill elimination entry is not correct; the consolidated balance for goodwill should be $223,513.
    E. The goodwill elimination entry is not correct; the consolidated balance for goodwill should be $131,000.
    F. The goodwill elimination entry is not correct; the consolidated balance for goodwill should be $39,891.
    G. The goodwill elimination entry is not correct; the consolidated balance for goodwill should be $239,861.

    (A) ○ (B) ○ (C) ○ (D) ○ (E) ● (F) ○ (G) ○ (H) ○

	(A)	(B)	(C)	(D)	(E)	(F)	(G)	(H)
3. The balance for PP&E is incorrect.	○	○	○	○	○	●	○	○

3. The balance for PP&E is incorrect.
   A. The correct balance should be $2,850,000.
   B. [Delete Text]
   C. The correct balance should be $4,050,000
   D. The correct balance should be $2,250,000
   E. The correct balance should be $3,381,345
   F. The correct balance should be $3,250,345

| 4. Pele and SSS... | ● | ○ | ○ | ○ | ○ | ○ | ○ | ○ |

4. Pele and SSS had an intercompany inventory transaction. Because of this transaction, several accounts require review to determine if the proper consolidated balances are presented correctly.
   - A. The consolidated ending balance for sales revenue is correct.
   B. [Delete Text]
   C. The consolidated ending balance for sales revenue is not correct. The correct balance should be $10,800 cr.
   D. The consolidated ending balance for sales revenue is not correct. The correct balance should be $2,000 dr.
   E. The consolidated ending balance for sales revenue is not correct. The correct balance should be $2,000 cr.
   F. The consolidated ending balance for sales revenue is not correct. The correct balance should be $2,500 dr.
   G. The consolidated ending balance for sales revenue is not correct. The correct balance should be $10,800 dr.
   H. The consolidated ending balance for sales revenue is not correct. The correct balance should be $15,800 cr.

| | ○ | ○ | ● | ○ | ○ | ○ | ○ | ○ |

   - A. The eliminating entry for cost of revenues is correct, however no there is no elimination of the profit in ending inventory. The eliminating entry should include a debit to inventory for $13,300.
   B. [Delete Text]
   C. The eliminating entry for cost of revenues and inventory is incorrect. The correct entry should credit cost of revenues for $12,170 and credit inventory for $1,130.
   D. The eliminating entry for cost of revenues and inventory is incorrect. The correct entry should debit cost of revenues for $12,170 and credit inventory for $12,170.
   E. The eliminating entry for cost of revenues and inventory is incorrect. The correct entry should debit cost of revenues for $11,970 and credit inventory for $1,800.
   F. The eliminating entry for cost of revenues and inventory is incorrect. The correct entry should credit cost of revenues for $2,000 and credit inventory for $1,330.
   G. The eliminating entry for cost of revenues is incorrect; the correct entry should be a credit of $11,970.

1. **(E)** GAAP requires consolidated financial statements of all entities under common control. Pele Inc. & Subsidiaries represent one economic entity, and as such, cannot report a receivable or payable to itself. The eliminating entry for both accounts receivable and accounts payable currently include the receivables/payables with both Soccer Strategies Specialists (SSS) and Low Far Post Sporting Goods Corp. Only the payables and receivables between the consolidated entities (Pele and SSS) should be eliminated in consolidation. The proper consolidated debit balance of Accounts Receivable should be $261,364 and the proper consolidated credit balance of Account Payable should be ($83,000.) The elimination entries to both accounts receivable and accounts payable should be a debit to A/P of $12,000 and a credit to A/R of $12,000.

2. **(E)** Goodwill is determined based on the difference between the acquisition price of SSS stock and the fair value of the identifiable net assets on the date of acquisition (June 30, 20X7). The acquisition price of SSS was $800,000. The net book value of SSS on the acquisition date was $469,000 (found on the June 30, 20X7 balance sheet). The only fair value adjustment needed is to land for $200,000 ($1,000,000 appraised value less $800,000 June 30, 20X7 balance sheet amount). The consolidated balance for goodwill should be $131,000 and is calculated as follows:

Price Paid	$800,000	
Goodwill (800,000 – 669,000)	$131,000	Unidentifiable asset
Net FV Assets and Liabilities	669,000	
Fair value adjustment of land (1,000,000 – 800,000)	$200,000	Identifiable assets revalued to FV (tangible and intangible)
Net BV (Acquisition Date)	$469,000	

3. **(F)** When SSS was purchased, the appraisal report indicated that the fair value of the land is $1,000,000. All assets acquired and liabilities assumed are reported at the acquisition date fair value. Therefore, land should be reported at $1,000,000. Upon consolidation, land is adjusted by $200,000 ($1,000,000 fair value less $800,000 book value on June 30, 20X7). The ending balance of PP&E should be $3,250,345 (2,250,345 + 800,000 + 200,000).

4. **(A)** SSS purchased 133 soccer posts from Pele at $100 each. Pele had paid $90 each for the items. SSS later sold 20 of those soccer posts to an outside party, Corner Kick, at $125 each. In consolidation, intercompany sales need to be eliminated so that only revenues with third parties are reported. Below is a diagram of the intercompany sales transaction.

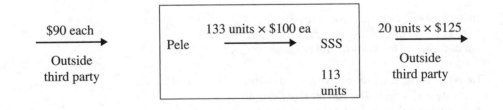

The table below presents the information related to the elimination of intercompany sales, cost of sales and inventory. The table below presents what should have been recorded as the consolidated balance versus what was recorded by both Pele and SSS. The difference is the eliminating entry. Intercompany revenues of $13,300 (133 × $100) need to be eliminated and the ending balance for sales revenue would be $2,500 (20 × $125).

	Should be	What is recorded by Pele + SSS	Difference (eliminating entry)
Sales revenue	2,500 cr. (20 × $125)	13,300 cr. + 2,500 cr. (133 × $100) (20 × $125)	13,300 cr.
Cost of revenue	1,800 dr. (20 × $90)	11,970 dr. + 2,000 dr. (133 × $90) (100 × $20)	12,170 cr.
Inventory	25,200 dr. (280 × 90)	15,030 dr. + 11,300 dr. (ending balance) (ending balance)	1,130 cr.

(C) SSS purchased 133 soccer posts from Pele, and SSS sold 20 of those soccer posts to an outside party, Corner Kick. In consolidation, intercompany inventory transactions need to be eliminated so that only transactions with third parties are reported. The table below presents what should have been recorded as the consolidated balance versus what was recorded by both Pele and SSS. The difference is the eliminating entry. The cost of revenue should be reduced by $12,170 and inventory should be reduced by $1,130.

	Should be	What is recorded by Pele + SSS	Difference (eliminating entry)
Sales revenue	2,500 cr. (20 × $125)	13,300 cr. + 2,500 cr. (133 × $100) (20 × $125)	13,300 cr.
Cost of revenue	1,800 dr. (20 × $90)	11,970 dr. + 2,000 dr. (133 × $90) ($100 × 20)	12,170 cr.
Inventory	25,200 dr. (280 × 90)	15,030 dr. + 11,300 dr. (ending balance) (ending balance)	1,130 cr.

Additional Explanation: Corrected Consolidation Worksheet

Consolidation Worksheet—Pele Inc. & Subsidiaries

Item	Pele Inc.	SSS Inc.	Eliminations	Consolidation Totals
Cash	1,024,516	164,274		1,188,790
A/R	237,000	36,364	a. (12,000)	261,364
Inventory	15,030	11,300	c. (1,130)	25,200
Other Current assets	200,000	2,875		202,875
PP&E, net	2,250,345	800,000	b. 200,000	3,250,345
Investment in SSS Inc.	892,513		b. (892,513)	-
Goodwill			b. 131,000	131,000
Accounts Payable	(75,000)	(20,000)	a. 12,000	(83,000)
Accrued Liabilities	(62,000)	(32,000)		(94,000)
Other Current Liabilities	(10,000)	(69,700)	d. 31,838	(47,862)
Non-Current Liabilities	(836,701)	(331,600)		(1,168,301)
Common stock	(600,000)	(25,000)	b. 25,000	(600,000)
APIC	(2,200,000)	(175,000)	b. 175,000	(2,200,000)
Ret. Earnings	(650,000)	(269,000)	b. 269,000	(650,000)
Service revenue	(475,556)	(297,500)		(773,056)
Sales revenue	(13,300)	(2,500)	c. 13,300	(2,500)
Income from SSS Inc.	(92,513)		b. 92,513	-
Cost of revenues	200,000	120,000	c. (12,170)	307,830
Other Expenses	100,000	39,828		139,828
Income Tax Expense	95,666	47,659	d. (31,838)	111,487
Total	$ -	$ -		$ -

Select Financial Statement Accounts

Long-Term Debt (Financial Liabilities): Bonds Payable

Bond Accounting Principles

Task-Based Simulation 4

aicpa.tbs.sm.bond.acc.prin.02_13

Accrual Basis Worksheet		
	Authoritative Literature	
		Help

Scroll down to complete all parts of this task.

On January 1, Year 1, Stopaz Co. issued 8%, five-year bonds with a face value of $200,000. The bonds pay interest semiannually on June 30 and December 31 of each year. The bonds were issued when the market interest rate was 4% and the bond proceeds were $235,931.

Stopaz uses the effective interest method for amortizing bond premiums/discounts and maintains separate general ledger accounts for each.

Select from the list provided the appropriate account name. An account may be used once or not at all for the entry. Enter the corresponding debit or credit in the appropriate column. Round all elements to the nearest dollar. All rows may not be required to complete the entry. If no journal entry is needed, choose "No entry required". For Wiley CPAexcel grading purposes, enter debits and credits in descending order based on dollar amount. Under the Account Name column, select "Blank" and under the Debit and Credit columns, enter a zero "0" in lieu of leaving any cell empty.

Prepare the journal entry to record the issuance of the bonds on January 1, Year 1.

Account name	Debit	Credit
	(A) (B) (C) (D) (E) (F) (G) (H) (I) (J)	(A) (B) (C) (D) (E) (F) (G) (H) (I) (J)
1. A. Bond interest expense B. Bond interest payable C. Bond issue cost expense D. Bonds payable E. Cash F. Discounts on bonds payable G. Premium on bonds payable H. Unamortized bond issue costs I. No entry required J. None	○ ○ ○ ○ ○ ○ ○ ○ ○ ○	○ ○ ○ ○ ○ ○ ○ ○ ○ ○
2. A. Bond interest expense B. Bond interest payable C. Bond issue cost expense D. Bonds payable E. Cash F. Discounts on bonds payable G. Premium on bonds payable H. Unamortized bond issue costs I. No entry required J. None	○ ○ ○ ○ ○ ○ ○ ○ ○ ○	○ ○ ○ ○ ○ ○ ○ ○ ○ ○
3. A. Bond interest expense B. Bond interest payable C. Bond issue cost expense D. Bonds payable E. Cash F. Discounts on bonds payable G. Premium on bonds payable H. Unamortized bond issue costs I. No entry required J. None	○ ○ ○ ○ ○ ○ ○ ○ ○ ○	○ ○ ○ ○ ○ ○ ○ ○ ○ ○

Prepare the journal entry to record the payment of interest on June 30, year 1:

Account name	Debit	Credit
1. A. Bond interest expense B. Bond interest payable C. Bond issue cost expense D. Bonds payable E. Cash F. Discounts on bonds payable G. Premium on bonds payable H. Unamortized bond issue costs I. No entry required J. None		
2. A. Bond interest expense B. Bond interest payable C. Bond issue cost expense D. Bonds payable E. Cash F. Discounts on bonds payable G. Premium on bonds payable H. Unamortized bond issue costs I. No entry required J. None		
3. A. Bond interest expense B. Bond interest payable C. Bond issue cost expense D. Bonds payable E. Cash F. Discounts on bonds payable G. Premium on bonds payable H. Unamortized bond issue costs I. No entry required J. None		

Calculate the amounts requested below for Stopaz. Enter amounts as positive values rounded to the nearest dollar. If your response is zero, enter a zero (0).

Bond interest expense accrual for the six months ended June 30, Year 2	

Premium amortized for the six months ended June 30, Year 2	

Task-Based Simulation 5 Solution

Accrual Basis Worksheet	
	Authoritative Literature
	Help

Account name	Debit (A) (B) (C) (D) (E) (F) (G) (H) (I) (J)	Credit (A) (B) (C) (D) (E) (F) (G) (H) (I) (J)
1. A. Bond interest expense B. Bond interest payable C. Bond issue cost expense D. Bonds payable E. Cash F. Discounts on bonds payable G. Premium on bonds payable H. Unamortized bond issue costs I. No entry required J. None	○ ○ ○ ○ ● ○ ○ ○ ○ ○	○ ○ ○ ● ○ ○ ○ ○ ○ ○
2. A. Bond interest expense B. Bond interest payable C. Bond issue cost expense D. Bonds payable E. Cash F. Discounts on bonds payable G. Premium on bonds payable H. Unamortized bond issue costs I. No entry required J. None	○ ○ ○ ○ ○ ○ ● ○ ○ ○	● ○ ○ ○ ○ ○ ○ ○ ○ ○
3. A. Bond interest expense B. Bond interest payable C. Bond issue cost expense D. Bonds payable E. Cash F. Discounts on bonds payable G. Premium on bonds payable H. Unamortized bond issue costs I. No entry required J. None	○ ○ ○ ○ ○ ○ ● ○ ○ ○	○ ○ ○ ● ○ ○ ○ ○ ○ ○

Account name	Debit	Credit
1. A. Bond interest expense B. Bond interest payable C. Bond issue cost expense D. Bonds payable E. Cash F. Discounts on bonds payable G. Premium on bonds payable H. Unamortized bond issue costs I. No entry required J. None	235,931	200,000
2. A. Bond interest expense B. Bond interest payable C. Bond issue cost expense D. Bonds payable E. Cash F. Discounts on bonds payable G. Premium on bonds payable H. Unamortized bond issue costs I. No entry required J. None	35,931	4,719
3. A. Bond interest expense B. Bond interest payable C. Bond issue cost expense D. Bonds payable E. Cash F. Discounts on bonds payable G. Premium on bonds payable H. Unamortized bond issue costs I. No entry required J. None	3,281	8,000

Bond interest expense accrual for the six months ended June 30, Year 2	$4,586

Premium amortized for the six months ended June 30, Year 2	$3,414

1. The bonds have a face value of $200,000 but were sold for $235,931; therefore, the premium on the bonds was $35,931.

2. On June 30, the first interest payment is made based on the stated annual rate of 8%. 8% × $200,000 × 6/12 months = $8,000. The interest expense equals the carrying value of the bond, $235,931 multiplied by the market rate of 4% for 6/12 months, or $4,719. The difference between the $8,000 and the $4,719 equals $3,281 and is the amortization of the premium.

3. To calculate the June 30, Year 2 interest expense, repeat the exercise of calculating the interest expense and amortization of the premium for December 31.

Year 1	Bond carrying value	$235,931	
	June 30 amortized premium	($3,281)	
	June 30 carrying value	$232,650	
	December interest expense: $4,653 ($232,650 × 4% × 6/12)		
	December amortized premium	(3,347)	$8,000 – $4,463
	December carrying value	$229,303	
Year 2	June 30 interest expense	$4,586	$229,303 × 4% × 6/12
	June 30 amortized premium	$3,414	$8,000 – $4,586

Select Transactions

Revenue Recognition

Special Issues in Revenue Recognition

Task-Based Simulation 5

tbs.revrecog.spec.iss.001_0318

Accrual Basis Worksheet		
	Authoritative Literature	
		Help

You are the senior on an audit engagement for Franco Corp., which is a manufacturer of cellphones. Currently, Franco Corp. manufactures and sells three types of cellphones: Zone-out, Zone-in, and Zone-plus. During 20X1, four retailers entered into contracts with Franco Corp.

On December 15, 20X1, at a recent meeting with the auditors, a director of Franco Corp. asked how the company's contracts and return policies would impact the year-end financial statements with respect to revenue recognition. You were asked to review the contracts for each retail customer and provide the accounting term for the contract that determines additional criteria for revenue recognition, if applicable. In addition, you were asked to provide journal entries related to certain transactions with the retailers. As an accounting policy, Franco Corp. has stated that it accounts for service warranty revenue using the proportion of warranty expense incurred over the total expected costs of fulfilling the warranty.

Exhibit 1: Agreement with Lee's Electronics

January 18, 20X1

Franco Corp.
25838 Parker Lane
Dallas, TX
75001

AGREEMENT

Dear Lee's Electronics:

Thank you for your recent purchase!

The cellphones you purchased are warranted free from defects in workmanship and materials upon purchase. If the cellphones are defective, then we will replace or repair them free of charge on return if returned within three months from the date of purchase. Proof and date of purchase from Franco Corp. is required.

This agreement is only available to the original purchaser and will be void if any of the following occur:

- The customer damages the cellphone.
- The cellphone has water damage from the customer.
- The cellphone has been altered by another vendor.
- The customer has added items to the cellphone that may have caused impairment to the cellphone.

If the cellphone is damaged and the terms are applicable, then please return the cellphone to the location listed above, and Franco Corp. will replace or repair the cellphone within one week.

Sincerely,

Carlos Franco

President, Franco Corp.
(972) 559-3838

Exhibit 2: Agreement with Gabbies Inc.

AGREEMENT

This agreement is being made between **Franco Corp.** and **Gabbies Inc**. on **February 7, 20X1**.

- Franco Inc. has delivered cellphones listed below to Gabbies Inc. for resale. The cellphones shall remain on property of Gabbies Inc. until sold. The delivery does not constitute a sale to Gabbies Inc.
- Gabbies Inc. agrees to make its best effort to sell Franco Inc.'s cellphones at the agreed-upon prices shown below.
- This agreement is effective and valid until October 31, 20X1.
- Upon termination of the agreement, Gabbies Inc. agrees to return any cellphones that have not been sold. The cellphones should be in the same condition that they were in upon delivery to Gabbies Inc. Franco Inc. warrants that the cellphones are free of physical damage.

Details of Agreement for Cellphones delivered to Gabbies Inc.
1. **300** Zone-out
   Price to be sold: **no less than $125.00**
   Fees for Gabbies Inc.: **10% of price**
2. **250** Zone-in
   Price to be sold: **no less than $250**
   Fees for Gabbies Inc.: **15% of price**
3. **200** Zone-plus
   price to be sold: **no less than $350**
   Fees for Gabbies Inc.: **20% of price**

Signed:
Carlos Franco

President, Franco Inc.

Gabriel Davies

Chief Executive Officer, Gabbies Inc.

Exhibit 3: Agreement with Talk to Us Corp.

April 3, 20X1

Franco Corp.
25838 Parker Lane
Dallas, TX
75001

NOTICE OF AGREEMENT

Dear Talk to Us Corp.:

Thank you for your recent purchase of the cellphones!

In addition, you have chosen to purchase protection for the cellphones for **$10,000**

If the cell phones you purchased are defective or damaged in any way for any reason, then we will replace or repair them free of charge, without charge on return if returned within two years from the date of purchase. Proof and date of purchase from Franco Corp. is required.

This agreement does not include lost or stolen merchandise.

If the cell phone needs to be replaced or repaired, then please return the cell phones to the location listed above and Franco Corp. will replace or repair the cell phones within two weeks.

Sincerely
Carlos Franco

Carlos Franco

President, Franco Corp.
(972) 559-3838

Exhibit 4: Agreement with Harvey's Inc.

May 14, 20X1

Franco Corp.
25838 Parker Lane
Dallas, TX
75001

NOTICE OF AGREEMENT

Dear Harvey's Inc.:

Thank you for your purchase!

You have chosen to purchase the cellphones as is and, in return, you have received 15% discount off our normal retail pricing.

If the cellphones are defective, then we will replace or repair them at a charge to Harvey's Inc. that will be determined and quoted to you at the time of return. There will not be any charge for the quote.

Sincerely
Carlos Franco

Carlos Franco

President, Franco Corp.
(972) 559-3838

Exhibit 5: Transactions with Retailers

Lee's Electronics					
Date	**Description**	**Item**	**Quantity**	**Price/Cost per item**	**Total**
January 18, 20X1	Cash sale to Lee Electronics (estimated returns/ repairs = 2% of sales)	Zone-plus	750	$300	$225,000
March 13, 20X1	Cash Repair	Zone-plus	30	$140	$4,200
Gabbies Inc.					
Date	**Description**	**Item**	**Quantity**	**Price/Cost per item**	**Total**
April 25, 20X1	Sale made by Gabbies— on account	Zone-plus	100	$360	$36,000
Talk to Us Corp					
Date	**Description**	**Item**	**Quantity**	**Price/Cost per item**	**Total**
April 3, 20X1	Cash sale	Zone-plus	300	$350	$105,000
April 3, 20X1	Warranty ($5,400 expected costs)	Warranty	1	$10,000	$10,000
June 25, 20X1	Cash replacement	Zone-plus	15%	$5400	$810
Harvey's Inc.					
Date	**Description**	**Item**	**Quantity**	**Price/Cost per item**	**Total**
May 14, 20X1	Cash sale	Zone-in	125	$212	$26,500
July 18, 20X1	Cash repair	Zone-in	25	$45	$1,125

Part One: For each retailer listed the table below, review the agreements with each retailer provided in the exhibits and choose the appropriate accounting term for the contract. Choose only one response for each item. If no term is applicable, then choose "N/A" from the list of items.

Retailer	Accounting Term							
	(A)	**(B)**	**(C)**	**(D)**	**(E)**	**(F)**	**(G)**	**(H)**

1. Lee's Electronics
  A. N/A
  B. Assurance-type warranties
  C. Bill-and-hold arrangements
  D. Extended assurance-type warranties
  E. Goods on consignment
  F. Nonrefundable up-front fee
  G. Sales with a right of return
  H. Service-type warranties
	○	○	○	○	○	○	○	○

2. Gabbies Inc.
  A. N/A
  B. Assurance-type warranties
  C. Bill-and-hold arrangements
  D. Extended assurance-type warranties
  E. Goods on consignment
  F. Nonrefundable up-front fee
  G. Sales with a right of return
  H. Service-type warranties
	○	○	○	○	○	○	○	○

3. Talk to Us Corp
  A. N/A
  B. Assurance-type warranties
  C. Bill-and-hold arrangements
  D. Extended assurance-type warranties
  E. Goods on consignment
  F. Nonrefundable up-front fee
  G. Sales with a right of return
  H. Service-type warranties
	○	○	○	○	○	○	○	○

4. Harvey's Inc.
  A. N/A
  B. Assurance-type warranties
  C. Bill-and-hold arrangements
  D. Extended assurance-type warranties
  E. Goods on consignment
  F. Nonrefundable up-front fee
  G. Sales with a right of return
  H. Service-type warranties
	○	○	○	○	○	○	○	○

Part Two: In the table below, provide the journal entries for the requested date that Franco Corp. would record related to its transactions with retailers. The journal entries are based on the transaction detail and terms of the agreements provided in the Exhibits tab. Franco Corp. uses the periodic method of recording inventory. From column A select the desired account title from the list provided. If none is required, select "None" from the list. You do not need to indent the account(s) to distinguish debits from credits. An account title or an amount may be used once, more than once, or not at all. You may not need all the lines provided. Enter the amount for each debit and credit. Do not use dollar signs but do use commas for thousand separators: e.g., 100,000. If no amount is required, enter "None." Record only in shaded boxes.

Entry to record January 18 transaction with Lee's Electronics:

Account titles	Debit amounts	Credit amounts
1. A. Blank B. Accounts receivable C. Cash D. Commission expense E. Cost of Goods Sold F. Inventory G. Repairs expense H. Sales revenue I. Service revenue J. Sales returns/discounts/allowances K. Unearned warranty revenue L. Warranty expense M. Warranty liability		
2. A. Blank B. Accounts receivable C. Cash D. Commission expense E. Cost of Goods Sold F. Inventory G. Repairs expense H. Sales revenue I. Service revenue J. Sales returns/discounts/allowances K. Unearned warranty revenue L. Warranty expense M. Warranty liability		
3. A. Blank B. Accounts receivable C. Cash D. Commission expense E. Cost of Goods Sold F. Inventory G. Repairs expense H. Sales revenue I. Service revenue J. Sales returns/discounts/allowances K. Unearned warranty revenue L. Warranty expense M. Warranty liability		
4. A. Blank B. Accounts receivable C. Cash D. Commission expense E. Cost of Goods Sold F. Inventory G. Repairs expense H. Sales revenue I. Service revenue J. Sales returns/discounts/allowances K. Unearned warranty revenue L. Warranty expense M. Warranty liability		

Entry to record March 13 transaction with Lee's Electronics:

Account titles	Debit amounts	Credit amounts
1. A. Blank B. Accounts receivable C. Cash D. Commission expense E. Cost of Goods Sold F. Inventory G. Repairs expense H. Sales revenue I. Service revenue J. Sales returns/discounts/allowances K. Unearned warranty revenue L. Warranty expense M. Warranty liability		
2. A. Blank B. Accounts receivable C. Cash D. Commission expense E. Cost of Goods Sold F. Inventory G. Repairs expense H. Sales revenue I. Service revenue J. Sales returns/discounts/allowances K. Unearned warranty revenue L. Warranty expense M. Warranty liability		

Entry to record April 3 transaction with Talk to Us Corp.:

Account titles	Debit amounts	Credit amounts

1.   A. Blank
     B. Accounts receivable
     C. Cash
     D. Commission expense
     E. Cost of Goods Sold
     F. Inventory
     G. Repairs expense
     H. Sales revenue
     I. Service revenue
     J. Sales returns/discounts/allowances
     K. Unearned warranty revenue
     L. Warranty expense
     M. Warranty liability		

2.   A. Blank
     B. Accounts receivable
     C. Cash
     D. Commission expense
     E. Cost of Goods Sold
     F. Inventory
     G. Repairs expense
     H. Sales revenue
     I. Service revenue
     J. Sales returns/discounts/allowances
     K. Unearned warranty revenue
     L. Warranty expense
     M. Warranty liability		

3.   A. Blank
     B. Accounts receivable
     C. Cash
     D. Commission expense
     E. Cost of Goods Sold
     F. Inventory
     G. Repairs expense
     H. Sales revenue
     I. Service revenue
     J. Sales returns/discounts/allowances
     K. Unearned warranty revenue
     L. Warranty expense
     M. Warranty liability		

4.   A. Blank
     B. Accounts receivable
     C. Cash
     D. Commission expense
     E. Cost of Goods Sold
     F. Inventory
     G. Repairs expense
     H. Sales revenue
     I. Service revenue
     J. Sales returns/discounts/allowances
     K. Unearned warranty revenue
     L. Warranty expense
     M. Warranty liability		

Entry to record April 25 transaction with Gabbies Inc.:

Account titles	Debit amounts	Credit amounts

1. A. Blank
   B. Accounts receivable
   C. Cash
   D. Commission expense
   E. Cost of Goods Sold
   F. Inventory
   G. Repairs expense
   H. Sales revenue
   I. Service revenue
   J. Sales returns/discounts/allowances
   K. Unearned warranty revenue
   L. Warranty expense
   M. Warranty liability		

2. A. Blank
   B. Accounts receivable
   C. Cash
   D. Commission expense
   E. Cost of Goods Sold
   F. Inventory
   G. Repairs expense
   H. Sales revenue
   I. Service revenue
   J. Sales returns/discounts/allowances
   K. Unearned warranty revenue
   L. Warranty expense
   M. Warranty liability		

3. A. Blank
   B. Accounts receivable
   C. Cash
   D. Commission expense
   E. Cost of Goods Sold
   F. Inventory
   G. Repairs expense
   H. Sales revenue
   I. Service revenue
   J. Sales returns/discounts/allowances
   K. Unearned warranty revenue
   L. Warranty expense
   M. Warranty liability		

4. A. Blank
   B. Accounts receivable
   C. Cash
   D. Commission expense
   E. Cost of Goods Sold
   F. Inventory
   G. Repairs expense
   H. Sales revenue
   I. Service revenue
   J. Sales returns/discounts/allowances
   K. Unearned warranty revenue
   L. Warranty expense
   M. Warranty liability		

Entry to record May 14 transaction with Harvey's Inc.:

Account titles	Debit amounts	Credit amounts
1. A. Blank B. Accounts receivable C. Cash D. Commission expense E. Cost of Goods Sold F. Inventory G. Repairs expense H. Sales revenue I. Service revenue J. Sales returns/discounts/allowances K. Unearned warranty revenue L. Warranty expense M. Warranty liability		
2. A. Blank B. Accounts receivable C. Cash D. Commission expense E. Cost of Goods Sold F. Inventory G. Repairs expense H. Sales revenue I. Service revenue J. Sales returns/discounts/allowances K. Unearned warranty revenue L. Warranty expense M. Warranty liability		

Entry to record June 25 transaction with Talk to Us Corp.:

Account titles	Debit amounts	Credit amounts
1. A. Blank B. Accounts receivable C. Cash D. Commission expense E. Cost of Goods Sold F. Inventory G. Repairs expense H. Sales revenue I. Service revenue J. Sales returns/discounts/allowances K. Unearned warranty revenue L. Warranty expense M. Warranty liability		
2. A. Blank B. Accounts receivable C. Cash D. Commission expense E. Cost of Goods Sold F. Inventory G. Repairs expense H. Sales revenue I. Service revenue J. Sales returns/discounts/allowances K. Unearned warranty revenue L. Warranty expense M. Warranty liability		
3. A. Blank B. Accounts receivable C. Cash D. Commission expense E. Cost of Goods Sold F. Inventory G. Repairs expense H. Sales revenue I. Service revenue J. Sales returns/discounts/allowances K. Unearned warranty revenue L. Warranty expense M. Warranty liability		
4. A. Blank B. Accounts receivable C. Cash D. Commission expense E. Cost of Goods Sold F. Inventory G. Repairs expense H. Sales revenue I. Service revenue J. Sales returns/discounts/allowances K. Unearned warranty revenue L. Warranty expense M. Warranty liability		

Entry to record July 18 transaction with Harvey's Inc.:

Account titles	Debit amounts	Credit amounts
1. A. Blank B. Accounts receivable C. Cash D. Commission expense E. Cost of Goods Sold F. Inventory G. Repairs expense H. Sales revenue I. Service revenue J. Sales returns/discounts/allowances K. Unearned warranty revenue L. Warranty expense M. Warranty liability		
2. A. Blank B. Accounts receivable C. Cash D. Commission expense E. Cost of Goods Sold F. Inventory G. Repairs expense H. Sales revenue I. Service revenue J. Sales returns/discounts/allowances K. Unearned warranty revenue L. Warranty expense M. Warranty liability		

Task-Based Simulation 5 Solution

| Accrual Basis Worksheet | Authoritative Literature | Help |

Retailer	(A)	(B)	(C)	(D)	(E)	(F)	(G)	(H)
					Accounting Term			
1. Lee's Electronics	○	●	○	○	○	○	○	○

A. N/A
B. Assurance-type warranties
C. Bill-and-hold arrangements
D. Extended assurance-type warranties
E. Goods on consignment
F. Nonrefundable up-front fee
G. Sales with a right of return
H. Service-type warranties

Retailer	(A)	(B)	(C)	(D)	(E)	(F)	(G)	(H)
2. Gabbies Inc.	○	○	○	○	●	○	○	○

A. N/A
B. Assurance-type warranties
C. Bill-and-hold arrangements
D. Extended assurance-type warranties
E. Goods on consignment
F. Nonrefundable up-front fee
G. Sales with a right of return
H. Service-type warranties

Retailer	(A)	(B)	(C)	(D)	(E)	(F)	(G)	(H)
3. Talk to Us Corp	○	○	○	○	○	○	○	●

A. N/A
B. Assurance-type warranties
C. Bill-and-hold arrangements
D. Extended assurance-type warranties
E. Goods on consignment
F. Nonrefundable up-front fee
G. Sales with a right of return
H. Service-type warranties

Retailer	(A)	(B)	(C)	(D)	(E)	(F)	(G)	(H)
4. Harvey's Inc.	●	○	○	○	○	○	○	○

A. N/A
B. Assurance-type warranties
C. Bill-and-hold arrangements
D. Extended assurance-type warranties
E. Goods on consignment
F. Nonrefundable up-front fee
G. Sales with a right of return
H. Service-type warranties

Account titles													Debit amounts	Credit amounts
(A)	(B)	(C)	(D)	(E)	(F)	(G)	(H)	(I)	(J)	(K)	(L)	(M)		
1. ○	○	●	○	○	○	○	○	○	○	○	○	○	225,000	0
2. ○	○	○	○	○	○	○	●	○	○	○	○	○	0	225,000
3. ○	○	○	○	○	○	○	○	○	○	○	●	○	4,500	0
4. ○	○	○	○	○	○	○	○	○	○	○	○	●	0	4,500

Account titles													Debit amounts	Credit amounts
(A)	(B)	(C)	(D)	(E)	(F)	(G)	(H)	(I)	(J)	(K)	(L)	(M)		
1. ○	○	○	○	○	○	○	○	○	○	○	○	●	4,200	0
2. ○	○	●	○	○	○	○	○	○	○	○	○	○	0	4,200

Account titles													Debit amounts	Credit amounts
(A)	(B)	(C)	(D)	(E)	(F)	(G)	(H)	(I)	(J)	(K)	(L)	(M)		
1. ○	○	●	○	○	○	○	○	○	○	○	○	○	115,000	0
2. ○	○	○	○	○	○	○	●	○	○	○	○	○	0	105,000
3. ○	○	○	○	○	○	○	○	○	○	●	○	○	0	10,000
4. ●	○	○	○	○	○	○	○	○	○	○	○	○	0	0

Account titles													Debit amounts	Credit amounts
(A)	(B)	(C)	(D)	(E)	(F)	(G)	(H)	(I)	(J)	(K)	(L)	(M)		
1. ○	●	○	○	○	○	○	○	○	○	○	○	○	28,800	0
2. ○	○	○	●	○	○	○	○	○	○	○	○	○	7,200	0
3. ○	○	○	○	○	○	○	●	○	○	○	○	○	0	36,000
4. ●	○	○	○	○	○	○	○	○	○	○	○	○	0	0

Account titles													Debit amounts	Credit amounts
(A)	(B)	(C)	(D)	(E)	(F)	(G)	(H)	(I)	(J)	(K)	(L)	(M)		
1. ○	○	●	○	○	○	○	○	○	○	○	○	○	26,500	0
2. ○	○	○	○	○	○	○	●	○	○	○	○	○	0	26,500

Account titles													Debit amounts	Credit amounts
(A)	(B)	(C)	(D)	(E)	(F)	(G)	(H)	(I)	(J)	(K)	(L)	(M)		
1. ○	○	○	○	○	○	○	○	○	○	○	●	○	810	0
2. ○	○	●	○	○	○	○	○	○	○	○	○	○	0	810
3. ○	○	○	○	○	○	○	○	○	○	●	○	○	1,500	0
4. ○	○	○	○	○	○	○	○	●	○	○	○	○	0	1,500

Account titles													Debit amounts	Credit amounts
(A)	(B)	(C)	(D)	(E)	(F)	(G)	(H)	(I)	(J)	(K)	(L)	(M)		
1. ○	○	●	○	○	○	○	○	○	○	○	○	○	1,125	0
2. ○	○	○	○	○	○	○	●	○	○	○	○	○	0	1,125

1. **(B)** Warranties offered by companies at no charge to the customer that offer the customer assurance that the product will function to agreed-upon specifications are termed assurance-type warranties.

2. **(E)** In a consignment arrangement, the consignor (owner of goods) uses the consignee's premises to sell its goods. In this situation, Franco Inc. is the consignor and Gabbies Inc. is the consignee.

3. **(H)** Warranties offered by companies at no charge to the customer that offer the customer assurance that the product will function to agreed-upon specifications are termed assurance-type warranties. If a warranty provides services in addition to assurance for an additional cost and the customer has the option to purchase the warranty, then it is termed a service-type warranty.

4. **(A)** In this situation, the customer has purchased the goods as is. There are no warranties or other concessions made for the retailer, and therefore there are no additional criteria to consider for revenue recognition. All performance obligations related to the sale of the cellphones have been met, and revenue will be recognized at the time the goods are transferred to the buyer. If Harvey's Inc. requires repairs or replacements, then a new performance obligation would arise and the amount would be determined at that time.

Entry to record January 18 transaction with Lee's Electronics: The warranty offered to Lee's Electronics is accounted for as an assurance-type warranty and is not considered a separate performance obligation. When the cellphones are transferred to Lee's Electronics, cash and revenue of $225,000 should be recorded. In addition, the estimated warranty expense of' $4,500 ($225,000 × 2%) and related liability should also be recorded.

Entry to record March 13th transaction with Lee's Electronics: The warranty offered to Lee's Electronics is accounted for as an assurance-type warranty and is not considered a separate performance obligation. When the revenue for the sale of the cellphones was recorded on January 18, the estimated warranty expense of' $4,500 ($225,000 × 2%) and related liability was also recorded. On March 13, actual cash warranty expenses paid will reduce the liability recorded earlier, and Franco Corp. will debit warranty liability and credit cash for the actual warranty expenses incurred and paid, which is $4,200.

Entry to record April 3 transaction with Talk to Us Corp.: The warranty offered to Talk to Us Corp. is accounted for as a service-type warranty and is considered a separate performance obligation. When the sale of the cellphones is made, revenue for the purchase price of the cellphones ($105,000) is recorded. In addition, a separate performance exists due to the warranty purchased, but because the obligation has not yet been met, a liability (unearned warranty revenue) will be recorded for $10,000, which represents the portion paid for the warranty.

Entry to record April 25 transaction with Gabbies Inc.: The agreement with Gabbies Inc. is a consignment arrangement. In a consignment arrangement, the consignor (owner of goods) uses the consignee's premises to sell its goods. Revenue was not recognized on February 7, 20X1, when the cellphones were transferred to Gabbies Inc., because no sale had taken place. On April 25, 20X1, the cellphones were sold by Gabbies Inc. on behalf of Franco Corp., and at that time, Franco Corp. recognizes revenue. According to the terms of the agreement, Gabbies Inc. will retain a percentage of each sale based on the type of cellphone sold. In this case, Gabbies Inc. will retain $7,200 ($36,000 × 20%) as its fee for sales of the Zone-plus and remits the remainder of $28,200 ($36,000 − $7,200) to Franco Corp. Franco Corp. recognizes the entire $36,000 as sales revenue, and Gabbies Inc.'s fee of $7,200 is recorded as commission expense.

Entry to record May 14 transaction with Harvey's Inc.: In this situation, Harvey's Inc. has purchased the goods as is. There are no warranties or other concessions made for the retailer, and therefore, there are no additional criteria to consider for revenue recognition. All performance obligations related to the sale of the cellphones are met, and revenue for the entire sale of $26,500 is recorded as sales revenue.

Entry to record June 25 transaction with Talk to Us Corp.: When the retailer pays for the service-type warranty, the seller initially records unearned warranty revenue (liability) for the portion of the transaction price allocated to the warranty. The unearned revenue is recognized as revenue as a proportion of the costs incurred to fulfill the warranty over the total expected costs to fulfill the warranty and warranty expense is recognized as incurred. On June 25, actual warranty costs of $810 were incurred and should be recorded. Franco Corp. expects to incur $5,400 of total warranty costs (as noted in the transaction detail). Therefore, since 15% of the total estimated warranty expenses are recorded (810 ÷ 5400), 15% of the unearned warranty revenue (liability) should be reversed, and revenue for the same amount of $1,500 (15% × $10,000) should also be recorded.

Entry to record July 18 transaction with Harvey's Inc.: Harvey's Inc. has purchased the goods as is. Therefore, any repairs or further replacements are considered a separate performance obligation and should be recorded as revenue when the obligation is met. Franco Corp. should record revenue for the entire amount of the repair, which is $1,125.